DELIVERING ON THE PROMISE
OF PRO-POOR GROWTH

DELIVERING ON THE PROMISE OF PRO-POOR GROWTH

Insights and Lessons from Country Experiences

Timothy Besley and Louise J. Cord, Editors

**A copublication of Palgrave Macmillan
and the World Bank**

A copublication of The World Bank and Palgrave Macmillan.

Palgrave Macmillan
Houndmills, Basingstoke, Hampshire RG21 6XS and
175 Fifth Avenue, New York, NY 10010
Companies and representatives throughout the world

Palgrave Macmillan is the global academic imprint of the Palgrave Macmillan division of St. Martin's Press, LLC and of Palgrave Macmillan Ltd.

Macmillan® is a registered trademark in the United States, United Kingdom, and other countries. Palgrave is a registered trademark in the European Union and other countries.

Rights and Permissions

ISBN-10: 0-8213-6515-0 (softcover)
ISBN-10: 0-8213-6670-X (hardcover)
ISBN-13: 978-0-8213-6515-1
eISBN-10: 0-8213-6516-9
eISBN-13: 978-0-8213-6516-8
DOI: 10.1596/978-0-8213-6515-1

Library of Congress Cataloging-in-Publications Data has been applied for.
Cover design: Paine Bluett Paine, Inc.

Contents

TABLES

FIGURES

Acknowledgments

This book was prepared under the auspices of the Operationalizing Pro-Poor Growth (OPPG) research program cosponsored by Agence Française de Développement (AFD), German Development Policy, the UK Department for International Development (DFID), and the World Bank. The members of the OPPG research program include Mandy Chatha, Tom Crowards, Will Gargent, Manu Manthri, and Christian Rogg (DFID); Jacky Amprou, Jean Marc Chataigner, Christian Flamant, and François Pacquement (AFD); Daniel Alker, Hartmut Janus, Annette Langhammer, Ulrike Maenner, Ute Möhring, Birgit Pickel, and Julius Spatz (German Development Policy); and Sabine Bernabè, Louise Cord, Ignacio Fiestas, and Humberto Lopez (World Bank).

The work was carried out under the direction of Adrian Wood (DFID), Luca Barbone, Danny Leipziger, and Sudhir Shetty (World Bank). The team also gratefully acknowledges Gobind Nankani and John Page (World Bank), who initiated this work.

The book reflects comments received during a workshop with the authors in Frankfurt in June 2004 and during workshops with the authors, the core donor team, and World Bank and DFID staff in London in December 2004 and in Washington in February 2005. These workshops also included academics, nongovernmental organization representatives, and representatives of other donor agencies. The book reflects valuable feedback received during the World Bank's 2005 Poverty Reduction and Economic Management Conference sessions, "Equity and Pro-Poor Growth" and "Making Growth Pro-Poor: Cases and Policies," which were organized jointly with the 2006 World Development Report team.

Many others provided helpful comments. They include Gary Fields (Cornell University); C. Peter Timmer (Center for Global Development); Alan Gelb, Indermit Gill, Daniela Gressani, Catherine Hull, Tamar Manuelyan Atinc, John Page, and Martin Ravallion (World Bank); Lionel Demery (consultant); Max Everest-Phillips and Arjan de Haan (DFID); and Marc Raffinot (AFD-Development, Institutions, and Long-Term Analysis).

The editors gratefully acknowledge production assistance provided by Aliya Husain, Nelly Obias, and Jae Shin Yang. They also acknowledge the support of Stephen McGroarty, Dina Towbin, and Nora Ridolfi from the World Bank Office of the Publisher.

Abbreviations

AFD	Agence Française de Développement
AGOA	African Growth Opportunity Act
BBS	Bangladesh Bureau of Statistics
DFID	UK Department for International Development
DHS	Demographic and Health Survey
FDI	foreign direct investment
GDP	gross domestic product
GEP	growth elasticity of poverty
GIC	growth incidence curve
GLSS	Ghana Living Standards Surveys
HCMC	Ho Chi Minh City
HCS	Household Consumption Survey
HEPR	National Program for Hunger Eradication and Poverty Reduction
HIES	Household Income Expenditure Survey
HIPC	Heavily Indebted Poor Country
IMR	infant mortality rate
NGO	nongovernmental organization
NSS	National Sample Survey
OPPG	Operationalizing Pro-Poor Growth Research Program
PNAD	Pesquisa Nacional por Amostra de Domicilios
RMG	ready-made garments
SMEs	small and medium-size enterprises
SOEs	state-owned enterprises
SUSENAS	national socioeconomic survey
TFP	total factor productivity
TFR	total fertility rate

1

Overview

Louise Cord

Broad-based growth is critical to accelerating poverty reduction. The most successful East Asian countries in the 1970s and 1980s showed that rapid growth, combined with low initial inequality and pro-poor distributional change, could significantly reduce poverty (World Bank 1993). Analysis of changes in poverty levels across a sample of developing countries in the 1980s and 1990s also highlights the importance of fast growth for poverty reduction (Dollar and Kraay 2002; Foster and Székely 2001; Kraay 2006; Ravallion and Chen 1997).

But income inequality also affects the *pace* at which growth is translated into poverty reduction. Growth is less efficient in lowering poverty levels in countries with high initial inequality or in which the distributional pattern of growth favors the nonpoor (Bourguignon 2004; Ravallion 1997, 2004). In the late 1990s the term *pro-poor growth* became popular as economists recognized that accelerating poverty reduction required both more rapid growth and lower inequality.[1]

Despite the attention given to the relative roles of growth and inequality in reducing poverty, we know little about how the microunderpinnings of growth strategies affect the ability of poor households to participate in and benefit from growth. This book contributes to the debate on how to accelerate poverty reduction by providing insights from studies of eight countries that have been relatively successful in delivering pro-poor growth: Bangladesh, Brazil, Ghana, India, Indonesia, Tunisia, Uganda, and Vietnam (figure 1.1). The studies analyze the distributional pattern of growth and the ways in which country policies and conditions affected it. They use an income-based

Figure 1.1 The Eight Countries

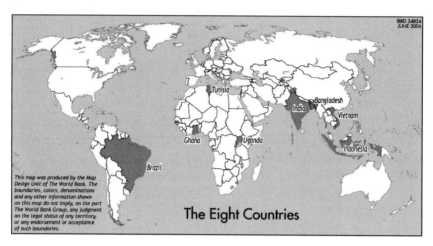

methodology built on Ravallion (2004) to analyze the distributional impact of growth. Because institutions and nonincome dimensions of poverty are considered highly relevant determinants of this, they are discussed where relevant.

Table 1.1 shows conditions in the eight countries in the early 1990s. The three middle-income countries (where gross domestic product [GDP] per capita exceeded $1,000 in 1990) and India experienced sustained long-term pro-poor growth. The studies of Indonesia, India, and Tunisia start in the 1950s and 1960s, while analysis of Brazil goes back to the 1980s. Growth has ebbed and flowed in these countries, reflecting exogenous forces and macro- and structural policies, as well as political and financial events, but overall these economies have shown a great deal of resiliency in delivering development.

In India and the three middle-income countries (Brazil, Indonesia, and Tunisia), governments have been able to promote public and private accumulation of physical and human capital across most households in the income distribution. (The exception may be Brazil, where capital accumulation occurred disproportionately at the middle and top end of the income distribution.) Yet these governments differ widely with respect to institutional qualities: Indonesia has a high level of corruption, whereas Tunisia has a low level. India has relatively strong democratic and federal traditions and stable public institutions, whereas Tunisia and Indonesia have largely centralized and autocratic systems of governments that are relatively effective but associated with lower levels of voice (citizen input) and accountability.

Table 1.1 *Initial Conditions in the Eight Countries Studied*

	Bangladesh	Brazil	Ghana	India	Indonesia	Tunisia	Uganda	Vietnam
Geography and level of economic development								
Population density (1990)	845.2	17.5	67.1	285.7	98.4	52.5	88.1	203.4
GDP per capita (early 1990s)	$291.5	$4,116.0	$356.6	$360.3	$1,113.2	$1,823.2	$260.3	$247.2
Dollar-a-day poverty (early 1990s)	49.7	61.6	51.7	36.0	15.4	6.7	55.7	58.1
Gini coefficient (early 1990s)	0.28	0.61	0.37	0.28	0.36	0.40	0.36	0.34
Share of urban population (1990)	20	75	36	26	31	58	11	20
Share of GDP in agriculture (1990)	30	8	45	31	19	16	57	39
Human development outcomes (1990)								
Fertility	4.1	2.7	5.5	3.8	3.0	3.5	7.0	3.6
Infant mortality	96.0	50.0	74.0	80.0	60.0	37.0	100.0	36.0
Male literacy	44.3	82.9	70.1	61.9	86.7	71.6	69.3	94.0
Female literacy	23.7	81.2	78.5	35.9	72.5	46.5	43.5	87.1
Macroeconomic stability and trade openness								
Average inflation rate (1985–90)	7.3	934.8	28.0	8.0	7.0	7.2	134.8	n/a
Trade openness (1989–91)	19.2	15.0	42.1	16.1	48.2	90.6	27.4	68.7
Public accountability and governance (2000)								
Voice and accountability	38.7	63.9	52.9	62.8	32.5	26.2	19.4	6.8
Corruption	33.9	59.7	44.6	49.5	11.3	78.0	17.7	27.4
Government effectiveness	35.5	47.3	59.1	52.7	38.7	86.6	48.9	43.0

Sources: Public accountability and governance data are from Mastruzzi, Kraay, and Kaufmann 2005; all other data are from the World Bank's *World Development Indicators* 2004.

Note: n.a. = not available.

In the four low-income countries (Bangladesh, Ghana, Uganda, and Vietnam) much of the progress toward poverty reduction has been spurred by peace dividends and one-off gains from macrostabilization along with structural reforms. Attractive world market conditions and trade liberalization also allowed these countries to benefit from export growth in agriculture and manufacturing, albeit somewhat sporadically in Uganda and Ghana. In addition, increased aid flows and public expenditures have helped these countries to promote human capital accumulation with investments in health and education and, to a lesser degree, to finance improvements in their infrastructure base.

Progress in delivering human and physical capital (particularly infrastructure) has been spotty in the more remote areas of these low-income countries. The difficulty of creating pro-growth environments in these more challenging areas may particularly explain the rise in inequality that these countries experienced in the 1990s. Moreover, only Vietnam and Bangladesh achieved any measure of structural transformation with growing agricultural productivity and the release of labor into dynamic industrial and services sectors. In Ghana and Uganda, the gains from economic policy reforms appear to be shorter-lived; the bulk of the population and in particular the poor remain in agricultural and low-return nonagricultural self-employment activities.

Poverty, Growth, and Inequality Trends in the 1990s and Early 2000s

Table 1.2 summarizes the main poverty, growth, and inequality trends in the countries studied. Vietnam was the most successful: it reduced poverty by almost 8 percent a year between 1993 and 2002, while Ghana, India, Uganda, and Tunisia all experienced falling poverty rates that were just under 4 percent a year in the 1990s and early 2000s. Poverty also fell in Bangladesh and Brazil but at a lower rate: just under 3 percent per year. It rose slightly in Indonesia, reflecting the 1998 financial crisis.[2] Although poverty tended to fall more rapidly in urban areas of the sample countries, most poverty reduction was in rural areas, where the share of poor households tended to be higher (figures 1.2 and 1.3). The exception was Brazil, where most poverty reduction occurred in urban areas, because only 30 percent of the poor resided in rural areas in 1990.

Driving these overall reductions in poverty was the rebound in growth in the mid-1990s, which led to a median growth rate for the countries of 3.1 percent in the late 1990s and early 2000s. This rate was slightly higher than the average of 2.5 percent for all low- and middle-income countries for

Table 1.2 *Basic Poverty, Growth, and Inequality Trends in the Eight Countries Studied*

	Survey year 1	Survey year 2	Initial GDP per capita ($)	Annual GDP growth rate (%)	Initial national poverty rate	Annual change in poverty rate (%)	Initial Gini coefficient	Annual change in Gini (%)
Bangladesh	1990	2000	292	3.03	49.7	−3.8	0.28	0.2
Brazil	1992	2002	4,116	3.34	61.6	−3.9	0.61	1.8
Ghana	1992	1999	357	1.63	51.7	−3.9	0.37	0.6
India	1994	2000	360	4.18	36.0	−3.8	0.28	0.6
Indonesia	1993	2002	1,113	5.70	15.4	−7.8	0.36	0.9
Tunisia	1996	2002	1,823	−0.81	6.7	0.7	0.40	−0.9
Uganda	1993	2001	260	1.47	55.7	−2.3	0.36	−0.2
Vietnam	1992	2000	247	3.09	58.1	−2.8	0.34	1.5
Median	n.a.	n.a.	360	3.06	50.7	−3.8	0.36	0.7

Source: With the exception of national Gini in Bangladesh and poverty data on India, poverty and inequality data come from country case studies, which used national household survey data as cited in the case studies. GDP data were obtained from *World Development Indicators 2004.*

Note: Country-based poverty data for seven of the countries are based on expenditure/consumption household surveys. Data for Brazil are based on income household surveys. Poverty rates are based on national poverty lines and are therefore not comparable across countries. n.a. = not applicable.

Figure 1.2 *Urban Poverty Fell More Rapidly than Rural Poverty except in Indonesia*

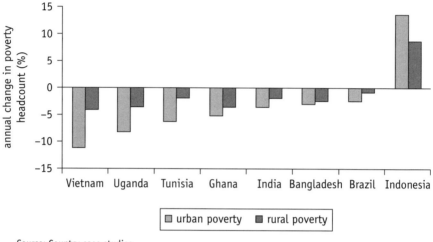

Source: Country case studies.

Figure 1.3 *Most Poverty Reduction Occurred in Rural Areas except in Brazil*

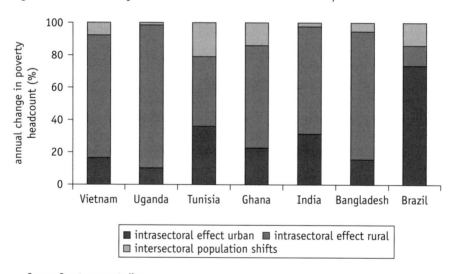

Source: Country case studies.
Note: In Brazil only 30 percent of the poor lived in rural areas in the early 1990s.

the same period. The economic recovery in the countries can be linked to the successful implementation of macrostabilization reforms, which were particularly effective in stimulating nonagricultural growth.[3] Beyond these policies, trade and exchange rate reforms, improvements in the investment

Figure 1.4 *Economic Growth Reduces Poverty*

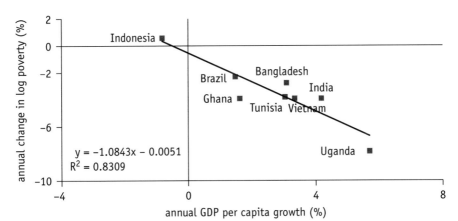

Sources: Country case studies and *World Development Indicators 2004.*

climate, attractive world market prices for key export commodities, and investments in education and infrastructure also increased the rate of agricultural and nonagricultural growth. Not surprisingly, countries that experienced the strongest growth also had the greatest poverty reduction. The correlation between changes in poverty and changes in GDP per capita growth (differences in logs) was positive and significant, with a regression coefficient of −1.1 (0.01) (figure 1.4).[4]

However, rising inequality offset the gains from growth in all countries but Brazil and Indonesia, where inequality fell, and Tunisia, where inequality was relatively constant. The increase in inequality was highest in Bangladesh, followed by Uganda and Vietnam. Comparing changes in average consumption with the rate of pro-poor growth (the mean growth rate of consumption for the poor) provides a more precise measure of the impact of growth on the well-being of the poor and nonpoor.[5] The regression coefficient between the logged changes in the rate of pro-poor growth and the mean growth rate in consumption is 0.89 (0.01) (figure 1.5). The latter implies that the rate of pro-poor growth is less than the average growth rate in mean consumption, indicating that on average inequality rose among the eight countries.

Although extremely important, these results underscore that growth (either in GDP or in consumption) does not explain all the variation in poverty reduction across the eight countries. Initial inequality and changes in inequality were also important factors. In Uganda the impact of changes in growth and inequality on poverty offset each other. More specifically, if

Figure 1.5 *Consumption by the Poor Generally Grew Slower than Average Consumption*

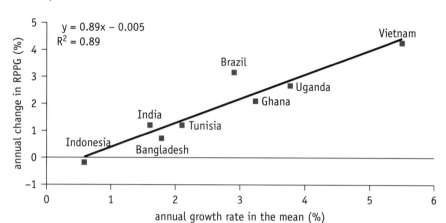

Source: Country case studies.
Note: RPPG = rate of pro-poor growth.

inequality had not increased in Uganda between 1992 and 2002, the country's poverty rate would have been 8 percentage points lower (headcount poverty would have been 30 percent instead of 38 percent). In Bangladesh rising inequality meant that poverty fell by only 9 percentage points, instead of 16 percentage points if growth had been distributionally neutral between 1992 and 2000. In Brazil, poverty levels in those states with higher levels of initial inequality were less responsive to growth in the 1980s and 1990s than poverty levels in states with lower levels of initial inequality.

The importance of distributional change in reducing poverty can become more important when the data are disaggregated into subnational groupings, because national averages may hide significant regional variations in the distributional pattern of growth. For example, in Ghana, the distribution component was very small at the national level and only slightly offset the positive effect of growth on poverty reduction. But at the regional level, the distributional effect not only varied (it was positive in some regions and negative in others), but also significantly affected regional poverty levels (figure 1.6). In Accra falling inequality—reflecting rising self-employment in trading, construction, transport, and communications for poorer workers—was almost as important as growth in reducing poverty. The other major region that experienced a rapid reduction in poverty was the rural forest zone, where workers benefited from rising cocoa prices and remittances. In contrast, rising inequality offset gains from growth,

Figure 1.6 *National Averages in Ghana Mask Significant Regional Variation in the Contributions of Growth and Inequality to Poverty Reduction*

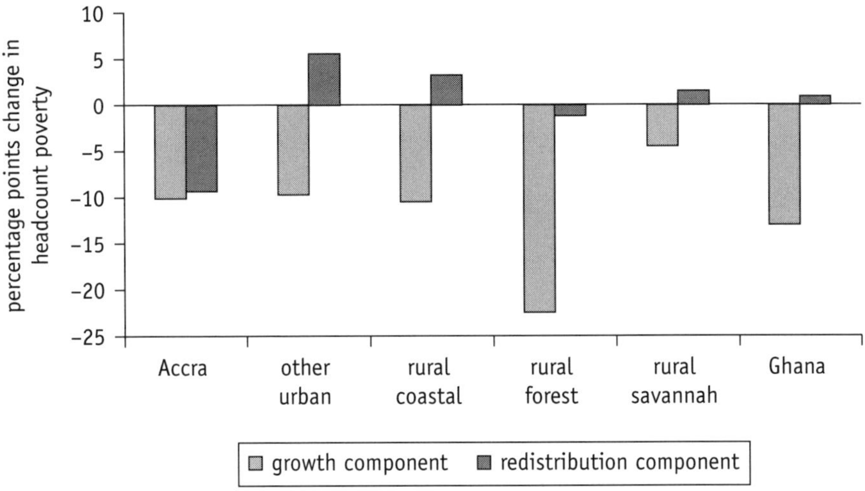

Source: Ghana case study.

depressing the rate of poverty reduction in the rural coastal region and other urban areas of Ghana.

Another indicator of the relationship between growth and poverty reduction is the growth elasticity of poverty, which measures how a 1 percent increase in the rate of growth affects the poverty rate. It offers insight into the efficiency of growth in reducing poverty, and how initial inequality and GDP per capita levels, distributional change, and other factors affect this efficiency. Although conceptually appealing, total growth elasticities should be interpreted with care, particularly when making cross-country comparisons, given the multitude of variables that affect them.[6] Examining variations in the sensitivity of poverty to growth across states within Brazil, Menezes-Filho and Vasconcellos in chapter 9 find that when the initial level of income is high and initial inequality is low, growth is more efficient in reducing poverty among Brazilian states.

The relationship between changes in growth and inequality among the eight countries in the 1990s reveals a significant and positive relationship between changes (logged differences) in growth and inequality, with a correlation coefficient of 0.32 percent (0.008) (figure 1.7). The three countries where inequality rose the most—Vietnam, Uganda, and Bangladesh—were also among the strongest growth performers. The positive correlation

Figure 1.7 *Changes in Growth and Inequality Are Related*

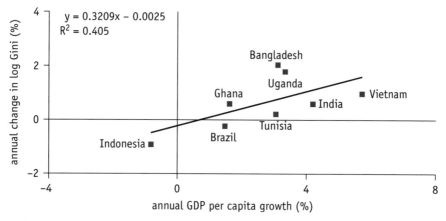

Source: Country case studies.

Figure 1.8 *Significant Poverty Reduction but Rising Inequality in Bangladesh, Uganda, and Vietnam*

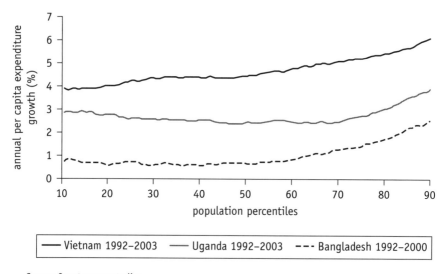

Source: Country case studies.

between changes in growth and inequality means that poor households benefited less than nonpoor households from growth.

The growth incidence curves for the three countries with the greatest increase in inequality indicate the average rate of consumption growth per capita for each percentile of the distribution (figure 1.8). They show that the high rate of economic growth generated significant poverty reduction (as shown by the positive rates of income growth across the bottom percentiles). But the upward slope of the curves also points to rising inequality, because the rate of income growth of individuals in the upper income percentiles was higher than the income growth rate of the poor.

The positive relationship between inequality and growth that existed among these eight countries in the 1990s challenges the consensus that no general relationship between inequality and growth exists, and certainly not one in which growth systematically widens inequality. The theoretical literature is divided on the relationship between growth and inequality, and the empirical literature on developing countries has found no consistent relationship between the two variables.[7] For example, Deininger and Squire (1998) found Kuznets's inverted-U in 10 percent of the countries they studied, an ordinary U in another 10 percent, and no statistically significant relationship in the remaining 80 percent.

But earlier papers did not control for potential changes in the relationship between changes in growth and inequality over time. Understanding the relationship between growth and inequality and the factors that affect it are a priority in designing pro-poor growth strategies. Lopez (2005a) explores whether, controlling for the effect of time, this relationship between per capita GDP growth and inequality holds more broadly among all developing and rich countries. His analysis indicates that the relationship between growth and inequality was negative in the 1970s and 1980s (for the 1970s it was not significant), but that it became positive and significant in the 1990s.[8] Recent analysis by Ravallion (2005) finds a similarly positive link (a correlation coefficient of 0.26 that is significant at the 5 percent level) between the growth rate of per capita consumption at the mean and (relative) inequality across 80 countries in the 1990s.

More analysis is needed to assess whether growth in the 1990s led to sustained increases in inequality, or whether the relationship reflects specific initial conditions present in the high-growth countries in the sample—such as low levels of initial inequality (Bangladesh, Uganda, Vietnam) or rapid structural transformation (Bangladesh and Vietnam). The chapter on Bangladesh examines rising inequality in rural and urban areas and concludes that it could have been avoided in urban areas with greater investments in human development but that it was inevitable in rural areas in the 1990s, because wealthier households were better placed, at least initially, to move into rapid growth sectors.

Although analyzing the aggregate relationships among poverty reduction, growth, and changes in inequality is analytically appealing, the case studies show that in an operational policy context, separating the growth and distributional impacts of policies on poverty reduction is often not possible. Most policies have both a growth and a distributional impact. From a policy perspective, the more relevant questions are how did poor households participate in growth, and what were the main channels? What policies and country conditions were effective in helping poorer households take advantage of and contribute to growth?

Increasing Poor Households' Participation in Economic Growth

The case studies presented in this volume offer several policy lessons for promoting broad-based growth.

Households can participate in economic growth through three main channels: employment, transfers (from public and private sources), and returns on investment. We focus on employment, because the most successful experiences in pro-poor growth occurred when government policy, combined with favorable exogenous events, supported creation of attractive jobs accessible to poor households.

In addition, employment income is between two-thirds and three-quarters of total income, and this share tends to be even larger for poor households with little income from nonlabor-related sources. Countries with relatively low levels of GDP per capita tend to have most employment concentrated in agriculture, but as productivity in that sector rises and nonagricultural activities expand, the workforce shifts out of agriculture and into attractive informal and formal employment in industry and services. Income generated from other assets (rental income, interest income) is not considered directly in the case studies, because the great majority of poor people have no assets aside from labor and land. Income transfers offer another channel for connecting the poor to growth, and they grew in importance in the 1990s. Nonetheless, they remain limited in scope, particularly in low-income countries.[9]

Making Agricultural Activities More Productive

Given the concentration of poor people in agriculture, most of the poverty reduction occurred among households engaged primarily (although not exclusively) in agriculture. Taking into account the indirect effects on non-agricultural households, agriculture (principally food crops) accounted for 44 and 77 percent of poverty reduction in the 1990s in Ghana and Uganda, respectively, and up to three quarters of the poverty reduction from 1984 to 1996 in Indonesia. In Vietnam 71 percent of workers who moved out of poverty between 1993 and 1997 either remained employed in agriculture or moved into agricultural employment.

In the eight study countries, five policy interventions helped raise the agricultural earnings of poor households in the 1990s:

- improving market access and lowering transaction costs,
- strengthening property rights to land,
- creating an incentive framework that benefited all farmers,
- expanding the technology available to smallholder producers, and
- helping poorer and smaller producers cope with risk.

Among the countries where agricultural earnings increased for the poor, these policies were implemented to various degrees. Moreover, because of different initial conditions and other influences in each country, not all of the policies increased the ability of the poor to participate in growth to the same extent.

Improving market access and lowering transaction costs were essential in Indonesia, Bangladesh, and parts of Vietnam for increasing the agricultural earnings of smaller and poor farmers. In his study of Indonesia, Timmer argues that public sector investments and regulatory improvements to lower transaction costs provided the crucial link between growth-oriented macroeconomic policies and broad-based participation by the poor in the market economy. Market access in these countries was facilitated by significant investments in rural roads and marketplaces (often implemented under food-for-work programs), by high population densities, and by the fact that smallholder export and food crops were often the same (rice). But high transaction costs constrained agricultural earnings in the more remote regions of the Asian and Latin American countries, where rural poverty is disproportionately high (such as in Bolivia, northeast Brazil, and the upland regions of Vietnam).

Among the low-income African countries in the sample, high transaction costs and low market access were among the most important constraints on expanding agricultural earnings, especially for small farmers and those in remote areas. With food markets in Africa expected to be the fastest growing of all agricultural markets in the continent over the next 20 years (Commission for Africa 2005), it will be important to link rural farmers to local and regional markets with better infrastructure and marketing associations. Contract farming with nongovernmental organizations (NGOs) and the private sector has facilitated market access in several African countries, particularly when complemented by organized grassroots involvement.

Strengthening land property rights improved incentives to increase production and diversify into higher-value crops in Vietnam. In 1988 land was decollectivized, and under the 1993 Land Law certificates of use were issued to all rural households, stimulating the intensification and diversification of agricultural production into higher value-added crops. For the poorer farmers in the African case studies, clear tenure and transparent land markets were important. Weak land market institutions—often reflecting the partial implementation of land laws (Uganda) and rapidly changing land tenure conditions, along with uncertain land market institutions (Ghana)—were key constraints on the ability of all farmers to invest in their land. Lack of secure tenure and of legally recognized ownership rights, particularly for inheritance, negatively affected poor rural women in the African countries. These women often are the primary producers of food crops. In Uganda, as in many African countries, improving security of land tenure for poorer farmers will require developing formal systems that strengthen and complement customary land practices.

In Brazil access to land is a major issue because of very unequal land distributions. Large-scale land reform is not politically viable, but expanding the access of smallholders and poorer farmers to long-term financing, and, in some cases, to grants for land purchases, has been successful. Similarly, in Tunisia land access for the poor remains a critical issue as a partially implemented land reform has led to unequal access to both private and public agricultural lands. In Bangladesh and India continuing restrictions on land rental markets to protect ownership rights make it difficult and costly for smaller farmers (particularly women and the landless) to rent land. In Indonesia land rights, particularly to forests, remain fairly undefined at the local level. (Land records cover only 20 percent of all land in Indonesia.) Opaque and costly systems of land administration and allocation in rural Indonesia are serious obstacles to expanding agricultural earnings, particularly for poorer farmers (Deininger and Zakout 2005).

Creating an incentive framework that benefited all farmers was an important part of the structural reforms by the African countries, Bangladesh, and Vietnam. The impact has varied, depending on the size of production units, access to capital, technical assistance, and markets (or transaction costs), and the crops grown. Trade liberalization, along with land reform, promoted Vietnam's rapid emergence as a major world exporter of rice and coffee in the 1990s, greatly benefiting smallholders. Trade liberalization in Bangladesh facilitated imports of low-cost inputs, increasing their use by poor farmers. Food crop farmers in Africa generally benefited less from trade liberalization than export crop farmers, whose poverty rates fell sharply. With the exception of coffee producers in Uganda, export farmers tended to make up a small share of the total and were mainly the better off. The private sector often did not fill the void left by reforms in food crop marketing, leaving many poor producers in remote areas of Africa without market access.

Subsidies and protection in India, Indonesia, and Tunisia characterized agricultural production, redirecting public resources and incentives from higher-value production toward less labor-intensive basic food grains. In Indonesia the tariff on rice imports raised prices for rice producers (many of whom are smallholders and poorer farmers) but hurt rice consumers and slowed poverty reduction. In India the reform of agricultural subsidies has been difficult, in large part because of their political appeal and high visibility (Keefer and Khemani 2003). Such reform must consider the transition costs to small farmers: they may receive only a small share of total subsidies, but these subsidies are a significant share of their total income. Implementation of trade and price reforms more generally must reflect understanding of the reforms' effects on different types of households. Moreover, poorer households will need roads, financial services, and marketing associations so that they can take advantage of the new opportunities.

Expanding the technology available to smallholder producers helped the Green Revolution raise agricultural earnings in Asia. In Indonesia Green Revolution technology and massive investments in agriculture catalyzed high rates of pro-poor growth from the 1960s to the 1980s. In sub-Saharan Africa the lack of adequate technologies for arid climates was a severe constraint on producers, particularly those in food crops, where the poor are concentrated. Increasing financial support to African research institutions and improving the delivery of extension services to food crop farmers, in particular women with private firms and NGOs, could lift agricultural earnings for poorer farmers.

Helping poorer and smaller producers cope with risk has stimulated adoption of higher-yielding agricultural techniques. Investments in flood infrastructure and flood season safety nets for poorer farmers (along with greater access to private irrigation) reduced risk and created incentives for diversification in Bangladesh. Information and communication technologies (such as mobile phones in Uganda) can provide smallholders with market information. In general, expanding the use of targeted safety-net programs (where administrative capacity exists or can be reinforced) would help farmers avoid severe deprivation from output and price variations and encourage them to adopt riskier technologies that offer higher returns.

Figure 1.9 *Nonagricultural Growth Was almost Triple Agricultural Growth*

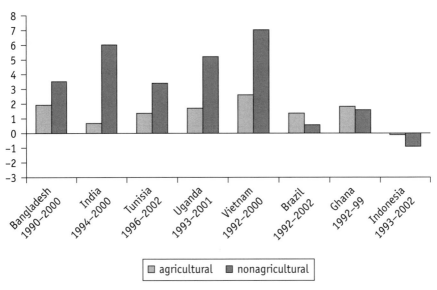

Source: Lopez (2005a), based on *World Development Indicators 2004.*
Note: Start and end years same as in table 1.1.

Taking Advantage of Nonagricultural and Urban Employment Opportunities

In the 1990s median nonagricultural growth was 3.4 percent a year, almost three times the 1.4 percent for the agricultural sector. Only in Ghana and Brazil did the agricultural sector outperform growth in services and industry (figure 1.9). Nonagricultural growth was particularly effective in reducing poverty in Bangladesh, India and Vietnam, where nonfarm activities became linked to rapid and more urban-based industrial and service sector growth, and in Bangladesh and Tunisia, where manufacturing employment grew.

Understanding the factors that can allow poor households to take advantage of nonagricultural jobs in rural areas and job opportunities in urban areas is crucial for a pro-poor growth strategy. In Vietnam trade liberalization and export promotion in labor-intensive manufacturing—combined with rising domestic demand stimulated in part by fairly high rates of agricultural growth—increased nonagricultural employment and earnings for poor households in urban and more connected rural areas. By contrast, in Uganda, though the share of the labor force in nonagricultural services (particularly trade) expanded, limited returns to these activities suppressed income growth and the impact on poverty.

More generally, the country cases underscored four broad policy options to enhance access to nonagricultural earnings for poor households:

- improving the investment climate,
- designing labor market regulations to create attractive employment opportunities,
- expanding access to secondary and girls' education, and
- increasing access to infrastructure.

As with policies to expand agricultural earnings for the poor, the relative priorities and the appropriate design and scope of these policy options vary across countries.

Improving the investment climate stimulated growth, influencing the size of the formal sector and the composition of formal employment. In Bangladesh, Tunisia, and Vietnam investment climate improvements, trade liberalization, and special incentives for manufacturing industries significantly increased unskilled manufacturing employment, particularly for women. By contrast, in Ghana, private investment remained low (undermined in part by persistently high inflation and a poor investment climate), causing manufacturing employment to contract in the late 1990s.

Designing labor market regulations to create attractive formal employment for poor workers helps expand their nonagricultural earnings, particularly in countries with fast growth. Labor market regulations, often designed to protect the interests of workers, can restrict formal labor markets and the market access of poor workers. In India states with "pro-worker" legislation recorded lower growth rates and less efficiency in reducing poverty. By contrast, Indonesia's high degree of labor market flexibility during the Suharto years promoted formal employment and labor-intensive growth. But since the 1997 Asian financial crisis, minimum wage increases prompted by union activity have left almost all employment growth to the informal sector, at wages below those in the formal sector.

Three caveats: First, labor market regulations are only one of a set of factors that affect the investment climate and the willingness of a firm to formalize. Other critical constraints include policy uncertainty, fiscal burdens, the cost of finance, corruption, and the quality of courts (World Bank 2005a). Second, loosening labor market regulations in some regions, particularly Africa, may have little impact on labor markets, especially if employment is mainly in agriculture (Uganda). Third, labor market regulations, though imperfect, constitute a form of social protection. The extent of labor market regulation needs to reflect a balance between workers' needs and employers' needs, a balance that hangs on a country's labor market conditions and level of development.

Expanding access to secondary and girls' education is important for nonagricultural growth and for facilitating poor households' participation in nonagricultural growth. In India and Brazil poor educational outcomes reduced growth among different states and the impact of that growth on poverty reduction. Female literacy, also important in reducing poverty, was the most important determinant of interstate differences in the efficiency of nonfarm growth in reducing poverty in India (Ravallion and Datt 1996). In Brazil the importance of education as a predictor of poverty has declined over time, given advances in educational levels that have occurred among the poor. But states that invested in college had more rapid growth, while states that invested in both secondary and tertiary education saw the greatest reductions in inequality and the greatest increases in the growth elasticity of poverty.

Educational differences were associated with rising inequality in Uganda: those with more education were better placed to take the more attractive nonagricultural jobs. But access to secondary education by the poor declined in Uganda throughout the 1990s and early 2000s, while it increased for children in the top quintile. Because the impact of education on household income growth is nondecreasing (Deininger and Okidi 2003), inequality in access to higher education will certainly perpetuate welfare inequality and remain a major constraint for the poor to exploit market-driven opportunities for participation in future growth.

Increasing access to infrastructure (especially the combination of roads and electricity) and linking rural areas to small towns and urban centers, along with strong nonagricultural growth, contributed to rising informal sector employment in rural Bangladesh, India, Tunisia, and Vietnam. In contrast, the lack of infrastructure in Africa, along with low population density, constrained access to attractive informal employment in rural areas and kept the rural poor engaged in more traditional and lower-return nonfarm activities linked to agriculture. Therefore, lifting infrastructure constraints to improve market access, as well as increasing access to electricity and education in high-density rural areas and small towns, may raise nonagricultural earnings for the poor. But improving access to infrastructure requires more than expanding public investments—it also requires higher institutional quality. Poor institutions in Uganda may have prevented improvements to the power infrastructure (Keefer 2000).

Overarching Messages

The eight country studies provide insights on how to better integrate short-term and long-term policies to increase the impact of growth on poverty

reduction. Perhaps most important, policy makers who seek to accelerate growth in the incomes of poor people and thus reduce overall poverty levels would be well advised to implement policies that enable their countries to achieve a faster rate of overall growth. A successful pro-poor growth strategy would thus need to have, at its core, measures for sustained and rapid economic growth. These measures include macroeconomic stability, well-defined property rights, trade openness, a good investment climate, an attractive incentive framework, well-functioning factor markets, and broad access to infrastructure and education. With the exception of Indonesia (whose 1998 financial crisis is not heavily covered in chapter 2 as it focuses on the Suharto period), the countries in this book were relatively successful in generating growth in the 1990s. However, moving beyond the one-time gains from peace dividends, macro and trade reforms, and favorable international markets to sustained productivity gains and structural shifts within the economy will be a challenge for some of the countries, particularly those in sub-Saharan Africa.

Because poverty reduction's sensitivity to growth can vary significantly across countries and growth spells, more favorable outcomes are observed where policies have been implemented to enhance the capacity of poor people to participate in and contribute to growth. This task requires a conscious and sustained effort on the part of governments to provide the basic conditions necessary for broad-based growth in the regions and sectors where the poor live and work. This effort can mean ensuring that the incentive framework for agriculture does not discriminate against the poor and delivers efficient market signals; that the property rights of the poor and in particular land rights are guaranteed and can be transacted; that basic levels of physical and human capital are present in rural areas and urban slums to unleash private investment and facilitate access to labor, financial, and product markets; and that risk is maintained at acceptable levels through investments in irrigation and flood infrastructure or the delivery of safety nets so as to protect basic incomes and support private investments in higher-risk activities.

The specific strategies adopted by the eight countries differed, as did the role of exogenous forces in affecting growth and hence poverty reduction. However, some common threads emerge—in particular, the need for good economic policies and political stability combined with public investments in physical and human capital. These ingredients—good policies, stability, and public goods—were essential in facilitating private initiatives and investments among the non-poor and especially the poor. Political regimes and the quality of institutions also affected outcomes, but drawing conclusions about their impact on growth and poverty reduction is difficult, as many countries were innovative in overcoming their institutional weaknesses.

The case studies suggest that pro-poor growth, even over sustained periods of time, can occur in a variety of contexts, including very unfavorable initial conditions. The experiences of Bangladesh, Indonesia, and Uganda testify that countries can achieve high rates of growth and poverty reduction even when faced with weak institutions, poor human development outcomes, and weak trading links and infrastructure assets. Vietnam provides an example of how a country with good initial conditions can lift itself out of extreme poverty within two decades by adopting economic policies that allow exploitation of growth potential in urban and rural areas. Understanding initial conditions and their effect on poor households' ability to contribute to growth requires careful examination of a country's growth and its distributional impact and how they affect poverty.

A pro-poor growth lens involves analyzing the specific constraints that poor households in different countries face in participating in growth. Depending on country circumstances, it may be that priority investments for electricity and secondary education should extend beyond the capital city to the surrounding areas, as well as to rural areas and small towns. Or it may require strengthening basic property rights for poor households by helping deliver titles that build on customary tenure systems in small towns and rural areas. Or it may require that governments facilitate nonagricultural growth through supportive infrastructure, lower transactions costs, and a better investment climate in both urban and rural areas.

Challenges for Further Analysis

The experience of the eight study countries in the 1990s underscores three challenges for the countries as they seek to accelerate poverty reduction through broad-based growth. First, movement from agricultural to nonagricultural employment helped raise the incomes of poor households in many countries, but the more educated and better-connected workers were more successful in this regard. The effects of education and labor market policies on sectoral mobility and the role of limited mobility in poverty traps are important areas for further research.

Second, the impact of growth was uneven across regions within countries. Public investment strategies that can address subregional growth and poverty are another important area for further analysis. The findings may differ for low- and middle-income countries and could be particularly important for countries with decentralized governments and for countries that face important regional disparities in growth and poverty reduction.

Third, political economy considerations often affect the distributional outcomes of structural and investment policies, at times at the expense of poor households. Public policies to enhance the ability of the poor to participate in and influence government processes is another area for further exploration.

Structure of the Book

Chapter 2 explores how Indonesia under Suharto implemented a three-tiered strategy that combined rapid economic growth with investments and policies to ensure that growth would reach the poor. This strategy integrated the macroeconomy with the household economy by lowering the transaction costs of operating in factor and product markets, which in turn facilitated links between the macro and micro levels of the economy. In addition, public investments in human capital and flexible and well-integrated labor markets expanded poor households' ability to contribute to growth.

Chapter 3 examines trends in growth and poverty reduction in postindependence India, where states' poverty performance depended on growth rates, policy regimes, and initial conditions. Because different states have experimented with different policies and have different initial conditions, India represents an ideal testing ground for use of micro and macro data to examine the link between growth and poverty. The chapter highlights the importance of several institutional variables in delivering high rates of pro-poor growth. States that had more accountable governments, more pro-business investment climates, and greater access to finance and human capital and that extended property rights to the poor and included women in economic growth have been more successful in reducing poverty.

Chapter 4 draws on macro and micro data to determine why growth has been so effective in reducing poverty in Bangladesh at the same time that income inequality has risen and institutional capacity has evolved so unevenly there. Despite the bleak development prospects that characterized Bangladesh at the time of independence, poverty has fallen dramatically since the early 1970s. Sharply improving human development indicators, particularly in rural areas; rising participation in rural input and land markets; an enhanced capacity to cope with climatic instability due to investments in rural infrastructure and safety nets; and rapid growth in nonagricultural exports explain the strong poverty reduction performance of the

1990s. The chapter also examines how the country was able to overcome its generally weak institutional environment through ring-fencing policies and institutions and by drawing on nongovernmental institutions. It concludes with an assessment of whether the rise in inequality was inevitable.

Chapter 5 explores why the growth process in Vietnam that began with the *doi moi* reforms of the late 1980s has been so effective in promoting a structural transformation of the economy and shrinking poverty levels. Critical to the success of Vietnam has been the creation of attractive employment opportunities accessible to low-income workers in both urban and rural areas. In the agriculture sector, workers benefited from land reform and trade liberalization and attractive world market conditions, as well as growing connections to urban areas. Economic and institutional reforms also facilitated the emergence of a viable private sector that, along with rapid nonagricultural growth, generated significant formal and informal employment in services and, more recently, industry. But despite the fall in aggregate poverty numbers, certain regions and groups continue to benefit less from economic development. Further development of a broad-based domestic private sector as well as public investments in improved infrastructure and a cautious strategy of local government reform are needed to address chronic poverty and to ensure continued broad-based growth.

The case study on Ghana in chapter 6 describes the impressive turnaround of an economy after more than 20 years of serious decline. Starting in 1984 improved policies and aid flows led to a more consistent economic framework and political stability, which along with remittances, helped catalyze steady growth and poverty reduction. However, strong spatial and sectoral policies influenced the distributional pattern of growth. Poverty reduction in the agriculture sector has been limited for those not engaged in export crop production or in urban areas other than Accra. In addition, growth has been associated with limited creation of wage jobs and little deepening of the formal sector, reflecting low private investment and a lack of basic structural change in the economy. More recently, the government has shown a strong commitment to macrostability, agriculture, and private sector development. However, making good on this commitment will require sustained political will as well as an effective decentralization policy to deliver critical services and goods for shared growth.

Chapter 7 examines the evolution of growth and poverty reduction in Uganda since the early 1990s. Strong economic growth, induced by the restoration of political and economic stability, along with large aid flows, was effective in the early to mid-1990s in reducing both poverty and inequality. Since then, poverty levels have risen, because the incomes of poor households have not responded to the continued (albeit slower) growth, leading to rising inequality. The chapter underlines several factors that contributed to the slower growth and rising inequality: the lack of investment in and structural transformation of agriculture, low and declining levels of secondary education among the poor, continued tensions in northern Uganda (the poorest region), a nontransparent public–private partnership, along with a weak rural and urban investment climate. Overall, Uganda's experience shows that despite the existence of good policies and programs, translation of policies into desired outcomes can be undermined by political economy inconsistencies and institutional weaknesses, leading to economic slowdown and uneven participation in growth.

Chapter 8 explores how Tunisia achieved relatively high growth and sharply reduced poverty between 1960 and 2000 with limited initial resources and a poor natural resource endowment. Four sets of factors played a particularly important role in affecting the capacity of the poor to participate in growth: macrostability and trade openness; integrated rural development programs that provided the infrastructure to develop agriculture; promotion of labor-using industries and services, which provided attractive job opportunities and eased rural labor markets; and significant investment in human capital in rural and urban areas and among men and women. Since 2000 Tunisia has continued its strong growth and made improvements in social indicators. But some uncertainties related to the institutional environment and to future job creation (given the moderately high unemployment rate and changes in global trading arrangements) are on the horizon. These uncertainties will need to be addressed if Tunisia's pro-poor growth experience is to be sustained.

The final chapter is on Brazil, which among the countries featured in this volume has the highest GDP per capita and the highest income inequality. As a result of the latter, growth has not evenly benefited the poor and the nonpoor, leading to persistent high rates of poverty. The chapter explores the contribution of education to growth and inequality during the 1980–2000 period. It concludes that investments in human capital were the most important drivers of poverty reduction, because they tended to make growth more pro-poor and increase the growth rate. Investments in high school education appear to be important in increasing growth's benefits to the poor but do not alone improve growth prospects, whereas investments in college education are important determinants of growth but are less effective in making growth more pro-poor. With respect to other policy variables, infrastructure investments were also important for pro-poor growth and for growth itself. In recognition of the importance of education in growth and reducing inequality, the government has expanded its efforts to encourage children from poorer households to attend school at the secondary and tertiary levels and to improve the quality of primary education. Recent trends showing falling inequality suggest that these efforts may be having some success.

Notes

The author gratefully acknowledges comments from Tim Besley and the Operationalizing Pro-Poor Growth donor team.

1. In attempting to give analytical and operational relevance to the concept of pro-poor growth, two broad definitions have emerged. The relative definition of pro-poor growth requires that the income share of the poor increase (Kakwani and Pernia 2000; White and Anderson 2001). This definition might favor interventions that reduce inequality regardless of their impact on growth. The absolute definition of pro-poor growth focuses on accelerating the rate of income growth of the poor and thus the rate of poverty reduction (DFID 2004; Ravallion 2004; Ravallion and Chen 2003). This approach would favor policies that accelerate growth and opportunities for the poor to participate in growth and is consistent with the broad definition of equality of opportunity contained in *World Development Report 2006: Equity and Development* (World Bank 2005b) and with the international community's commitment to the first Millennium Development Goal of halving poverty by 2015.

2. The country studies track the evolution of poverty during the early 1990s and late 1990s to early 2000s using national poverty lines, which do not permit cross-country comparisons of poverty levels.

3. Lopez (2005b) examines the impact of macro reforms on growth and various macro aggregates. He finds that the macrostability brought about by the reforms had payoffs in higher economic growth (particularly for the nonagricultural sector), reduced output volatility, and generally higher investment levels (including foreign direct investment, remittances, and aid, particularly for countries initially underperforming within their regions, such as Uganda and Ghana).

4. Numbers in parentheses provide standard errors.

5. There is significant noise in the measurement of both GDP and household consumption, and GDP trends also reflect other variables not necessarily captured by household consumption data (investment, government spending, net exports).

6. The growth elasticity of poverty can also vary depending on how the population is clustered around the poverty line and as a result of country-specific measurement issues with the national accounts and with the consumption aggregate used to measure poverty trends. Consequently, comparing the overall efficiency of the growth process in reducing poverty across the eight countries was not possible.

7. Several theoretical papers conclude that inequality is detrimental to growth. They argue that redistributive policies, sociopolitical instability, and credit constraints

(particularly for poor households) are associated with high levels of inequality and are bad for growth (Aghion, Caroli, and Garcia-Peñalosa 1999; Alesina and Perotti 1996; Alesina and Rodrik 1994; Galor and Zeira 1993). Other models predict that inequality is likely to enhance growth by drawing on the greater ability and propensity of rich people to invest and the need for unequal wage structures to provide incentives for outstanding achievement (Mirrlees 1971). Although the empirical literature has found no consistent relationship between changes in growth and income inequality, there is some evidence that asset inequality is detrimental to growth (Deininger and Olinto 2000; Birdsall and Londoño 1997).

8. His sample included 23 countries in the 1970s, 42 in the 1980s, and 21 in the 1990s.

9. Although safety nets and conditional cash transfers were effective in improving the welfare of recipients in Bangladesh and Brazil, only in middle-income Brazil was the scope of the transfers sufficiently large to make a dent on poverty and inequality levels. Remittances were associated with poverty reduction in Bangladesh, Vietnam, and Tunisia. In Bangladesh and Ghana, but not Tunisia, they were also associated with rising inequality.

References

Aghion, P., E. Caroli, and C. Garcia-Peñalosa. 1999. "Inequality and Economic Growth: The Perspective of the New Growth Theories." *Journal of Economic Literature* 37 (4): 1615–60.

Alesina, A., and R. Perotti. 1996. "Income Distribution, Political Instability, and Investment." *European Economic Review* 40 (6): 1203–28.

Alesina, A., and D. Rodrik. 1994. "Distributive Politics and Economic Growth." *Quarterly Journal of Economics* 109 (2): 465–90.

Birdsall, N., and J. L. Londoño. 1997. "Asset Inequality Matters: An Assessment of the World Bank's Approach to Poverty Reduction." *American Economic Review Papers and Proceedings* 87 (2): 32–37.

Bourguignon, F. 2004. "The Poverty-Growth-Inequality Triangle." Paper presented at the Indian Council for Research on International Economic Relations, New Delhi, February 4.

Commission for Africa. 2005. *Our Common Interest*. Report of the Commission for Africa. London: Penguin.

Deininger, K., and J. Okidi. 2003. "Growth and Poverty Reduction in Uganda, 1992–2000: Panel Data Evidence." *Development Policy Review* 21 (4): 481–509.

Deininger, K., and P. Olinto. 2000. "Asset Distribution, Inequality, and Growth." Policy Research Working Paper 2375, World Bank, Washington, DC.

Deininger, K., and L. Squire. 1998. "New Ways of Looking at Old Issues: Inequality and Growth." *Journal of Development Economics* 57: 259–87.

Deininger, K., and W. Zakout. 2005. "Land Policy, Management, and Administration." Indonesia Policy Briefs, World Bank, Washington, DC.

DFID (U.K. Department for International Development). 2004. "What Is Pro-Poor Growth and Why Do We Need to Know?" Pro-Poor Growth Briefing Note 1, Policy Division, DFID, London.

Dollar, D., and A. Kraay. 2002. "Growth Is Good for the Poor." *Journal of Economic Growth* 7: 195–225.

Foster, J., and M. Székely. 2001. "Is Economic Growth Good for the Poor? Tracking Low Incomes Using General Means." Research Department Working Paper 453, Inter-American Development Bank, Washington, DC.

Galor, O., and J. Zeira. 1993. "Income Distribution and Macroeconomics." *Review of Economic Studies* 60 (1): 35–52.

Kakwani, N., and E. Pernia. 2000. "What Is Pro-Poor Growth?" *Asian Development Review* 18: 1–16.

Keefer, P. 2000. "Growth and Poverty Reduction in Uganda: The Role of Institutional Reform." Working paper, World Bank, Washington, DC.

Keefer, P., and S. Khemani. 2003. "Democracy, Public Expenditure, and the Poor." Policy Research Working Paper 3164, World Bank, Washington, DC.

Kraay, A. 2006. "When Is Growth Pro-Poor? Evidence from a Panel of Countries." *Journal of Development Economics* 80 (1): 198–227, June.

Lopez, H. 2005a. "Growth and Inequality: Are They Connected?" Working paper, World Bank, Washington, DC.

———. 2005b. "Pro-Poor Growth: How Important Is Macroeconomic Stability?" Working paper, World Bank, Washington, DC.

Mastruzzi, M., A. Kraay, and D. Kaufmann. 2005. "Governance Matters: Governance Indicators for 1996–2000." Policy Research Working Paper 3630, World Bank, Washington, DC.

Mirrlees, J. 1971. "An Exploration in the Theory of Optimum Income Taxation." *Review of Economic Studies* 38: 175–208.

Ravallion, M. 1997. "Can High-Inequality Developing Countries Escape Absolute Poverty?" *Economics Letters* 56: 51–57.

———. 2004. "Pro-Poor Growth: A Primer." Policy Research Working Paper 3242, World Bank, Washington, DC.

———. 2005. "A Poverty-Inequality Trade-Off." *Journal of Economic Inequality* 3 (2): 169–81.

Ravallion, M., and S. Chen. 1997. "What Can New Survey Data Tell Us about Recent Changes in Distribution and Poverty?" *World Bank Economic Review* 11 (2): 357–82.

_____. 2003. "Measuring Pro-Poor Growth." *Economics Letters* 78 (1): 93–99.

Ravallion, M., and G. Datt. 1996. "How Important to India's Poor Is the Sectoral Composition of Economic Growth?" *World Bank Economic Review* 10: 1–26.

White, H., and A. Anderson. 2001. "Growth vs. Redistribution: Does the Pattern of Growth Matter?" *Development Policy Review* 19 (3): 167–289.

World Bank. 1993. *The East Asian Miracle: Economic Growth and Public Policy.* New York: Oxford University Press.

_____. 2004. *World Development Indicators 2004.* Washington, DC: World Bank.

_____. 2005a. *A Better Investment Climate for Everyone.* Washington, DC: World Bank.

_____. 2005b. *World Development Report 2006: Equity and Development.* Washington, DC, and Oxford: World Bank and Oxford University Press.

2

How Indonesia Connected the Poor to Rapid Economic Growth

C. Peter Timmer

Economic growth has been the main source of sustained poverty reduction in Indonesia. Income equality increased during some growth episodes and decreased during others. Indonesia has experienced both "relative" and "absolute" pro-poor growth. The poor were never absolutely worse off during sustained periods of economic growth. During economic decline and crises, the impact on the poor has been severe.

Indonesia's pro-poor performance from the late 1960s to the mid-1990s was based on a conscious strategy that combined rapid economic growth with investments and policies that ensured the growth would reach the poor. This strategy integrated the macroeconomy with the household economy by lowering the transaction costs of operating in the factor and product markets, which provide links between the two levels of the overall economy. This strategy was designed and implemented by highly skilled economic planners (the "technocrats") at the urging of President Suharto.

The success of the strategy depended partly on good luck, as highly productive new agricultural technology became available in the late 1960s, just as the country was implementing its economic strategy and rural investments. In the 1980s foreign direct investment (FDI) arrived from northeast Asia, just as Indonesia needed to restructure its manufacturing sector to be more labor intensive and export oriented.

Bad luck has also been important. The drought that struck the country in 1997 was the worst in a century; the Asian financial crisis caught Indonesia particularly ill-equipped to fix rapidly its badly flawed system of corporate governance; and the collapse of the Suharto regime in 1998 left no political institutions in place for efficient public governance. The transition to democracy has been rapid, but economic growth has not returned to previous high levels.

Long-term overall distribution of household expenditures in Indonesia has changed relatively little; the average Gini coefficient is about 0.33 (compared with about 0.32 for India, 0.45 for the Philippines and Thailand, and 0.50 for Malaysia). The Gini does change somewhat during short periods, reflecting changes in variables that affect how well the poor connect to economic growth. This short-run variance in the growth elasticity of poverty is caused mostly by changes in real rice prices, but these changes are largely driven by macroeconomic policy, especially control of inflation and management of the real exchange rate, and by rice import policy. Over the long run, the income growth of the poor has depended almost entirely on overall income growth.

The interaction between macroeconomic policy and poverty reduction is especially important in Indonesia because of the relatively smooth interface between the tradable and nontradable sectors (and between the formal and informal economies). Rapidly rising demand for the goods and services produced by the nontradable, informal sector, especially in rural areas, has been an important short-run mechanism for pulling people out of poverty. The close integration of rural and urban labor markets, facilitated by rural financial market intermediation, especially on Java, has made economic growth pro-poor.

Investments in agricultural infrastructure have also had a major impact. When productivity-enhancing agricultural technology was available and profitable—from the late 1960s through the mid-1980s—growth could be "strongly" pro-poor (rapid growth with improving income distribution). Much of the rural infrastructure was built using labor-intensive techniques. The jobs created were "self-targeted" to the poor because of the low wages paid, a conscious government policy. Thus investments in rural infrastructure were doubly pro-poor.

Financing for these projects came mostly from the central government, whose budget until the early 1980s depended heavily on two sources of revenue: donor funding in the early years (especially from the World Bank) and oil revenues after the mid-1970s. The 1970s saw the most massive rural investments, and these provided the foundation for broadly based rural development. But large oil revenues also caused "Dutch Disease" in the mid-1970s, which in Indonesia's case was especially anti-poor. At the time, the poor depended heavily on tradable agriculture as the driver of income growth in the rural economy. Only the preemptive devaluation in November 1978 put the economy back on a path of pro-poor growth.

"Pro-poor" public expenditures and targeted subsidies to the poor have played a minor role in poverty reduction in Indonesia. Only the labor-intensive public works programs might claim to be sufficiently large, well targeted to the poor, and productive in the creation of rural infrastructure to have linked public expenditures to poverty reduction and pro-poor economic growth. The direct impact of public expenditures on poverty reduction has been very limited, both because of small sums and poor targeting.

The political economy of pro-poor growth is now complicated by the transition to democracy and the absence of effective institutions to insulate economic policy making from populist rhetoric. The country has been through massive upheavals since 1998, including decentralization of political and economic authority to the district level in 2001. Nonetheless, the country has survived and even recovered economic growth at a modest pace. But effective leadership will be needed to reestablish rapid growth and a strong connection to the poor.

Indonesia's Pro-Poor Growth in Historical Perspective

Indonesia has long been a laboratory for understanding the long-run interactions among markets, politics, and institutions in determining the rate of poverty reduction (Boeke 1946). First, market-driven processes determine the proximate distribution of consumption-based equity. Next, political processes, and the engagement of the poor in these processes, determine the policy framework in which all markets work. Finally, institutions dominate in determining the long-run conditions of governance in which both markets and politics operate. Long periods are needed to observe and identify these complex interactions, especially because sustained economic growth is the main vehicle for poverty reduction.

Indonesia has experimented with all three of the basic poverty reduction approaches. Under President Sukarno, most attention was on redistributive measures, including efforts at a systematic land reform in 1960. After 1967, the focus shifted under the "New Order" regime of President Suharto to active implementation of pro-poor growth strategies because, in the famous words of one of the economic technocrats who came to power in the late 1960s, "There is nothing to re-distribute; we have to make the pie bigger." Under the democratic governments in power since 1999, most of the effort to help the poor has been through direct fiscal transfers involving loosely targeted distribution of rice, school vouchers, and cards granting access to health facilities.

Only the pro-poor growth strategy, implemented after 1967, has sustained any progress in reducing poverty. Indonesia is one of the few developing countries that consciously attempted to design and implement a strategy of pro-poor growth over many years. Although the terminology at the time did not include "pro-poor growth," planners sought to use economic growth to reach the poor, especially in rural areas, and this effort quickly became a key objective of the New Order government of President Suharto. The political economy behind this commitment has been the object of much speculation and analysis, but the results speak for themselves.

The first reliable data on income distribution were not collected until 1967, and the first estimate of poverty levels was made in 1976. Since then a large, nationally representative, high-quality expenditure survey (SUSENAS, or national socioeconomic survey) has been conducted every three years, and it has attracted extensive analytical (and political) attention (for example, Ravallion and Huppi 1991). The story told by the survey is little short of amazing: between 1967 and 1996, income per capita increased by 5 percent per year. The incomes of the bottom quintile of the income distribution—incomes of individuals who lived below the national poverty line until the 1990s and who still subsist on less than $2 per day—grew at the same rate (or possibly slightly faster).

The distribution of household expenditures has been remarkably stable and even; the overall Gini coefficient has stayed within a narrow range, between 0.31 and 0.36. Rural inequality has actually declined significantly since the 1970s, when access to unequally distributed land allowed substantial benefits to be reaped from the Green Revolution. By the mid-1980s, however, the labor market became the primary determinant of income in rural areas and thus drove rural income inequality down. The financial crisis sharply lowered inequality, as urban real estate and financial markets collapsed, but the dramatic reduction in GDP—over 13 percent in 1998 alone—caused poverty rates to triple. Only after 2002 did poverty rates return to their previous lows observed in 1996. They did not return to the trend rate of decline that was disrupted in 1998 until 2004.

For Indonesia, the main economic growth story is clearly about overall growth rates rather than dramatic changes in income distribution. Even when viewed from the perspective of the worst years of the past three decades—1996 to 2002—the growth incidence curve is remarkably flat and pro-poor. A surprising "anti-rich" tail in the top 10 percent of the income distribution was perhaps caused by the depth of the financial crisis and its lasting effect on the portfolios of the wealthy. But overall, even during these difficult years, the poor have done quite well in terms of protecting their real incomes (see figure 2.1).

But focusing analysis solely on growth would miss two important parts of the story. First, short-term episodes of significant income distribution change have occurred (see figure 2.2). Second, the relatively stable long-run

Figure 2.1 *Indonesia's Growth Incidence Curve, 1996–2002*

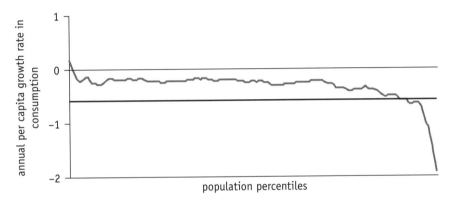

Source: Alatas, Arulpragasam, and McCulloch 2004.
Note: For further growth curves and calculations of pro-poor growth for subperiods, see annex 4 of the full country study (Timmer 2005b).

Figure 2.2 *Income Growth for Bottom Quintile Plotted against Growth for Average Per Capita Incomes, Indonesia, 1967–2002*

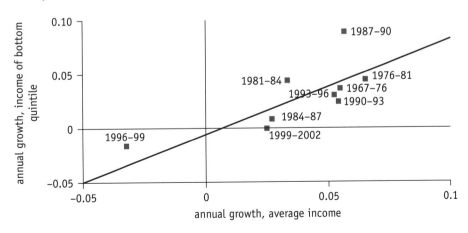

Source: Timmer 2004.

distributional outcome is arguably a result of conscious efforts by policy makers to correct for any tendencies of distribution to worsen significantly (Afiff 2004; Prawiro 1998). If so, the mechanisms that generate stability of income distribution are just as interesting for pro-poor growth strategies as would be the mechanisms that lead to rapid changes in distribution.

Indonesia's experience with pro-poor growth was very much the outgrowth of conscious policy attention to achieving precisely such growth. The task was extraordinarily difficult, as it began in 1967 with a wrecked economy, hyperinflation, an absence of effective political or legal institutions, and a hostile regional environment dominated by the war in Vietnam:

> ... Indonesia's record may have wider lessons. Most obviously, it shows what can be achieved despite unfavorable initial conditions, some weak institutions, and flawed microeconomic policies. Given that the country grew rapidly for three decades, so that per capital GDP rose more than fourfold, it is clear that the necessary conditions for successful economic development are not quite as demanding as often suggested. (Temple 2001)

The weak starting conditions significantly influenced how economic planners approached the task of linking growth to the poor. In retrospect, it appears that they designed a three-tiered strategy for pro-poor growth that linked sound macroeconomic policy to market activities that were facilitated by progressively lower transactions costs, which in turn were linked to household decisions about labor supply, agricultural production, and investment in the nontradable economy (see figure 2.3). The rate of poverty reduction driven by this strategy then depended on the pace of growth in GDP, which was a function of macroeconomic policy (and the external environment), and on the extent to which poor households were connected to this growth.

That connection depended on the array of assets controlled by the poor: their labor, human capital, social capital, and other forms of capital, including access to credit. Those dimensions could also be influenced by appropriate government policies, especially in health and education, which fostered human capital investments by the poor. Thus the "road to pro-poor growth" started from desperately poor economic conditions, weak institutions, and a decade of political instability. It seemed that everything needed to be done at once. The key was to focus on restarting and then sustaining rapid economic growth, empowering poor households to enter the market economy, and reducing the costs and risks of doing so by investments to lower transactions costs. If all this appears obvious now, it was not so at the time (IBRD 1968; Prawiro 1998; Thee 2003). Perhaps more to the point, the issue was not what to do but how to do it. The historical record provides important guidelines for implementing a pro-poor growth strategy.

Figure 2.3 *Road to Pro-Poor Growth*

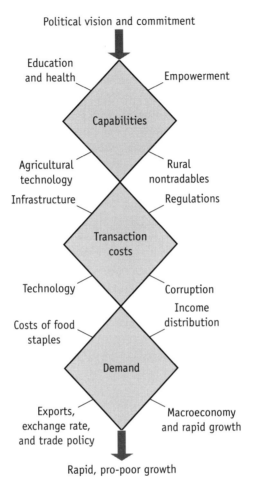

Source: Timmer 2004.

The "New Order" Government of Suharto

In its early, pre-OPEC years (1966–73), the Suharto government needed to establish stability and consolidate political power.[1] In this process, the food logistics agency (Bulog) played an important role in stabilizing rice prices, as did donors, especially in providing food aid. Major investments were made to stimulate agriculture: irrigation rehabilitation, the introduction of high-yielding varieties of rice from the International Rice Research Institute (IRRI), fertilizer imports and distribution, and the BIMAS program of extension and farm credits. Because median farm size was less than a hectare, rice intensification had widespread benefits, although larger farmers (those who cultivate about one hectare of land) benefited the most in the early years, leading to concerns about a skewing of rural income distribution (Afiff and Timmer 1971; Collier and Sajogyo 1972).

Macroeconomic stability was achieved through a balanced budget and donor-provided foreign borrowing, with all proceeds going to the Development Budget (Hill 1996; IBRD 1968). Poverty fell rapidly as the economy stabilized and grew 5 to 6 percent per year in per capita terms, and as food production and overall food supplies rose sharply. Still, absolute poverty was thought to be about 60 percent in 1970. The first official poverty estimates, based on the 1976 SUSENAS, indicate a national poverty rate of about 40 percent.

Even for an oil exporter, coping with high oil prices (1973–83) is not the luxury it might appear. To be sure, the economy expanded as the role of the state expanded, but much of this growth was in inefficient public sector investments. Accompanying the real appreciation of the rupiah was declining profitability of tradable goods production, especially in agriculture (Warr 1984). During the mid-1970s income inequalities and severe poverty in rural areas appeared to be growing, although the regional and commodity dimensions of the poverty masked its macroeconomic roots.

Income distribution deteriorated sharply between 1976 and 1978, confirming growing anxieties (see table 2.1). To improve income distribution and maintain rapid growth, the technocrats took a highly original approach to what was then diagnosed as "Dutch Disease." Devaluation of the rupiah in November 1978 came as a big surprise to financial markets. Afterward, tradable goods production recovered rapidly, especially in agriculture. Poverty rates fell after 1978, driven by a significant recovery in the share of income garnered by the bottom 40 percent of the distribution.

Politics clearly played a major role in these policy responses, despite the authoritarian nature of the Suharto regime. After the 1974 Malari riots, ostensibly in response to a visit by the Japanese prime minister but in fact a reaction to the visibly widening income distribution, especially in urban areas, the government responded. First, it brutally put down the riots and imprisoned the student leaders. Then it mounted a serious effort to figure out how to make the economy more equitable. The result, stimulated as well by the World Food Crisis in 1973–74, was a major shift in priorities toward rural development and a push toward increasing domestic rice production. Behind this push was the stabilization objective as well as the equity objective. To lose control of the rice economy was to lose control of what mattered to Indonesian society.

Table 2.1 Income Distribution and the Share of the Poor in National Income, 1964/65–2002

Year	Gini			Percentage of national income shared by poorest 40 percent		
	Urban	Rural	National	Urban	Rural	National
1964/65	0.34	0.35	0.35	n.a.	n.a.	n.a.
1970	0.33	0.34	0.35	19.5	19.6	18.6
1975	n.a.	n.a.	n.a.	n.a.	n.a.	n.a.
1976	0.35	0.31	0.34	19.6	21.2	19.6
1977	n.a.	n.a.	n.a.	n.a.	n.a.	n.a.
1978	0.38	0.34	0.38	17.4	19.9	18.1
1979	n.a.	n.a.	n.a.	n.a.	n.a.	n.a.
1980	0.36	0.31	0.34	18.7	21.2	19.6
1981	0.33	0.29	0.33	20.8	22.8	20.4
1982	n.a.	n.a.	n.a.	n.a.	n.a.	n.a.
1983	n.a.	n.a.	n.a.	n.a.	n.a.	n.a.
1984	0.32	0.28	0.33	20.6	22.3	20.8
1985	n.a.	n.a.	n.a.	n.a.	n.a.	n.a.
1986	n.a.	n.a.	n.a.	n.a.	n.a.	n.a.
1987	0.32	0.26	0.32	21.5	24.3	20.9
1988	n.a.	n.a.	n.a.	n.a.	n.a.	n.a.
1989	n.a.	n.a.	n.a.	n.a.	n.a.	n.a.
1990	0.34	0.25	0.32	19.7	24.4	21.3
1991	n.a.	n.a.	n.a.	n.a.	n.a.	n.a.
1992	n.a.	n.a.	n.a.	n.a.	n.a.	n.a.
1993	0.33	0.26	0.34	20.5	25.1	20.3
1994	n.a.	n.a.	n.a.	n.a.	n.a.	n.a.
1995	n.a.	n.a.	n.a.	n.a.	n.a.	n.a.
1996	0.36	0.27	0.36	19.0	23.2	20.3
1997	n.a.	n.a.	n.a.	n.a.	n.a.	n.a.
1998	n.a.	n.a.	n.a.	n.a.	n.a.	n.a.
1999	0.32	0.24	0.31	21.5	25.0	21.7
2000	n.a.	n.a.	n.a.	n.a.	n.a.	n.a.
2001	n.a.	n.a.	n.a.	n.a.	n.a.	n.a.
2002	0.33	0.25	0.33	20.3	25.8	20.9

Source: Assembled by Papanek (2004) from Badan Pusat Statistik (BPS) data.
Note: n.a.=not available.

Table 2.2 Percentage of Employment by Major Sector, Urban and Rural Areas, Formal and Informal Sectors, Indonesia, 1986–2004

	Distribution				Growth rates		
					1986/87–	1996/97–	1999/00–
	1986/87	1996/97	1999/00	2003/04	1996/97	1999/00	2003/04
All sectors							
Agriculture	55	43	44	45	−0.4	2.3	1.5
Manufacturing	8	13	13	13	6.5	1.8	−0.7
Other	37	45	43	42	4.2	−0.3	1.2
Total	100	100	100	100	2.2	1.1	1.1
Nonagricultural							
Urban	42	53	59	64	7.0	3.9	2.2
Rural: nonfarm	58	47	41	36	2.5	−4.6	−1.5
	100	100	100	100	4.6	0.2	0.8
Wage	46	50	48	44	5.5	−1.0	−1.5
Nonwage	54	50	52	56	3.9	1.3	2.8
	100	100	100	100	4.6	0.2	0.8
Total employment (000)	69.370	86.376	89.321	93.266			

Source: Adapted from Alisjahbana and Manning forthcoming.

The restructuring of Indonesia's development approach after 1974, and especially the preemptive devaluation of the rupiah in 1978, signaled the government's determination to include the poor in the development process. The stability of the Gini coefficient seen from the late 1960s to the present should not be taken as the result of market-driven forces in the face of given technology, but rather as a conscious government effort, led from the macroeconomic arena by the technocrats but blessed by the president, to stimulate what is now called pro-poor growth (Timmer 2004).

By the early 1980s the oil boom was over. Restructuring of the economy in response to low commodity prices in world markets became necessary from 1983 to 1993. Agriculture continued to grow, and rice prices were stable (this stability amounted to protection against the low prices in world markets). The government pursued aggressive exchange rate protection through further rupiah devaluations in 1983 and 1986 (Hill 1996; Thorbecke

1995). Massive investments in rural infrastructure from earlier oil revenues began to pay off in higher production and in lower transactions costs for marketed goods (and improved labor mobility). Industrial output, led by labor-intensive manufactured exports, surged in the latter part of the period.

The manufacturing sector contributed 29.2 percent of the growth in GDP between 1987 and 1992, a radical increase from the 10 percent contributed during the recovery from 1967 to 1973, and most of this increase came from labor-intensive subsectors such as shoes, garments, and electronics assembly (Hill 1996). Large-scale and sustained economic deregulation led to better incentives for exports, and these incentives were matched by incentives for FDI. Manufactured exports responded even faster than policy makers had hoped and contributed almost *half* of all exports by 1992, up dramatically from the 3 percent in 1980. The fortuitous "push" in FDI from Japan and the "pull" from the attractive climate in Indonesia thus allowed manufactured exports to play a significant role in employment generation by the end of the 1980s.

Importance of the Nontradable Economy

The nontradable economy, which is not directly reflected in national income accounts, also experienced a boom. When the export economy was flourishing in the late 1980s and early 1990s, and overall GDP was growing by nearly 7 percent per year, roughly half of that growth was made up of nontradable goods and services. According to the Mellor model of poverty reduction (Mellor 2000), production of nontradable goods and services, especially in rural areas, provides the economic link between higher incomes from both agriculture and manufacturing wages, and pulls people out of underemployment in rural areas—and out of poverty.

The Mellor model stresses the role of producing rural nontradables that are locally consumed—processed foods, construction, trade, and small-scale manufactures—as the "ladder" for underemployed workers in agriculture to begin the climb to modern jobs at higher wages. In most poor, rural economies this nontradable sector is demand constrained. That is, expanding the sector, and the number of jobs it creates, does not depend on better access to capital or to management skills, but on greater purchasing power among local consumers. Thus Mellor emphasizes rising profitability of agriculture—through higher productivity, not higher prices. Higher prices for agricultural output, especially food, do not contribute much to added demand for nontradable goods and services because the higher prices choke off demand for nonfood items except from farmers with significant surpluses to sell. The growing wages of workers in a rapidly expanding manufacturing export sector also contribute to higher demand for the output from the nontradables sector (if the wages are not all spent on imports).

This Mellor model is basically a three-sector version of the standard Lewis model of the dual economy. In Mellor's version there are two "commercial" sectors—industry and agriculture. The latter has come to use modern technology and is market driven, a departure from the traditional rural economy envisioned by Lewis (1954). Relatively separate from the commercial sectors is the "nontradable" sector, which is informal and mostly rural. The two commercial sectors are the "engines of growth" because of their potential for rapid productivity gains. Connecting them to the "nontradable" sector, however, is the key to a high "elasticity of connection" between overall economic growth and rapid poverty reduction. This sector is the one in which most of the poor make a living (Timmer 1997, 2002). Unless demand from rising incomes in the commercial sectors spills over to this nontradables sector, the poor tend to be left out of the growth process.

The combined boom in agriculture, manufacturing, and nontradables meant the period from the late 1970s to the mid-1990s was one of the most "pro-poor growth" episodes in modern economic history. This result is a surprise to many. The extensive economic restructuring that took place in the 1980s was expected to create widespread unemployment and lead to lower wages for unskilled labor.[2] Instead, agricultural growth continued, labor-intensive exports surged, and poverty continued to decline throughout the period of restructuring (Ravallion and Huppi 1991).[3]

End of the Run of Pro-Poor Growth

Corruption and increasing distortions in resource allocation from 1993 to 1998 followed the interests of the Suharto family, especially the children (and grandchildren). These interests distorted trade policy and public sector investments and had visible effects on competitiveness, which were partly masked by the inflow of FDI (Cole and Slade 1996). As the economy boomed, deregulation lost steam, first in the Bulog commodities, then more broadly. Productivity growth in the overall economy rapidly deteriorated.[4]

The three decades of superb economic results were over. The Asian financial crisis hit in late 1997. Investors started to lose confidence in the ability of the Suharto government to cope, especially after the new cabinet, packed with Suharto cronies and relatives, was named in April 1998. The crisis caused a massive depreciation of the rupiah, which eventually led to chaos in the domestic rice market (Schydlowsky 2000). Spiraling rice prices late in 1998 led to huge increases in poverty, which is estimated to have reached over 30 percent of the population by the peak in late 1998 or early 1999. Thus began a dismal period for economic growth and poverty reduction (see figure 2.2).

When the Asian financial crisis hit in 1997 and President Suharto was forced to resign in 1998 in the face of widespread rioting, the country was entirely unprepared in either political or institutional terms to cope with the rapid changes needed in corporate and public governance. Four presidents later, the country appears to be resolutely embarked on a democratic political path. In 2004 Indonesia held its first direct presidential election, which resulted in the largest one-day voter turnout in world history. The current president (Susilo Bambang Yudhoyono) was inaugurated in October 2004.

Representative democracy has brought a new political economy of economic policy. Populist voices ostensibly speak on behalf of the poor. An important test is under way to determine whether Indonesia's pro-poor growth experience under a highly centralized and politically dominant regime put down sustainable, even irreversible, roots, or whether the very foundations of the strategy will come undone under political challenge (MacIntyre 2001).

Why Economic Growth in Indonesia Has Been So Pro-Poor

From a policy perspective, Indonesia's pro-poor growth record after the late 1960s presents two puzzles. First, what measures turned around the *overall* rate of growth after the Suharto regime took power? Second, in view of the initial equitable distribution of income (almost inevitable because nearly everyone was desperately poor), how did policy makers ensure that the poor were connected to this growth and that income distribution did not deteriorate significantly?

Agriculture specifically, and the rural economy more broadly, play a key role in answering both questions. The availability of new seed technology from IRRI sharply raised the potential productivity of Indonesia's millions of small-scale rice farmers. The initial spurt of growth after 1967 was led by agriculture. This growth was especially pro-poor, because food supplies increased significantly and with income growth widely distributed, food intake also rose sharply, raising millions above the poverty line (defined in terms of food energy intake) in just a few years. The rural economy continued to play an equalizing role even when it was no longer the main source of growth, and massive investments in rural infrastructure both absorbed rural labor and stimulated further productivity gains (McCawley 2002). The key to rapid, pro-poor growth was constant attention to keeping labor-intensive activities profitable. Until the 1980s, most of these activities were in the rural economy, so a focus on rural growth was also a focus on labor-intensive growth. After the mid-1980s, managing the labor intensity of economic growth became more complicated.

Growth Drivers and How They Changed over Time

Economic growth since the mid-1960s can be traced to three major sources: economic recovery and rehabilitation of the existing capital stock and infrastructure; rapid growth in agricultural productivity because of new technology and massive new investments in rural infrastructure; and, eventually, the emergence of a dominant manufacturing sector, stimulated by FDI and exports (Rock 2002).[5]

As standard growth theory would suggest, all three sources of growth drew on the abundance of unskilled labor in Indonesia (Manning 1998). A high labor intensity of output, on average and at the margin, characterized the most pro-poor episodes of Indonesia's growth. When labor intensity slipped, and the capital-output ratio rose, poverty reduction slowed dramatically, as was the case in the mid-1970s, during the oil boom. But from the late 1960s to the early 1990s, the "secret" of Indonesia's pro-poor growth was the labor intensity of its generally rapid growth. In the 25 years between 1967 and 1992, Indonesia's population grew 2.1 percent per year, total GDP (in real rupiahs) grew by 6.7 percent per year, and employment grew by 3.0 percent per year. As best the data can say, poverty rates fell from roughly two-thirds of the population to less than an eighth.

Since the early 1990s, and especially since the crisis in 1998, the story has been quite different (Islam 2002). From 1990 to 1997, overall GDP continued to grow rapidly, by 7.0 percent per year, but the Gini coefficient increased from 0.32 in 1990 to 0.36 in 1996. The crisis in 1998 caused GDP to fall by over 13 percent, and growth averaged less than 4 percent per year from 1999 until 2003.

One of the key stories of the crisis is the reversal of long-run structural trends in the Indonesian economy (see table 2.2). From 1990 to 1997, employment in the agriculture, forestry, and fisheries sector declined by 2.3 percent per year, reflecting rapid growth during that period and a successful structural transformation in both the economy and labor force. But employment in agriculture surged 13.3 percent between 1997 and 1998, as many workers in the urban economy returned to their rural families and

Table 2.3 Factors Affecting Changes in the Headcount Index of Poverty

	Annual % change in per capita income	Annual % change in poverty index	Growth elasticity of poverty	Annual % change in real rice prices
1967–76	5.48	−6.0	−1.09	2.5
1976–80	6.37	−8.1	−1.27	−3.5
1980–84	4.23	−6.8	−1.61	3.0
1984–87	2.69	−7.0	−2.60	−2.5
1987–90	5.66	−4.6	−0.81	5.5
1990–93	5.41	−4.6	−0.85	−1.6
1993–96	5.23	−6.2	−1.19	5.8
1996–99	−3.25	9.9	−3.05 (+)	19.2
1999–2002	2.49	−8.2	−3.29	−7.1

Source: Timmer 2005b.

Note: The growth elasticity of poverty (GEP) is calculated as the ratio of the percentage reduction in the headcount poverty index relative to the percentage change in per capita incomes (in $PPP) from the World Bank Database on Pro-Poor Growth. An OLS regression of GEP on the change in the real rice price (DRRP) explains 80 percent of the variance in GEP, with highly significant coefficients. The results are as follows (*t*-statistics in parentheses):

$$\text{GEP} = -1.57 + 0.209\ \text{DRRP} \qquad R\text{-squared} = 0.8325 \qquad (1)$$
$$\phantom{\text{GEP} = }(5.8)\quad(5.9) \qquad\qquad \text{Adj. } R\text{-squared} = 0.8086$$

Alternatively, changes in per capita incomes (DPCI) and in real rice prices can both be used to explain changes in the poverty index (DPI). This specification has the following results:

$$\text{DPI} = -2.42 - 0.853\ \text{DPCI} + 0.445\ \text{DRRP} \qquad R\text{-squared} = 0.9108 \qquad (2)$$
$$\phantom{\text{DPI} = }(1.68)\quad(2.93)\quad\quad(3.95) \qquad\qquad \text{Adj. } R\text{-squared} = 0.8811$$

When the intercept term is constrained to be zero (thus *assuming* there is no exogenous trend in poverty reduction), the result is something of a blend between equations 1 and 2, as equation 3 indicates:

$$\text{DPI} = -1.285\ \text{DPCI} + 0.3205\ \text{DRRP} \qquad R\text{-squared} = \text{na} \qquad (3)$$
$$\phantom{\text{DPI} = }(8.37)\quad\quad(3.36) \qquad\qquad \text{Adj. } R\text{-squared} = \text{na}$$

sought productive employment, even at low wages, or just shared meals and housing. Thus the crisis was not one of massive unemployment, despite the closure of much of the formal banking and industrial sectors, but of falling wages and real incomes. The rural economy was the main safety net for millions of workers previously employed in the urban economy. Without this rural resilience, the impact of the crisis on poverty would have been much deeper.

The second striking trend after the crisis is the growing divergence between the formal and informal economies (Islam 2002). Because minimum wage legislation had minimal impact during the Suharto regime, and mobility of labor was high geographically and across sectors, the formal and informal labor markets had been reasonably well integrated (Agrawal 1995; Mason and Baptist 1996). After the crisis, and in the face of aggressive labor activity and responses from newly democratic regional governments, increases in the minimum wage have led to a substantial divergence between trends in the formal and informal economy (see figure 2.5 in annex 2b in Timmer 2005b).[6] Virtually all of the job growth since 1997, accordingly, has been in the informal sector (Aaron and others 2004; Manning 2000). Employment growth in the formal sector has been negative since 2000, as documented by Alisjahbana and Manning (forthcoming):

> The *first* trend is the slow growth in non-agricultural jobs in general, including non-farm work, both in manufacturing and other sectors since the crisis (Table 2). This is in contrast with rapid employment growth of around 6 and 4 percent respectively during the pre-crisis period of 1986/87 to 1996/97. The bulk of employment growth since crisis has been in the agriculture sector which grew at 2.3 percent over the period of the crisis, and absorbed many of those displaced from non-agricultural work. However, even after the initial recovery period, jobs in agriculture continued to grow almost twice as fast as non-agricultural employment from 1999/2000 onwards (see last column in Table 2).

Finally, the change since 1990 in the composition of manufactured exports according to factor use has been striking. Natural–resource–intensive exports, such as wood and cork products, have declined from a third to a tenth of manufactured exports. Labor-intensive exports have also declined as a share, but their total value has increased impressively, from $5 billion in 1990 to over $11 billion in 2002. Increases in human–capital–intensive and technology-intensive exports also have been substantial. Exports of telecommunications and electrical machinery showed especially large increases. These export areas are directly competitive with China's growing capacity. Further growth will require serious attention to reducing costs and improving productivity, and both tasks have proven difficult historically.

Growth Elasticity of Poverty

The strength of economic growth's connection to the poor varies substantially in the short run. The impact of rice prices on short-run poverty levels is dramatic, as might be expected for a commodity that still makes up half the average Indonesian's food energy intake (see table 2.3). For each of nine growth episodes from 1967 to 2002 (episodes for which reasonably comparable SUSENAS data are available), the growth elasticity of poverty (GEP) is calculated as the annual percentage change in the headcount poverty index relative to the annual change in real per capita incomes. The simple average of the absolute values of GEP for the nine periods is 1.75, well above the East Asia and Pacific average of 1.00 reported by Besley and Burgess (2003). By this measure, Indonesia's post-1967 growth record has been especially pro-poor (Kraay 2004).

The GEP also varies a great deal, as it ranges from a low of 0.81 in the 1987–90 period, to a high of 3.29 from 1999 to 2002. Much of this variance is explained by changes in domestic rice prices during each growth episode, as is shown in table 2.3. A simple regression that explains GEP as a function of an intercept term (1.57) and changes in the real price of rice (coefficient of −0.21, with a *t*-statistic of 5.9), explains over 80 percent of the variance in GEP between 1967 and 2002 (see equation 1 in table 2.3). Even if the observation for 1996 to 1999, during the worst of the financial crisis, is dropped, the regression explains over 40 percent of the (much-reduced) variance. These results indicate the pro-poor nature of economic growth in Indonesia but also the vulnerability of the poor to instability in their economic environment, particularly in incomes and the price of their major foodstuff.

Regional Incidence of Poverty

Disaggregating the incidence of poverty geographically is important, because much of Indonesia's growth story is regional. Differences in agricultural potential and efficiency of market connections are the basic causes of geographical variance in poverty rates. One striking difference is between urban and rural areas. Four times as many poor people live in rural areas as in urban areas, despite the rapid urbanization of the population over the past four decades. Java, however, contains 75 percent of the urban poor and just 55 percent of the rural poor. Diverse job opportunities are available on densely settled Java that are not available to rural households on the Outer Islands. The importance of good infrastructure to connect rural households to nonfarm employment opportunities is reflected in these numbers. Provision of good infrastructure in areas with low population densities is equally important.

The dominance of Java in the total numbers of poor people, and of the Eastern Islands in poverty incidence, is readily apparent. Java has 59.9 percent of the poor and a poverty incidence of 15.3 percent. Eastern Indonesia (excluding Maluku and Papua) has 9 percent of the poor but a poverty incidence of 36.9 percent. Strategies for reducing poverty must cope with this obvious bimodal distribution of the problem.[7]

The bimodality of poverty stems from the success of economic growth on Java compared with the lagging growth in eastern Indonesia. In the 1960s and 1970s, poverty was concentrated on Java in both absolute terms and in incidence. In the mid-1960s, some districts in central Java would have been among the most impoverished anywhere in the world (Timmer 1975). Today, this region of Java is exporting handcrafted furniture to demanding markets in the West.

Sectoral Growth and Poverty Reduction

Early work by Ravallion and Huppi (covering the entire Indonesian economy for the 1984 to 1987 period) and recent work at the provincial level for the period from 1984 to 1996 by Sudarno Sumarto and Asep Suryhadi of the Social Monitoring and Early Response Unit highlight the powerful impact of growth in agricultural productivity on the reduction of poverty. Linking sectoral growth patterns to a long-run reduction in poverty is controversial, because mobile factors of production should make the overall growth rate the ultimate determinant.[8] Formal analysis of the Indonesia-specific dimensions of the role of agriculture and the rural economy in the country's generally successful record on poverty reduction date to Ravallion and Huppi (1991), although much of the earlier work in the late 1960s and early 1970s, which the Agricultural Development Council sponsored through the Agro-Economic Survey based at the Bogor Institute of Agriculture (Institut Pertanian Bogor), addressed this broad theme as well (Collier and Sajogyo 1972).

More recently, Timmer (1996b, 1997, 2002), Warr (2002), and Sumarto and Suryhadi (2003) have examined the contribution of growth in the agricultural sector to poverty reduction. Warr's results, which explain aggregate poverty rates in East Asia (Taiwan), Southeast Asia (Indonesia, Malaysia, the Philippines, and Thailand), and South Asia (India), revealed that the southeast Asian countries depend mostly on agricultural and services growth for poverty reduction. Growth had no significant impact on the industrial sector.

Sumarto and Suryhadi (2003) pursued this sectoral disaggregation of the sources of poverty reduction. They used panel data at the provincial level from 1984 to 1996 to examine the local poverty impact according to the sector of growth in the province. The results are startling: agricultural growth accounts for most of the reduction in poverty. Roughly two-thirds of the reduction observed during the period of fastest growth in manufactured exports was due to growth in agricultural output at the provincial level. This result is surprising. Most observers thought that agriculture's key role had been played in the previous two decades and that the "engine of growth and poverty alleviation" had passed to manufacturing (Papanek 2004). The manufacturing export boom had a *direct* impact on only a handful of provinces—all of them on Java. At the local level, the direct impact on poverty probably continued to come through the local agricultural economy.

Human Capital and Gender

As illustrated in figure 2.3, investments in human capital were a core component of raising the capabilities of the poor. Gross enrollment rates in primary school increased from about 70 percent of the eligible age group in the mid-1960s to 86 percent in the mid-1970s. Nearly all eligible students now finish primary school. Similarly, under-five child mortality declined from 91 per 1,000 in 1990 to 41 per 1,000 in 2003. Naturally, the education and health indicators have both a supply and a demand element. With the state making massive investments in rural schools and health clinics, local residents were able to make their own investments in their children.

On the international stage, profiles of poverty by gender indicate that important differences remain in several areas, including literacy. Gender and poverty is not the major issue in Indonesia that it is in Africa, the Middle East, or parts of Asia. Net primary school enrollment rates reached gender parity in 2002, a significant improvement from the 78:67 ratio of males to females in the 1970–75 period. Female life expectancy continues to outdistance that of males. The gap has grown from three years (53 versus 50) in the 1970–75 period to four years (69 versus 65) in 2002. Important exceptions to this good record include maternal mortality rates. The 373 maternal deaths per 100,000 live births are high by regional standards and even by the standard of Indonesia's average income level.

Implementing a Strategy of Pro-Poor Growth

Because global inflation was high and the United States was deeply engaged in Vietnam, the external environment was not particularly hospitable when the Suharto government started designing and implementing its economic policies in the late 1960s. But this environment permitted the Indonesian government to develop its own strategy for economic growth. Thus Indonesia had substantial "policy space" (Rodrik 2004). Because neither Suharto nor the technocrats had any experience in policy making, they had to design the mechanisms of economic governance almost from scratch and to put in place a workable set of relationships and division of responsibilities. Despite a surprising "constitutionalism" in Suharto's approach to governing, the government made no serious effort to open economic governance into a more democratic process (Liddle 1991, 1996).

In retrospect, the pro-poor strategy encompassed the three basic levels shown in figure 2.3. Macroeconomic policy was directly in the hands of the technocrats and, as always, they sought to maximize the overall rate of economic growth. This rate was subject to maintaining stability, however, so controlling inflation through fiscal and monetary discipline was also important. The exchange rate was an instrument of policy, not an objective except in the very short run. Policy makers managed the rate to maintain the profitability of producing tradable goods, especially in agriculture (Thorbecke 1995). Active management of the exchange rate was especially important in dealing with "Dutch Disease" (Warr 1984).

Such a growth-oriented macroeconomic policy should call forth investments from the private sector that become the actual engine of economic growth, but the institutional foundations for rapid expansion of the private sector in Indonesia were not in place until the reforms of the 1980s. A more active public role was deemed necessary to stimulate appropriate investments. Apart from the mid-1970s, during the peak of the oil boom, the public role was not primarily investments in state enterprises but rather in the supporting infrastructure, soft and hard, for private sector enterprises.

These investments in infrastructure lowered the costs of market connections that generated jobs and raised the productivity of the poor. Indeed, public sector investments and regulatory improvements to lower transaction costs as an approach to market development are arguably the crucial link between growth-oriented macroeconomic policy and widespread participation by poor households in the market economy. In Indonesia these investments were in roads (especially farm-to-market roads), communications networks, market infrastructure and ports, and irrigation and water systems. Many of the projects were built as labor-intensive public works, making millions of jobs available to unskilled labor willing to work at local market wages (Papanek 2004).

Directly measuring transaction costs is difficult, especially because the costs and risks of engaging in market exchanges are to a large degree

Table 2.4 Roads and Trucks in Indonesia, 1939–98

Year	Kilometers of roads (all conditions, 000 km)	Number of trucks registered (all sizes), 000 vehicles	Trucks per km of road
1939	75.1	~60.0	0.80
1960	80.8	75.5	0.93
1965	83.2	83.8	1.01
1970	84.3	102.3	1.21
1977	122.8	279.0	2.27
1993	344.9	1160.5	3.36
1998	355.4	1592.6	4.48
Average annual percentage increase			
1939–60	0.3	1.1	0.7
1960–70	0.4	3.1	2.7
1970–98	8.3	16.5	7.5

Sources: Statistical Pocketbook of Indonesia, various issues, and author's calculations.

perceptual. But some rough statistics illustrate the commitment of the government, in policy terms and budget revenues, to reducing transaction costs. For example, statistics on the kilometers of roads and the number of registered trucks are available and on the "density" of trucks for many years before and during the Suharto era can be calculated (see table 2.4).

Virtually no progress was made in road building between the waning years of the Dutch administration and the early years of the Suharto regime. Average annual increases in kilometers of roads were just 0.3 percent per year between 1939 and 1960, and 0.4 percent from 1960 to 1970. Investment in new trucks was modest between 1960 and 1970; virtually all of it occurred after 1965. Transformation of Indonesia's network of highways took off and accelerated through the 1990s. Kilometers of total roads expanded 8.3 percent per year between 1970 and 1998. Not shown in table 2.4 (because earlier breakdowns are not available) is a surge in "local" roads after the late 1970s. These roads would have been mostly farm-to-market roads. They expanded from 8,500 kilometers in 1977 to 31,900 kilometers in 1998.

Investments in trucks show a similar, but even more dramatic, surge after 1970. The total number of registered trucks increased by 16.5 percent per year. This explosion in the truck population increased the "density" of trucks on highways from just 1 truck per kilometer in 1965 to 4.48 trucks per kilometer in 1998. The capacity to move goods around the country was radically transformed in two decades, and that component of transaction costs was lowered.

A similar story can be told about communications costs. In 1990 nearly 77 million domestic long-distance telephone calls were placed, an increase of 13 percent per year from the 7.58 million calls placed in 1971. After a restructuring of calling services in 1989–90 that made most calls "local" instead of long distance, the number of local calls increased by more than 25 percent per year through 1997; in that year it totaled 50 billion (or 250 calls for every man, woman, and child in Indonesia). Through investment in a modern telecommunications system, Indonesia made the communications component of transactions easy and reliable.

The final component of transaction costs involves the risks of doing business. These risks range from normal market fluctuations that all businesses face, to the prospect of expropriation or demand for "special fees" when a business becomes visibly successful. Lack of transparency, highly corrupt rule of law, and lucrative opportunities handed to Suharto's children and cronies obviously raised the cost of doing business for legitimate firms. On this count, the Suharto regime appears to have *raised* transaction costs.

Market engagement raises another element of risk: whether price behavior is reasonably predictable and price margins are within normal business costs. Because of the Suharto regime's emphasis on price stability, most day-to-day business activities became more predictable—hence less risky. A farmer could sell rice during the harvest and be confident that, six months later, rice would be available for purchase in the market at a reasonable price. A trader could buy and store rice and be pretty sure that price behavior would provide normal returns to storage. Urban consumers did not have to hoard rice in anticipation of unexpected shortages. The rice market in particular, and most commodity trading in general, became routine and operated on relatively thin margins (Timmer 1996a). Lower transportation and communications costs contributed greatly to these lower transaction costs, but so too did an environment of lower risks from normal market activities.

Lower transaction costs mean more market opportunities and faster economic growth, but they also mean easier access for the poor to markets and better connections to economic growth. To ensure that access translates into participation, the capacity of poor households to enter the market economy needs to be enhanced. Investments in human capital—education, public health clinics, and family planning centers—improve the "capabilities" of the poor to connect to rapid economic growth.

There is little evidence that the incidence of public expenditures in these social sectors was deliberately pro-poor. In the early years, the needs were so great that simply building schools and clinics was the first priority. Not surprisingly, the relatively better off took advantage of these facilities and reaped the benefits of the subsidies spent before the poor. But pioneering research by the World Bank has shown that the poor have begun to benefit in very important ways (Lanjouw and others 2001). For both education and health expenditures, the marginal incidence of spending on the poor is substantially higher than the average.

Political Economy and Governance

Why President Suharto's government carried out the pro-poor strategy as aggressively as it did remains a mystery of modern political economy, although a personal concern for the welfare of farmers seems to be at least part of the explanation. This personal engagement may also have inhibited more flexible policies as the economy evolved and matured. Hull (2004) notes the continued tendency of the elite to think of peasants as illiterate, which matched President Suharto's memories of growing up among peasants in rural Central Java. The president's determination that civil servants receive rice in kind, as part of their salaries, extended far beyond the early and sensible justification for the program—local rice markets were thin and subject to highly unstable prices. Thus the personal influence of the president clearly played a major role in the evolution of policy, and this role became counterproductive as Indonesian society became more affluent and sophisticated and as the economy became more complex. Both farmers and civil servants were well equipped to deal with new technologies and market fluctuations, without heavy intervention by the state, by the 1990s.

Part of Suharto's commitment to the rural economy appears to stem from the highly visible politics, and power, of food security. The drive for higher agricultural productivity—a key ingredient in pro-poor growth—was fueled at least in part by the desire for households, and the country, to have more reliable supplies of rice than historically had been available from world markets. When the world rice market quite literally disappeared for several months during the world food crisis in 1973, Indonesia's dependence on imported rice to stabilize domestic prices highlighted its vulnerability to external markets beyond its control—the opposite of food security in the minds of most Indonesians—and showed how important increasing rice production was (Timmer 2000, 2005a). A ratcheting up of policy attention to agriculture and budget support for rural infrastructure followed the traumatic loss of control of rice prices in 1972–73. But here, too, the world has changed. A drive for rice self-sufficiency that made technical and economic sense in the late 1970s and early 1980s would be folly today.

What is next? The political appeal of the new strategy for dealing with poverty—direct fiscal transfers to the poor—is obvious. In principle, these transfers have an immediate and visible impact on the recipients, and the political "pitch" for the programs makes it sound as though the government is actively committed to poverty reduction. Although democracy has probably increased the size and influence of the political coalition concerned about poverty, it has greatly undermined the coalition supporting economic growth as the main mechanism for dealing with poverty. The problem, of course, is not with democracy itself, but with the lack of democratic institutions that provide real accountability of government to constituents. The decentralization that was designed and implemented shortly after Suharto's fall as a device to prevent another centralized political regime has delayed development of these institutions. At the same time, the decentralization is clearly broadening experimentation with different forms of political institutions and mechanisms for accountability.

It should be remembered that Indonesians coped with three massive shocks in the span of just a year. If 1966, in the famous words of President Sukarno, was "the year of living dangerously," what was 1998? The emerging answer is "the year of transformation to a freer and fairer society." This transformation is not the stuff of headlines. The headline grabbers are the Bali and Marriott hotel bombings, judicial ineptitude and outright corruption, human rights abuses by the military, the tsunami disaster in Aceh, and continuing games played by Jakarta's political elite (McBeth 2003).

Little noticed is the steady progress that Indonesia is making. If occasional jabs at foreign companies by local courts still roil investors, the competence of the new constitutional court is unreported. The petty (and not so petty) corruption of newly empowered local governments makes news and is troublesome. But the open competition to create good business environments at the local level might have more long-run impact (Ramage 2004).

Amid the gloom and doom, the historical resilience and successes of Indonesian society need to be appreciated and valued. From a long-term perspective, the Indonesian experience with pro-poor growth provides genuine hope that desperately poor societies can escape from the worst manifestations of their poverty in a generation, provided appropriate policies are followed. This message is critically important for the Indonesia of the future, unsure as the country is over what path to follow during its democratic transition. In its broadest outlines, that path is clear. The three-tiered strategy of growth-oriented macroeconomic policy, linked to product and factor markets through progressively lower transaction costs, which in turn are linked to poor households whose capabilities are being increased by public investments in human capital, is a general model accessible to all countries, including the future Indonesia.

Notes

1. An excellent summary of experience with economic growth from the Suharto era to the present is Hofman, Rodrick-Jones, and Wie (2004). For an "insider's" view of how the technocrats consciously managed both the growth process and its link to poverty reduction, see Afiff (2004). Papanek (2004) assesses the impact on the poor of economic policies under Sukarno and Suharto and the governments that followed the New Order regime.

2. World Bank (1987) notes that ". . . Indonesia's growth rate continues to be extremely low in relation to past performance and barely above the rate of population growth. With the added loss of purchasing power from lower oil prices, the impact on personal incomes and employment was severe" (p. vii).

3. It should be noted that the rice sector in particular was protected from the worst pressures of low prices in world markets, and the substantial rupiah devaluations in 1983 and 1986 enhanced profitability for the rest of the tradable sector.

4. The full story of how the Suharto regime came apart has yet to be told, but Stern (2003, 2004) provides details from the perspective of a long-term advisor to the Ministry of Finance. The regular "Survey of Recent Developments," published in each issue of the *Bulletin of Indonesian Economic Studies,* also provides a blow-by-blow account. Booth's (2002a) comparison of the growth collapses in Indonesia in the 1930s and 1990s provides important historical insights.

5. The best analysis of economic growth during the Suharto era is in Hill (2000). Hofman, Rodrick-Jones, and Wie (2004) describe institutional development and failures over the same period. Because of the size of its lending program in Indonesia, the World Bank has been a close observer of and participant in economic policy making since 1968. The Indonesian Country Assistance Strategy paper (World Bank 2003b) reflects this involvement.

6. The World Bank (2003a) report to the Consultative Group on Indonesia included a table on regional minimum wages for the first time.

7. This problem was stressed as early as the HIID report on poverty for BAPPENAS in 1992 (Timmer, Falcon, Wiebe, and Mason 1992).

8. For an especially thoughtful and technically sophisticated review of this issue on a global scale, see Bravo-Ortega and Lederman (2004). Sarris (2001) and Booth (2002b) also provide useful insights.

References

Aaron, Carl, Lloyd Kenward, Kelly Bird, Mehir Desai, Haryo Aswicahyono, Chatib M. Basri, and Choesni Tubagus. 2004. "Strategic Approaches to Job Creation and Employment in Indonesia." Report prepared for the U.S. Agency for International Development, Jakarta, Indonesia.

Afiff, Saleh. 2004. "Scaling Up Poverty Reduction in Indonesia." Paper presented at "Scaling Up Poverty Reduction," Shanghai, China, May 27–29.

Afiff, Saleh, and C. Peter Timmer. 1971. "Rice Policy in Indonesia." *Food Research Institute Studies in Agricultural Economics, Trade, and Development* 10 (2): 131–59.

Agrawal, Nisha. 1995. "Indonesia: Labor Market Policies and International Competitiveness." Policy Research Working Paper 1515, World Bank, Washington, DC.

Alatas, Vivi, Jehan Arulpragasam, and Neil McCulloch. 2004. "Poverty Rates and Growth Incidence Curves for Indonesia, 1990–2002." Working paper, World Bank, Jakarta, Indonesia.

Alisjahbana, Armida, and Chris Manning. Forthcoming. "Employment, Labour Standards and Flexibility: Getting the Balance Right."

Besley, Timothy, and Robin Burgess. 2003. "Halving Global Poverty." *Journal of Economic Perspectives* 17 (3): 3–22.

Boeke, Jan H. 1946. *The Evolution of the Netherlands Indies Economy.* New York: Institute of Pacific Relations.

———. 2002a. "Growth Collapses in Indonesia: A Comparison of the 1930s and the 1990s." Working paper, School of African and Oriental Studies, University of London, London.

Booth, Anne. 2002b. "Rethinking the Role of Agriculture in the 'East Asian' Model: Why Is Southeast Asia Different from Northeast Asia?" *ASEAN Economic Bulletin* 19 (1): 40–51.

Bravo-Ortega, Claudio, and Daniel Lederman. 2004. "Agriculture and National Welfare around the World: Causality and International Heterogeneity since 1960." Draft paper for the Latin America and Caribbean Region Department, World Bank, Washington, DC.

Bulletin of Indonesian Economic Studies. "Survey of Recent Developments." Various issues.

Cole, David C., and Betty F. Slade. 1996. *Building a Modern Financial System: The Indonesian Experience.* Melbourne: Cambridge University Press.

Collier, William L., and Sajogyo. 1972. "Employment Opportunities Created by the High Yielding Rice Varieties in Several Areas on Java." *Ekonomi dan Keuangan Indonesia* [Economy and Finance in Indonesia] 20 (2): 105–32.

Hill, Hal. 1996. *The Indonesian Economy since 1966.* Cambridge: Cambridge University Press.

———. 2000. *The Indonesian Economy since 1966.* 2nd ed. Cambridge: Cambridge University Press.

Hofman, Bert, Ella Rodrick-Jones, and Thee Kian Wie. 2004. "Indonesia: Rapid Growth; Weak Institutions." Paper prepared for "Scaling Up Poverty Reduction," Shanghai, May 27–29.

Hull, Terence H. 2004. "Indonesia's Demographic Turning Point." Working paper, Australian National University, Canberra, Australia.

IBRD (International Bank for Reconstruction and Development). 1968. "Economic Development in Indonesia: Volume I, Main Report." AS-132a, IRBD, Washington, DC.

Islam, Iyanatul. 2002. "Poverty, Employment and Wages: An Indonesian Perspective." Paper prepared for ILO-JMHLW-Government of Indonesia Seminar on Strengthening Employment and Labour Market Policies for Poverty Alleviation and Economic Recovery in East and Southeast Asia, Jakarta, April 29–May 1.

Kraay, Aart. 2004. "When Is Growth Pro-Poor? Cross-Country Evidence." Policy Research Working Paper 3225, World Bank, Washington, DC.

Lanjouw, Peter, Menno Pradhan, Fadia Saadah, Haneen Sayed, and Robert Sparrow. 2001. "Poverty, Education, and Health in Indonesia: Who Benefits from Public Spending?" Working paper, World Bank, Washington, DC.

Lewis, W. Arthur. 1954. "Economic Development with Unlimited Supplies of Labor." *The Manchester School* 22: 3–42.

Liddle, R. William. 1991. "The Relative Autonomy of the Third World Politician: Suharto and Indonesian Economic Development in Comparative Perspective." *International Studies Quarterly* 35 (4): 403–27.

———. 1996. *Leadership and Culture in Indonesian Politics.* Sydney: Allen and Unwin, in association with the Asian Studies Association of Australia.

MacIntyre, Andrew. 2001. "The Politics of Agricultural Policy-Making: The Importance of Institutions." In *The Evolving Roles of State, Private, and Local Actors in Asian Rural Development,* ed. Ammar Siamwalla, 243–70. Hong Kong: Oxford University Press.

Manning, Chris. 1998. *Indonesian Labour in Transition: An East Asian Success Story?* Cambridge: Cambridge University Press.

———. 2000. "Labour Market Adjustments to Indonesia's Economic Crisis: Context, Trends and Conclusions." *Bulletin of Indonesian Economic Studies* 36 (1): 105–36.

Mason, Andrew D., and Jacqueline Baptist. 1996. "How Important Are Labor Markets to the Welfare of Indonesia's Poor? Policy Research Working Paper 1665, World Bank, Washington, DC.

McBeth, John. 2003. "Leadership: The Betrayal of Indonesia." *Far Eastern Economic Review* 116 (25), June 26.

McCawley, Peter. 2002. "Economic Policy during the Suharto Era: A Balance Sheet." In *Ekonomi Indonesia di Era Politik Baru: 80 Tahun Mohammad Sadli* [The Indonesian Economy in the New Political Era: Mohammad Sadli's 80 Years], ed. Mohamad Ikhsan, Chris Manning, and Hadi Soesastro, 259–70. Jakarta: Penerbit Buku Kompas.

Mellor, John W. 2000. "Agricultural Growth, Rural Employment, and Poverty Reduction: Nontradables, Public Expenditure, and Balanced Growth." Prepared for World Bank Rural Week 2000, March.

Papanek, Gustav. 2004. "The Poor during Economic Decline, Rapid Growth and Crisis: The Case of Indonesia." Prepared for the USAID Project on Pro-Poor Growth conducted by Development Alternatives, Inc., and BIDE, Bethesda, MD.

Prawiro, Radius. 1998. *Indonesia's Struggle for Economic Development: Pragmatism in Action*. Kuala Lumpur: Oxford University Press.

Ramage, Douglas. 2004. "The Political Dynamics of Indonesia's Elections." Presentation to Asia Society and U.S. Indonesian Association (USINDO), Washington DC, April 29.

Ravallion, Martin, and Monika Huppi. 1991. "Measuring Changes in Poverty: A Methodological Case Study of Indonesia during an Adjustment Period." *World Bank Economic Review* 5 (1): 57–82.

Rock, Michael T. 2002. "Exploring the Impact of Selective Interventions in Agriculture on the Growth of Manufactures in Indonesia, Malaysia, and Thailand." *Journal of International Development* 14 (4): 485–510.

Rodrik, Dani. 2004. "How to Make the Trade Regime Work for Development." Harvard University. http://Aksghome.harvard.edu/~drodrik/How%20to% 20Make%20Trade%20Work.pdf.

Sarris, Alexander H. 2001. "The Role of Agriculture in Economic Development and Poverty Reduction: An Empirical and Conceptual Foundation." Prepared for the Rural Development Department of the World Bank, Washington, DC.

Schydlowsky, Daniel M. 2000. "Misperceived Corporate Exchange Risk and Hyperinflation in Indonesia 1998–99." American University and Boston Institute of Developing Economies, Ltd.

Stern, Joseph J. 2003. "The Rise and Fall of the Indonesian Economy." Working Paper 100, Center for International Development, Harvard University, Cambridge, MA.

———. 2004. "The Impact of the Crisis—Decline and Recovery." Working Paper 103, Center for International Development, Harvard University, Cambridge, MA.

Sumarto, Sudarno, and Asep Suryhadi. 2003. "The Indonesian Experience on Trade Reform, Economic Growth and Poverty Reduction." Paper presented at the Trade, Growth and Poverty Conference, London, December 8–9.

Temple, Jonathan. 2001. "Growing into Trouble: Indonesia after 1966." Working paper, Department of Economics, University of Bristol, Bristol.

Thee, Kian Wie, ed. 2003. *Recollections: The Indonesian Economy, 1950s–1990s*. Singapore and Canberra: Institute of Southeast Asian Studies and Research School of Pacific and Asian Studies, Australian National University.

Thorbecke, Erik. 1995. "The Political Economy of Development: Indonesia and the Philippines." The Frank H. Golay Memorial Lecture, Cornell Southeast Asia Program, Cornell University, Ithaca, NY.

Timmer, C. Peter. 1975. "The Political Economy of Rice in Asia: Indonesia." *Food Research Institute Studies* 14 (3): 197–231.

_____. 1996a. "Does BULOG Stabilise Rice Prices in Indonesia? Should It Try?" *Bulletin of Indonesian Economic Studies* 32 (2): 45–74.

_____. 1996b. "Economic Growth and Poverty Alleviation in Indonesia." In *Research in Domestic and International Agribusiness Management*, vol. 12, ed. Ray A. Goldberg, 205–34. Greenwich, CT: JAI Press.

_____. 1997. "How Well Do the Poor Connect to the Growth Process?" Paper prepared for U.S. Agency for International Development/CAER project, Harvard Institute for International Development, Harvard University.

_____. 2000. "The Macro Dimensions of Food Security: Economic Growth, Equitable Distribution, and Food Price Stability." *Food Policy* 25: 283–95.

_____. 2002. "Agriculture and Economic Growth." In *The Handbook of Agricultural Economics*, vol. 2, ed. Bruce Gardner and Gordon Rausser, 1487–546. Amsterdam: North-Holland.

_____. 2004. "The Road to Pro-Poor Growth: The Indonesian Experience in Regional Perspective." *Bulletin of Indonesian Economic Studies* 40 (2): 173–203.

_____. 2005a. "Food Security and Economic Growth: An Asian Perspective." *Asian-Pacific Economic Literature* 19 (1): 1–17.

_____. 2005b. "Operationalizing Pro-Poor Growth: A Country Case Study of Indonesia," PREM/World Bank, Washington, DC.

Timmer, C. Peter, Walter P. Falcon, Franck Wiebe, and Andrew D. Mason. 1992. "An Approach to Poverty Alleviation in Indonesia: Overview." In "Approaches to Poverty Alleviation in Indonesia," Harvard Institute for International Development Report 136/92/255, Cambridge.

Warr, Peter G. 1984. "Exchange Rate Protection in Indonesia." *Bulletin of Indonesian Economic Studies* 20 (2): 53–89.

_____. 2002. "Poverty Reduction and Sectoral Growth: Evidence from Southeast Asia" Draft, Economics Division, Research School of Pacific and Asian Studies, Australian National University, Canberra Australia.

_____. 2005. "Industrialization, Trade Policy, and Poverty Reduction: Evidence from Asia." In *Trade Policy Reforms and Development: Essays in Honour of Peter Lloyd*, vol. 2, ed. Sisira Jayasuriya. Cheltenham, U.K., and Northampton, MA: Edward Elgar.

World Bank. 1987. "Indonesia: Strategy for Economic Recovery." Country Study, World Bank, Washington, DC.

_____. 2003a. "Indonesia: Beyond Macro-Economic Stability." World Bank Brief for the Consultative Group on Indonesia, Jakarta, December.

_____. 2003b. "Indonesia: Country Assistance Strategy, FY 2004–2007." World Bank, Jakarta.

3

The Policy Origins of Poverty and Growth in India

Timothy Besley, Robin Burgess, and Berta Esteve-Volart

India contains about one-third of the world's population living on less than a dollar a day. Since India became a federal democracy in 1947, its states have experienced very different patterns of poverty reduction. The share of the population in poverty in Bihar, for example, remained stagnant at above 60 percent from 1958 to 2000. In Kerala, by contrast, poverty fell from about 60 percent to 15 percent over the same period. Differences in growth rates have also been striking, in particular during the past two decades.

A recent body of research has exploited the heterogeneity of the Indian experience to investigate how and why Indian states have or have not achieved growth and poverty reduction. This research is facilitated by the fact that Indian states retained responsibility for many policies in the Indian constitution, which came into force in 1950, and by India's establishment of the National Sample Survey (NSS), a database for analysis of socioeconomic issues. Through the NSS, India has collected poverty figures since 1958.[1]

This chapter analyzes links among poverty, growth, and policy in India over the 1958–2000 period in 16 states in which more than 95 percent of the Indian population lives. These states are larger than many of the countries that appear in typical cross-country analyses. But because these states operate under a single government, many of the unobserved factors that confound these analyses can be controlled.

The present analysis considers human capital and access to finance—classic themes in studies of growth and poverty reduction. It also considers voice and accountability, regulation, property rights, and gender—factors that are crucial to understanding the growth and poverty reduction experiences of Indian states. Thus the analysis emphasizes accumulation of physical and human capital but also focuses on institutional reforms that expand opportunities for households (and individuals), improve the climate for doing business, and increase the accountability of elected officials. Central to the analysis is the institutional and political context in which policy and accumulation decisions are made.

The analysis begins by relating poverty to growth. It then introduces the idea of a growth elasticity of poverty, applied state by state. On the basis of cross-state evidence, the study identifies six policy and institutional factors that have affected poverty reduction and growth and the relationship between them.

Poverty and Growth

Figure 3.1 depicts both the headcount measure of poverty—the standard deviation of log income inequality measure—and the log of income per capita between 1958 and 2000 for each of the 16 states in the analysis.[2] The poverty numbers show total (official) poverty and total adjusted (Sundaram and Tendulkar 2003c) poverty for 1994 and 2000.[3] Though the pattern of poverty change is unclear in the early years, most states have experienced a decline in poverty from the early 1970s onward. By contrast, inequality as measured by the Gini shows no consistent patterns of change. The data also show a slow but steady upward trend in income per capita from the 1970s in most states.

The most striking feature of figure 3.1, however, is cross-state heterogeneity in these patterns.[4] As noted above, poverty fell precipitously in Kerala but was impervious to change in Bihar. Economic performance also varies greatly from state to state. Growth rates divide the 16 main states of India into two groups of equal size: in one group economic growth has been limited, but in the other it has been intensifying.[5] Patterns of inequality vary across states but not in a systematic fashion. Figure 3.1 reveals that the relationship between income per capita and growth across states is heterogeneous. A simple way to summarize the relationship between poverty and growth is to run regressions of the form:

$$p_{st} = \alpha_s + \beta_s y_{st} + \varepsilon_{st},$$

where s denotes an Indian state t and denotes a year, α is a state fixed effect, p_{st} is the log of the poverty headcount ratio, and finally y_{st} is the log of

Figure 3.1 *Changes in Total Real Income Per Capita, Total Official Poverty, and Inequality, by Indian State, 1957–2000*

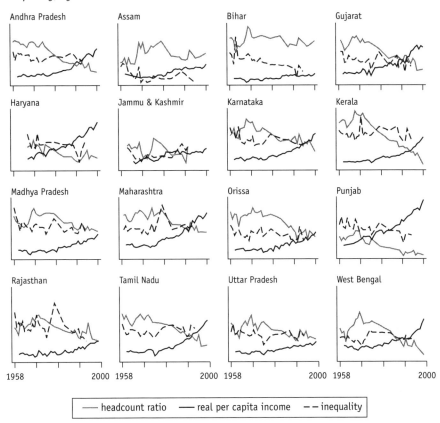

Source: Authors' estimations.
Note: The inequality index used is the standard deviation of the logarithm of income.

income per capita. These regressions were run for each of the 16 Indian states for the 1958–2000 period.

The coefficient β represents the poverty reduction efficiency of growth within states. Because both poverty and income per capita are measured in logs, this coefficient is the growth elasticity of poverty. It reveals what percentage fall in poverty was achieved for each percentage increase in income per capita. States with a higher value of β (in absolute terms) have experienced growth spells that have yielded greater poverty reduction. Thus having a high β provides a plausible notion of more effective poverty-reducing growth. Understanding which economic, social, and political factors are associated with high β provides a way of thinking about how to operationalize poverty-reducing growth.

The explained component of poverty reduction between any two time periods in a given Indian state will be a function of both the state growth elasticity of poverty β and the state growth rate g_s:

$$\Delta\hat{p}_{st} = \beta_s\, g_{s'}$$

where the coefficient β represents the poverty efficiency reduction of growth within states. This coefficient loosely summarizes how much growth within a state is poverty reducing.

Table 3.1 shows poverty elasticities with respect to growth for India's states. In every state the estimated elasticities are negative, confirming that increases in income per capita are associated with poverty reduction. This finding is consistent with the findings of other studies (Besley and Burgess 2003; Bourguignon 2002; Dollar and Kraay 2002; Ravallion 2004). The estimated average elasticity for India is -0.65, with an average (robust) standard error of 0.08. The size of the coefficient means that an increase in growth of 1 percent is associated with a reduction in poverty of 0.65 percent. That is, growth reduces poverty less than proportionally. But an average is less interesting than determining whether some states are more efficient than others in reducing poverty through growth. Table 3.1 shows that elasticities range from -0.30 for Bihar to -1.23 for Kerala.[6] Therefore, within the same country Bihar would need four times as much economic growth as Kerala to achieve the same level of poverty reduction. This finding is a good indication that the poor in Bihar are less included in the growth process than are the poor in Kerala.

Superior poverty reduction performance in an Indian state will come from either higher growth elasticity of poverty (for a given rate of growth) or higher economic growth (for a given growth elasticity of poverty). Table 3.1 divides overall poverty reduction in the 16 states into these two components (see columns 3 and 4). As the table shows, state performance is quite heterogeneous.

Table 3.2 classifies each state according to growth performance and poverty reduction for a given amount of growth. Some states, such as Kerala, have achieved rapid poverty reduction by combining relatively high economic growth rates with a high growth elasticity of poverty. Others, such as West Bengal, compensate for low growth with a high growth elasticity of

Table 3.1 Poverty and Growth across Indian States

coefficients from regression of	poverty on GDP				poverty on inequality
	β_s	g_s	$\bar{g}(\beta_s - \bar{\beta})$	$\beta_s(g_s - \bar{g})$	γ_s
State	(1)	(2)	(3)	(4)	(5)
Andhra Pradesh	−0.76**	0.028	0.17	0.24	−2.13**
Assam	−0.38**	0.021	−0.41	−0.07	−0.86
Bihar	−0.30**	0.012	−0.53	−0.23	−0.94**
Gujarat	−0.66**	0.027	0.02	0.18	0.34
Haryana	−0.57**	0.031	−0.12	0.32	1.43**
Jammu and Kashmir	−0.57**	0.018	−0.12	−0.19	−0.25
Karnataka	−0.53**	0.024	−0.19	0.02	−1.06*
Kerala	−1.23**	0.026	0.90	0.21	0.34
Madhya Pradesh	−0.39**	0.022	−0.39	−0.03	0.49
Maharashtra	−0.40**	0.029	−0.38	0.15	1.25**
Orissa	−0.69**	0.021	0.06	−0.12	0.96
Punjab	−1.03**	0.030	0.61	0.46	1.30*
Rajasthan	−0.43**	0.018	−0.33	−0.15	0.20
Tamil Nadu	−0.59**	0.029	−0.09	0.24	0.11
Uttar Pradesh	−0.64**	0.015	−0.01	−0.34	−0.56
West Bengal	−1.17**	0.021	0.82	−0.21	1.32
Average	−0.65**	0.023	0.001	0.03	0.12

Source: Özler, Datt, and Ravallion 1996.

Note: Data are from 1960–98. Significance levels were obtained using robust standard errors, where * indicates significance at the 5 percent level and ** indicates significance at the 1 percent level. Column 1 reports the coefficients from a regression, for each state individually, of log poverty headcount on log real GDP per capita. Column 2 reports each state's rate of real per capita GDP growth over the period. Column 3 reports each state's deviation from the average in terms of growth poverty elasticity. Column 4 reports the same in terms of the growth rate. Elements in columns 3 and 4 have been divided by the average amount of poverty reduction ($\bar{\beta}\,\bar{g}$). Column 5 reports the coefficient on standard deviation of log income from a regression of log poverty headcount regressed on log real GDP per capita and standard deviation of log income.

poverty (and vice versa for Maharashtra and other states in the bottom right-hand quadrant). Laggard states such as Bihar that have achieved relatively little poverty reduction have below average rates of growth and growth elasticities of poverty.

Table 3.2 *Classification of States according to Total Poverty Elasticity and Growth Components*

	(+) High growth	(−) Low growth
(+) High poverty elasticity	Andhra Pradesh	Orissa
	Gujarat	West Bengal
	Kerala	
	Punjab	
(−) Low poverty elasticity	Haryana	Assam
	Maharashtra	Bihar
	Tamil Nadu	Jammu and Kashmir
		Karnataka
		Madhya Pradesh
		Rajasthan
		Uttar Pradesh

Source: Özler, Datt, and Ravallion 1996.

Column 5 of table 3.1 introduces a measure of inequality to effectively estimate

$$p_{st} = \alpha_s y_{st} + \gamma_s \sigma_{st} + \varepsilon_{st},$$

where σ_{st} denotes the standard deviation of the logarithm of income.

The poverty-inequality elasticity varies a lot in size and sign. For example, for Haryana and Maharashtra, more income inequality is associated with *greater* poverty; Andhra Pradesh, Bihar, and Karnataka show significantly negative elasticities—an increase in income inequality is associated with poverty reduction. For the remaining states, as well as for the average of all states, the inequality elasticity is not significantly different from zero. The pattern of variation between inequality and poverty is therefore much less clear than that between economic growth and poverty. This is not to say that inequality is unimportant. However, the data do not associate inequality reduction with poverty reduction in the same robust way that they link economic growth and poverty reduction.

Six Propositions on Poverty Reduction and Growth

How can the heterogeneous pattern of growth and poverty across Indian states be explained? Cross-state regression analyses suggest six policy-relevant lessons concerning poverty reduction and growth in India.

Voice and Accountability

How can government be encouraged to respond to the needs of the poorest citizens? Besley and Burgess (2002) analyze this issue in the context of public food distribution and calamity relief in India and find that mass media and political competition are important in ensuring that the government responds effectively to the needs of vulnerable citizens when they face natural disasters.

They use 1958–92 panel data from India's states to explore the role of the media and political competition in mitigating political agency problems by providing information to voters. They focus on the public food distribution and calamity relief systems in India, which were established, in part, to deal with the threat posed by famine and natural calamities (such as droughts, floods, earthquakes, and cyclones). The public food distribution system, which involves large-scale procurement, storage, transportation, and distribution of food grains, is a key means of responding to drops in food production caused by droughts. Calamity relief expenditure covers a variety of direct relief measures, such as drinking water supply, medicine and health, clothing and food, veterinary care, and assistance for repair of damaged property and is a means for state governments to respond to crop damage caused by floods.

Besley and Burgess (2002) pose two main questions. First, in the event of a fall in food production caused by drought, does having greater newspaper circulation or stronger political competition imply that state governments will be more responsive in terms of distributing greater amounts of food through the public food distribution system? Second, in the event that a flood damages crops, does having greater newspaper circulation or stronger political competition imply that state governments will be more responsive in terms of spending more on calamity relief?

They find that when food production falls, states with higher per capita newspaper circulation and more intense political competition are more responsive in terms of public food distribution. Similarly, when floods damage crops, the states with higher per capita newspaper circulation and more intense political competition spend more on calamity relief.

In examining the role of the media in greater detail, Besley and Burgess (2002) find that regional newspapers appear to be associated with more responsive governments. These newspapers (printed in regional languages) report more localized events, and their readers tend to be people who rely on action by state governments for protection.

Another political economy issue with relevance to poverty reduction efforts is representation of disadvantaged groups. Scheduled castes and scheduled tribes, which constitute lower classes, as recognized by the Indian constitution, represent roughly 16 and 8 percent of the Indian population, respectively. But the incidence of poverty in these two groups is one and a half times that in the rest of the population. Hence, poverty reduction could be affected more than proportionally by enhancing the groups' political power.

Pande (2003) exploits the institutional features of political reservation—the setting aside of seats in state legislatures for scheduled castes and scheduled tribes—as practiced in Indian states from 1960 to 1992, to examine the role of mandated political representation in giving disadvantaged groups influence over policy making. Her study is of practical importance, because a quarter of all legislators in India, at both the national and state level, come from reserved jurisdictions. She uses changes in the extent of political reservation, which are specific to a given state, to identify how changes in the group shares of minority legislators affect policy outcomes. Her main finding is that political reservation has increased redistribution of resources to the groups that benefit from the reservation.

Pande (2003) finds that scheduled caste (SC) reservation increases job quotas (in particular, a 1 percent rise in SC reservation increases job quotas by 0.6 percent), whereas scheduled tribe (ST) reservation increases spending on ST programs (a 1 percent increase in ST reservation increases the share devoted to ST welfare programs by 0.8 percentage points). This finding is consistent with the nature of the SC and ST groups: because SC individuals are more educated and geographically more dispersed than ST individuals, they have higher returns from individual-specific policies as job quotas; ST individuals, who are less dispersed, benefit more from geographically localized welfare programs. In sum, changes in legislator identity in India have exerted a significant influence on state-level policies.

Regulation

Labor regulations are an important element of the investment climate in India (Sachs, Varshney, and Bajpai 1999; Stern 2001). Besley and Burgess (2004) examine whether labor can help explain differences in urban poverty and manufacturing performance across Indian states. Manufacturing has historically played a large role in the structural change accompanying economic development and has been a key driver in reducing poverty. Between 1960 and 1995 the share of manufacturing in GDP increased threefold in many East Asian countries (from 8 percent to 26 percent in Malaysia). These countries also experienced sharp reductions in poverty.

However, manufacturing in India only increased from 13 percent to 18 percent in the same period. The manufacturing sector in India consists of two subsectors: registered (formal, about 9 percent of GDP) and unregistered (informal, about 5 percent of GDP) manufacturing. Firms are required to register if they employ more than 10 individuals and use electric power, or if they do not use electric power but employ more than 20 individuals.

The analysis of Besley and Burgess (2004) exploits two important facts: (1) labor regulations apply only to firms in the registered manufacturing sector, and (2) the Indian constitution empowers state governments to amend central legislation. The main piece of central legislation is the Industrial Disputes Act of 1947. State governments extensively amended this act during the postindependence period. Besley and Burgess read the text of each amendment and coded each as pro-worker (+1), neutral (0), or pro-employer (−1).

Besley and Burgess then check whether regulatory changes affect urban and rural poverty and manufacturing development in the registered and unregistered sectors. They find that regulating in a pro-worker direction is associated with increases in urban poverty but does not affect rural poverty. This finding reflects the fact that the adverse effects of pro-worker labor regulation are on the growth of registered manufacturing, which is mainly located in urban areas. These effects are large—for example, had West Bengal, a state with substantial pro-worker legislation, passed no amendments, its urban poverty would have been 11 percent lower in 1990. Andhra Pradesh, in contrast, would have had 12 percent higher urban poverty had it not moved in a pro-employer direction. These results suggest that attempts to redress the balance of power between capital and labor can end up hurting the poor. They also show that states with more pro-worker labor regulations tend to have larger informal manufacturing sectors. This finding makes sense: workers can extract more of the rents from production in the registered sector; capitalists prefer to remain in the unregistered sector where labor has no power.

As Besley and Burgess (2004) show, the labor regulation choices of state governments in India have greatly affected manufacturing performance. Policies like labor regulation that are, in part, under the control of subnational governments have a strong bearing on whether or not manufacturing develops in areas under the governments' jurisdiction. These policies affect the ability of the poor to participate in manufacturing and to exit poverty. The institutional environment affects the investment and location decisions that entrepreneurs make and can have an important bearing on the pattern of poverty reduction in a state. Countries or regions wishing to develop manufacturing and reduce poverty must pay attention to the policies that affect the business climate. Ways in which these policies can be made more inclusive and pro-poor are an important area for future research.

The Besley and Burgess findings are particularly resonant for the post-1991 liberalization period, during which the negative consequences of a poor investment climate have been magnified. When manufacturing industries were exposed to domestic and foreign competition through delicensing and tariff reductions, Aghion and others (2005) found that the industries located in pro-employer states performed significantly better than those located in pro-worker states.

Access to Finance

Access to finance can enable people to exit poverty by transforming their production and employment activities. Understanding which factors drive structural change by facilitating the emergence of small businesses and other nonagricultural activities is a major challenge in efforts to reduce poverty. Burgess and Pande (2005) took it on by evaluating whether the massive expansion of rural branch banks in India affected rural poverty and economic growth. In the 1961–2000 period over 30,000 new branches were opened in rural areas. The rationale for the program was simple. The government identified lack of access to finance as a significant reason for stagnant growth and persistent poverty in rural areas. The failure of banks to enter rural areas was viewed as an impediment to entrepreneurship and the emergence of new production activities. To address this problem, the Indian central bank first nationalized commercial banks in 1969 and then imposed a license rule in 1977. The rule stated that for each branch opened in a banked (typically urban) location four more branches had to open in a location (typically rural) without a bank. This rule was removed in 1990, and branch building in rural areas came to a halt. As a result of the imposition of the 1:4 rule, states that had fewer banks per capita before the program began in 1961 received more bank branches between 1977 and 1990, leading to both a reduction and an equalization in population per bank branch. The rural banks made lending to entrepreneurs, small businessmen, and agriculturalists, as well as lower caste and tribal households, a priority.

To evaluate the program, Burgess and Pande (2005) use the 1977 and 1990 trend breaks in the relationship between initial financial development and rural branch expansion attributable to license regime shifts as instruments for the number of branches opened in the rural locations without banks. They show that rural branch expansion reduced rural poverty but had no effect on urban poverty. They also find that the wages of agricultural laborers are positively affected by rural branch expansion, perhaps because a rise in nonagricultural activities reduced the supply of labor to the agriculture sector, driving up the wages of the remaining agricultural laborers. Hence, these laborers, among the poorest in India and often having little access to land and nonagricultural employment activities, might benefit from rural branch expansion even if they do not transact directly with banks.

Burgess and Pande (2005) also find that rural branch expansion positively affected economic growth across Indian states by driving up nonagricultural output. Agricultural output, in contrast, was unaffected. The (albeit forced) entry of banks into the rural areas of India is thought to have spurred entrepreneurship, structural change, and poverty reduction. Again, access to finance may be critical in enabling poor, rural residents to begin new economic activities and thereby exit poverty.

Human Capital

Human capital is often viewed as a constraint on economic growth and poverty reduction in India. Average literacy rates in India are low. According to the 1991 Census of India, the literacy rate is 63 percent for males and 36 percent for females. These rates are lower than those in many East and Southeast Asian countries 40 years ago and are no higher than modern-day rates in sub-Saharan Africa (Dreze and Sen 1995). Moreover, educational achievements vary greatly across Indian states—male literacy rate ranges from 50 percent in Andhra Pradesh and Bihar to 93 percent in Kerala, and female literacy rates range from 17 percent in Rajasthan and 20 percent in Uttar Pradesh to 84 percent in Kerala (Census of India 1991). Disparities in the educational achievements of females and males, between rural and urban areas, and among castes are also large.

In the Indian constitution, education is mainly the responsibility of states. Therefore, the large differences in outcomes are due in part to the fact that efforts to expand education have varied enormously across states. Initial conditions are also important. For example, in Kerala, the region with the highest educational attainments in India, widespread literacy existed well before British rule, and mass literacy since then has been achieved through a mass social movement to promote schooling (Dreze and Sen 1997). By contrast, in Uttar Pradesh endemic teacher absenteeism and shirking are linked to poor schooling outcomes (Dreze and Gazdar 1997).

Trivedi (2002) exploits this heterogeneity in educational outcomes across Indian states by building up a panel data set on male and female secondary school enrollment rates for the period 1965 to 1992. He examines whether these rates are related to economic growth and finds a positive and significant relationship between both male and female enrollment rates and the annual rate of growth in per capita state income. Moreover, consistent with other evidence for India (for example, Esteve-Volart 2004), but in stark contrast with results from cross-country studies,[7] Trivedi (2002) finds that female human capital has a larger impact on economic growth than male human capital.

These results suggest that investments in human capital may represent a key means of increasing economic growth in Indian states. How such increases in human capital will be achieved remains an open question that can be addressed only through microeconomic evaluation of specific innovations in the delivery of education in India. School governance and accountability will need to be improved to tackle systemic failures such as widespread teacher absenteeism. Promising initiatives include promoting parental and community involvement, changing incentives for teachers and students, and involving nonstate actors and nongovernmental organizations in education provision. Duflo and Hanna (2005), for example, show that when primary school teachers are required to photograph themselves with a certain number of students each day, teacher attendance increases. Pedagogical innovations that improve the quality and relevance of education, in particular for poor and disadvantaged children, through curriculum reform, employment of female teachers for girl-friendly schools, hiring of assistant teachers to deal with large classes, and new teaching methods and materials are also likely to be relevant (see Banerjee and others 2004).

Property Rights

Given that the majority of India's poor reside in rural areas, rural development is key to India's success in reducing poverty. Under the Indian constitution, states are empowered to enact and implement land reforms. These reforms fall into four categories: tenancy reform, abolition of intermediaries, imposition of ceilings on landholdings (to redistribute land to the landless), and consolidation of disparate landholdings.

Besley and Burgess (2000) assigned each land reform act passed in an Indian state to one of these categories and analyzed how the act affected poverty and growth using state-level data from 1958 to 1992. They found that land reform taken as a whole is associated with reductions in rural poverty and that tenancy reforms and the abolition of intermediaries account for this effect. These results suggest that more moderate reforms that improve the property rights and bargaining power of tenants (and marginal farmers) may have had significant effects on rural poverty, whereas attempts to directly redistribute land had no effect, because powerful landed elites tended to block or evade them. There appears to be a trade-off between tenancy reforms and growth of agricultural output. Though they reduce poverty, tenancy reforms are negatively associated with the growth of real agricultural output per capita.

Other studies confirm the importance of secure property rights to poverty reduction. Links between property rights and economic performance have been proffered in the cross-country literature. Microeconomic studies now complement this evidence. Some of these studies extend beyond agricultural property rights—for example, to property rights over land in urban areas (see Field 2004). This area is ripe for future research on India.

The work by Besley and Burgess (2000) focuses on land reform after independence. But by 1950, interesting and important differences among historical landholding institutions already existed, and these differences could be important to subsequent performance. Landholding institutions that favored landlords dominated some states but not others, depending on choices made by British administrators during the colonial period. In landlord-based areas, landlords collected land revenues, whereas in non-landlord areas British officials or a village community body collected them. Banerjee and Iyer (2002) constructed an index of landholding institutions on the basis of the area in a state not under a landlord tenure system and showed that districts with systems of land-revenue collection that remained in indigenous hands have tended to experience better public goods provision.

Gender

Gender inequality in literacy in India is among the highest in developing countries. Heterogeneity in female literacy rates across India's states is also significant, as noted above. Northern states (most notably Rajasthan and Bihar) are characterized by relatively low female literacy rates; southern states have traditionally had higher female literacy rates. Indeed, northern regions tend to be more patriarchal and feudal (and have lower female-to-male sex ratios and therefore more "missing women" as calculated by Sen [1992]) than southern regions, where generally women have more freedom and a more prominent presence in society (Dreze and Sen 1995).

In India the participation of women in productive sectors is relatively low. Female labor participation was lower in 1991 (20 percent) than in

1901–51. As is the case with literacy and sex ratios, southeastern states tend to have larger rates of female labor force participation than northwestern states. In general, women in the middle classes tend not to participate in the labor force, whereas women from poorer households must engage in productive activity outside the home. That is, female labor participation in India is the result of the interaction between social norms (enforced by social stigma that obliges men to provide for their families) and economic conditions. The larger the family income, the more binding are the social norms.

Esteve-Volart (2004) uses state panel data for the period 1961 to 1991 to examine the aggregate costs, in terms of development, of gender discrimination in the labor market. She finds that these costs are substantial. She shows positive relationships between the ratios of female-to-male managers and female-to-male workers and per capita real output. She also shows that female literacy is positively associated with development, whereas male literacy is not statistically significant. She deals with endogeneity concerns by instrumenting both the female-to-male managers and workers with the ratio of prosecutions launched relative to complaints received by inspectors under the Maternity Benefits Act of 1961. Gender inequality in access to labor markets impedes development, and the efficiency costs of such inequality are large.

Summary of Findings

The Indian experience is specific in many ways. Moreover, the data are, by definition, backward looking. However, isolating the forces that shape the variety of Indian experiences observable at the state level is tremendously valuable. Identifying the policy origins of growth and poverty in India is key to informing the current debate and to shaping future policy.

Table 3.3 connects the policy analysis above to the earlier discussion of growth-poverty links. It ranks Indian states by their growth elasticity of poverty, growth rates, rates of poverty reduction, and performance in each of the six areas of policy discussed above. The table thus allows an informal look at how policy performance is linked to the growth elasticity of poverty and growth and hence to a state's overall record in reducing poverty. The first three columns identify the states that have been most effective at reducing poverty. These states have tended to have high growth elasticities of poverty and fast growth rates. Poverty reduction is greatest in states like Kerala, Punjab, and Andhra Pradesh, where higher-than-average growth elasticities of poverty have been combined with higher-than-average

Table 3.3 *Rankings of Growth Elasticities of Poverty, Growth Rates, and Policies of Indian States, 1958–2000*

State	Poverty reduction	Growth rate	Growth elasticity of poverty	Voice and accountability	Regulation	Access to finance	Human capital	Property rights	Gender
Kerala	1	7	1	1	4	8	5	2	1
West Bengal	2	11	2	4	11	4	11	1	10
Punjab	3	2	3	5	7	3	3	15	15
Andhra Pradesh	4	5	4	10	1	9	12	12	4
Orissa	7	12	5	16	8	14	6	3	6
Gujarat	6	6	6	6	9	6	7	7	8
Uttar Pradesh	10	15	7	8	7	12	16	6	13
Tamil Nadu	5	3	8	3	2	2	10	4	5
Haryana	9	1	9	13	7	7	2	16	14
Jammu and Kashmir	15	13	9	11	7	10	1	13	16
Karnataka	8	8	10	7	5	5	8	8	3
Rajasthan	12	14	11	9	3	13	9	14	11
Maharashtra	11	4	12	2	10	1	13	11	7
Madhya Pradesh	13	9	13	12	6	11	14	9	9
Assam	16	10	14	15	7	15	4	10	2
Bihar	14	16	15	14	7	16	15	5	12
Rank correlation: policy and growth elasticity of poverty				0.48 (0.06)	0.03 (0.91)	0.39 (0.13)	0.25 (0.36)	0.29 (0.27)	0.04 (0.89)
Rank correlation: policy and growth rate				0.41 (0.11)	0.13 (0.62)	0.74 (0.01)	0.33 (0.20)	−0.33 (0.22)	0.17 (0.52)
Rank correlation: policy and poverty reduction				0.62 (0.01)	0.12 (0.65)	0.58 (0.02)	0.08 (0.78)	0.37 (0.17)	0.21 (0.43)

Sources: Besley and Burgess 2000, 2002, 2004; Burgess and Pande 2005; Esteve-Volart 2004.
Note: Rankings are based on the average variable of interest over the period (1 = highest). Voice and accountability = newspaper circulation per capita. Regulation = labor regulation, ranked from most pro-employer to most pro-worker. Access to finance = total credit per capita. Human capital = education expenditure per capita. Property rights = land reform legislation. Gender = female-to-male workers. Poverty reduction uses official headcount ratio indexes. Significant levels for correlations are in parentheses.

growth. Poverty reduction is lowest in states like Bihar, Assam, and Madhya Pradesh, where both elasticities and growth rates are low.

The remaining columns correlate poverty elasticity, growth, and poverty reduction with policy indicators. These columns indicate how the state experience of pro-poor growth is linked to policy themes.

In the column on voice and accountability, a higher newspaper circulation per capita is associated with a higher growth elasticity of poverty, a higher growth rate, and a higher overall reduction in poverty. In the column on regulation, states are ranked from most pro-employer (Andhra Pradesh) to most pro-worker (West Bengal). More pro-worker regulation is associated with lower growth elasticities of poverty, lower growth rates, and less poverty reduction. A similar pattern is found in the access to finance column, where states are ranked by per capita credit extended by commercial banks. States with greater access to finance have higher growth rates, higher elasticities of poverty to growth, and more rapid reductions in poverty. The same pattern of correlations is recorded for human capital as proxied by state education expenditures per capita in the next column.

Property rights are proxied by the number of land reform acts passed in a state. The correlation of this variable with the growth elasticities of poverty is positive though that with growth rates is negative. In other words, states that have passed more land reforms are more efficient at converting growth into poverty, however a growth cost appears to be associated with land reforms. The overall association between the passage of land reforms and poverty reduction is, however, positive, suggesting that the growth costs are not of sufficient magnitude to overturn the poverty-reducing effects of land reform.

Finally, in the column on gender, inclusion of females in the labor force, as proxied by the ratio of female-to-male workers, is positively correlated with a higher growth elasticity of poverty, higher growth rates, and more rapid poverty reduction.

Although not admitting a causal interpretation, this table indicates the different policy origins of poverty reduction and growth in India.[8] Broadly speaking, states with more accountable governments, more pro-business investment climates, greater access to finance and human capital, greater extension of property rights to the poor, and greater inclusion of women in economic growth have been more successful in reducing poverty. The positive association between policy variables and growth elasticities of poverty and growth rates helps clarify the variables' overall effect on poverty. The policies we have identified may be poverty reducing because they positively affect growth *and* enhance the poverty effect of growth. These policies are powerful because they enhance growth and include the poor in the growth process.

There are grounds for optimism about future poverty reduction in India. First, the Indian economy is growing at an unprecedented rate, and historical experience suggests that this growth will lead to a widespread reduction in absolute poverty. Second, the building blocks of sustained economic growth and poverty reduction are known. The evidence from cross-state studies is consistent with basic messages from modern growth theory. Physical and human capital must be accumulated, institutional reforms that expand opportunities for households (and individuals) must be implemented, the business climate must be improved, and the accountability of elected officials must be increased.

Notes

1. Estimates of poverty derived from the NSS data use the urban and rural poverty lines developed by India's Planning Commission (Government of India 1979). The most common measure of poverty is the headcount ratio, which estimates the proportion of the relevant population living in households with consumption or income below the poverty line.

2. Measurement of poverty and inequality in India has particularly benefited from the work of a World Bank team headed by Martin Ravallion, who used tabulated NSS data to put together poverty and inequality series (Özler, Datt, and Ravallion 1996).

3. Surveys up to 1993/94 (50th round) generate relatively uncontroversial estimates, but changes in the survey design and sampling have raised questions about the comparability of the quinquennial 50th and 55th rounds of the Consumer Expenditure Survey. As a consequence, the accuracy of official estimates reflecting a steep reduction in poverty in all but 2 of the 16 study states (Assam and Bihar) in the 1990s is unclear. Considerable debate has led to adjusted numbers (Deaton and Dreze 2002; Lal, Mohan, and Natarajan 2001; Sundaram 2001; Sundaram and Tendulkar 2003a, 2003b, 2003c).

4. For a more complete analysis, see Datt and Ravallion (1998, 2002).

5. The former group includes Assam, Bihar, Jammu and Kashmir, Madhya Pradesh, Orissa, Rajasthan, Uttar Pradesh, and West Bengal; the latter group includes Andhra Pradesh, Gujarat, Haryana, Karnataka, Kerala, Maharashtra, Punjab, and Tamil Nadu.

6. Compare these numbers with estimates for other countries and regions. Besley and Burgess (2003) estimate the poverty elasticity with respect to income per capita to be -0.73 (with a robust standard error of 0.25) for a sample of 88 low- and middle-income countries. This elasticity is about the same as the estimated elasticity for Andhra Pradesh, for which the elasticity equals -0.76 (with a standard error of

0.05), and is similar to that of Orissa and Gujarat. Indeed, the average estimated elasticity for Indian states is -0.65, just slightly below the estimated global average elasticity. Although India's average elasticity is somewhat modest in international terms, the estimates by state show the variety across India's states: in particular, Kerala and West Bengal exhibit remarkable larger-than-one elasticities, as large as the elasticity for East Asia and the Pacific. On the more negative side, some Indian states (namely, Bihar, Assam, Madhya Pradesh, Maharashtra, and Rajasthan) have elasticities as low as those of Sub-Saharan Africa. Hence, table 3.1 exhibits variation in poverty-growth elasticities among India's states that is approximately as big as the variation at the global level.

7. For a review and results, see Krueger and Lindahl (2001).

8. To underline the illustrative nature of these results, observe that the correlations for gender, human capital, and pro-poor regulation reported in table 3.3 are not significantly different from zero.

References

Aghion, Philippe, Robin Burgess, Stephen Redding, and Fabrizio Zilibotti. 2005. "The Unequal Effects of Liberalization: Evidence from Dismantling the License Raj in India." Working paper, Institute for International Economic Studies, London School of Economics, University College, London.

Banerjee, Abhijit, Shawn Cole, Esther Duflo, and Leigh Lindon. 2004. "Remedying Education: Evidence from Two Randomized Experiments in India." Working paper, Department of Economics, Massachusetts Institute of Technology, Cambridge, MA.

Banerjee, Abhijit, and Lakshmi Iyer. 2002. "History, Institutions, and Economic Performance: The Legacy of Colonial Land Tenure Systems in India." Working paper, Department of Economics, Massachusetts Institute of Technology, Cambridge, MA.

Besley, Timothy, and Robin Burgess. 2000. "Land Reform, Poverty, and Growth: Evidence from India." *Quarterly Journal of Economics* 115 (2): 389–430.

———. 2002. "The Political Economy of Government Responsiveness: Theory and Evidence from India." *Quarterly Journal of Economics* 117 (4): 1415–51.

———. 2003. "Halving Global Poverty." *Journal of Economic Perspectives* 17 (3): 3–22.

———. 2004. "Can Labor Regulation Hinder Economic Performance? Evidence from India." *Quarterly Journal of Economics* 119 (1): 91–134.

Bourguignon, François. 2002. "The Growth Elasticity of Poverty Reduction: Explaining Heterogeneity across Countries and Time Periods." Working paper, Département et laboratoire d'Economie Théorique et Appliquée (DELTA), Paris, France.

Burgess, Robin, and Rohini Pande. 2005. "Do Rural Banks Matter? Evidence from the Indian Social Banking Experiment." *American Economic Review* 95: 780–95.

Census of India. 1991. Registrar General and Census Commissioner, government of India.

Datt, Gaurav, and Martin Ravallion. 1998. "Why Have Some Indian States Done Better than Others at Reducing Rural Poverty?" *Economica* 65 (257): 17–38.

———. 2002. "Is India's Economic Growth Leaving the Poor Behind?" *Journal of Economic Perspectives* 16 (3): 89–108.

Deaton, Angus, and Jean Dreze. 2002. "Poverty and Inequality in India: A Re-Examination." *Economic and Political Weekly* (September 7): 3729–48.

Dollar, David, and Aart Kraay. 2002. "Growth Is Good for the Poor." *Journal of Economic Growth* 7 (3): 195–225.

Dreze, Jean, and Haris Gazdar. 1997. "Uttar Pradesh: The Burden of Inertia." In *Indian Development: Selected Regional Perspectives,* ed. Jean Dreze and Amartya Sen. Oxford: Oxford University Press.

Dreze, Jean, and Amartya Sen. 1995. *India: Economic Development and Social Opportunity.* Delhi: Oxford University Press.

———. eds. 1997. *Indian Development: Selected Regional Perspectives.* Delhi: Oxford University Press.

Duflo, Esther, and Rema Hanna. 2005. "Monitoring Works: Getting Teachers to Come to School." Working paper, Massachusetts Institute of Technology, Cambridge, MA.

Esteve-Volart, Berta. 2004. "Gender Discrimination and Growth: Theory and Evidence from India." Development Discussion Paper 42, Suntory and Toyota Centres for Economics and Related Disciplines, London School of Economics.

Field, Erica. 2004. "Entitled to Work: Urban Property Rights and Labor Supply in Peru." Working paper, Harvard University, Cambridge MA.

Government of India. 1979. *Report of the Task Force on Projections of Minimum Needs and Effective Consumption.* New Delhi: Planning Commission.

Krueger, Alan, and Mikael Lindahl. 2001. "Education for Growth: Why and for Whom?" *Journal of Economic Literature* 39 (4): 1101–36.

Lal, Deepak, Rakesh Mohan, and I. Natarajan. 2001. "Economic Reforms and Poverty Alleviation: A Tale of Two Surveys." *Economic and Political Weekly* 36 (March 24): 1017–28.

Pande, Rohini. 2003. "Can Mandated Political Representation Increase Policy Influence for Disadvantaged Minorities? Theory and Evidence from India." *American Economic Review* 93 (4): 1132–51.

Özler, Berk, Gaurav Datt, and Martin Ravallion. 1996. "A Database on Poverty and Growth in India." World Bank, Washington, DC. http://web.worldbank.org/WBSITE/EXTERNAL/TOPICS/EXTPOVERTY/0,,contentMDK:20289079~menuPK:497971~pagePK:148956~piPK:216618~theSitePK:336992,00.html

Ravallion, Martin. 2004. "Pro-Poor Growth: A Primer." Policy Research Working Paper, No. 3242, World Bank, Washington, DC.

Sachs, Jeffrey, A. Varshney, and N. Bajpai, eds. 1999. *India in the Era of Economic Reforms*. Delhi: Oxford University Press.

Sen, Amartya. 1992. "Missing Women." *British Medical Journal* 304 (6827): 587–88.

Stern, Nicholas. 2001. *A Strategy for Development*. Washington DC: World Bank.

Sundaram, K. 2001. "Employment and Poverty in the 1990s: Further Results from NSS 55th Round Employment-Unemployment Survey, 1999–2000." *Economic and Political Weekly* (August 11): 3039–49.

Sundaram, K., and Suresh D. Tendulkar. 2003a. "Poverty Has Declined in the 1990s: A Resolution of Comparability Problems in NSS Consumer Expenditure Data." *Economic and Political Weekly* (January 25): 327–37.

_____. 2003b. "Poverty in India in the 1990s: An Analysis of Changes in 15 Major States." *Economic and Political Weekly* (April 5): 1385–93.

_____. 2003c. "Poverty in India in the 1990s: Revised Results for All-India and 15 Major States for 1993–94." *Economic and Political Weekly* (November 15): 4865–72.

Trivedi, Kamakshya. 2002. "Educational Human Capital and Levels of Income: Evidence from States in India, 1965–92." Working paper, Oxford University, Oxford, UK.

4

Explaining Pro-Poor Growth in Bangladesh: Puzzles, Evidence, and Implications

Binayak Sen, Mustafa K. Mujeri, and Quazi Shahabuddin

Bangladesh is one of the most vulnerable economies in the world. It has an extremely high population density, a low resource base, a high incidence of natural disasters, and sociopolitical instability, especially since gaining independence in 1971.[1] During the 1970s, negative images of the country were fed by social upheavals, economic mismanagement, and the absence of democratic governance. Observers considered the country to be locked in a below-poverty-level equilibrium trap impervious to any policy-based solution short of radical restructuring (see Alamgir 1978). Bleak development indicators of the period supported such a view. Analysts examined diverse theoretical explanations for Bangladesh's inability to make the transition to modernity during the 1980s (see, for example, Abdullah and others 1991; Sobhan 1991).

In recent years, Bangladesh has made that transition at a low level of per capita income (see Stern 2002) and in many respects is regarded as a lead performer among the least developed countries. Improvements in human development have been particularly remarkable: by 2004 Bangladesh had a

The authors are grateful to comments and suggestions from Louise Cord, Adrian Wood, John Toye, Christian Rogg, Shanta Devarajan, Christine Wallich, and Anthony Bottrill. The authors are also thankful to Catherine Hull for editorial assistance and to Syed Rashed Al-Zayed Josh for research support.

lower infant mortality rate than India and had eliminated the gender bias in primary education (Drèze 2004). On the economic front, it has made significant gains in poverty reduction and per capita GDP growth. Moreover, it achieved a poverty-reducing pattern of growth despite endemic vulnerability to natural disasters. Underlying the aggregate growth statistics is significant success in overcoming the threat of famine.[2]

This chapter considers how Bangladesh has overcome difficult initial conditions that constrained its options for growth and poverty reduction. Placing Bangladesh's experience in a postindependence historical context, the chapter focuses its empirical analysis on the 1980s and 1990s, decades of significant economic achievements. Progress has been achieved through macroeconomic stability and openness, which created fiscal space for sustained investments in rural infrastructure and social services. Improved vulnerability management and a generally constructive relationship between the government and civil society have allowed the country to overcome its challenging environment.

Bangladesh's achievements should not be overplayed, however. Modest gains in GDP leave the country firmly within the bracket of least developed country (LDC) status. These gains not only need to be sustained but increased. Rising inequality trends offer further cause for concern. Bangladesh's institutional environment remains weak, increasing the risk that policy mistakes, bad luck, or lack of political leadership may reverse recent gains.

Thus in considering the evidence on pro-poor growth in Bangladesh and highlighting the remarkable gains made in income and nonincome indicators in the 1990s, the chapter notes worrisome inequality trends. It examines how macroeconomic policy, public expenditures, and policy choices enabled Bangladesh to achieve its respectable rates of pro-poor growth in spite of a relatively weak institutional environment. It also examines rising inequality from both an urban and rural perspective and considers whether the trend was inevitable in each context. Finally, it identifies lessons from Bangladesh's experience and outlines priority policies to sustain pro-poor growth.

Evidence on Pro-Poor Growth

Income and nonincome indicators of poverty, as well as improvements in GDP (both in terms of levels and decreasing volatility), provide evidence of sustained poverty reduction in Bangladesh. However, increases in inequality in the 1990s hindered the extent to which growth benefited the poor.

Trends in Poverty: Income Dimensions

Data on the income dimensions of poverty show that Bangladesh has made significant progress on poverty reduction since independence and that these gains were particularly pronounced during the 1990s, though subject to considerable unevenness between urban and rural areas (table 4.1). Household Income Expenditure Survey (HIES) data are the major source of information for estimating trends in income dimensions of poverty. However, data inconsistency problems plague poverty comparisons between specific years.[3] Given these problems, this chapter restricts poverty comparisons to the poverty series starting with 1983/84 and skips the urban estimate for 1995/96 as the average level of urban per capita expenditure is considered to be grossly overestimated for this period.

The HIES data lead to several observations. First, Bangladesh has made notable progress in income-poverty reduction since independence. The proportion of the national population living below the poverty line was

Table 4.1 *Trends in Foster-Greer-Thorbecke Measures of Poverty: Consumption Expenditure Data*

	1983/84	1988/89	1991/92	2000
Rural				
H	53.8	49.7	52.9	43.6
P(1)	15.0	13.1	14.6	11.3
P(2)	5.9	4.8	5.6	4.0
Urban				
H	40.9	35.9	33.6	26.4
P(1)	11.4	8.7	8.4	6.7
P(2)	4.4	2.8	2.8	2.3
National				
H	52.3	47.8	49.7	39.8
P(1)	14.5	12.5	13.6	10.3
P(2)	5.7	4.6	5.1	3.6

Sources: Estimates for 1983/84 through 1991/92 are taken from Ravallion and Sen (1996); estimates for 2000 are authors' estimates.

Note: National poverty estimates are population-weighted poverty measures obtained separately for rural and urban sectors. The rural population shares are 88.7 percent (1983/84), 86.6 percent (1988/89), 83.4 percent (1991/92), and 78 percent (2000). These measures use mean consumption expenditure as reported in table 2.03 in successive HIES reports and are based on the suitable parameterized Lorenz curve as estimated from the grouped distribution data ranked by per capita consumption expenditure. The above estimates use the 1983/84 nonfood poverty line as the base-year nonfood poverty line.

as high as 74 percent in 1973/74. The most recent estimate available (for 2000) is 40 percent, indicating long-term progress in poverty reduction.[4] The income-poverty trends since the early 1990s show the following pattern. Between 1991/92 and 2000, the incidence of national poverty declined from 50 to 40 percent, indicating a reduction rate of 1 percentage point per year. The declining trend is robust to the choice of Foster-Greer-Thorbecke class of poverty measures.

Second, the data broadly indicate that the pace of poverty reduction was faster during the 1990s than during the 1980s because of accelerated economic growth. This growth is evidenced by trends in consumption expenditure data (on which the poverty estimates are based) and by national accounts data on GDP growth. The annual per capita HIES consumption expenditure growth at the national level, which was 0.83 percent between 1983/84 and 1991/92, rose to 2.38 percent between 1991/92 and 2000.

Third, the poverty reduction process in the 1980s was marked by considerable instability. The incidence of rural poverty declined in 1983–85, increased in 1985–88, declined again in 1988–91, and dropped little between 1983 and 1991. Much of these fluctuations were related to the damaging effects of floods in 1987 and 1988 on agricultural output. By contrast, the incidence of rural poverty dropped consistently throughout the 1990s, notwithstanding the adverse impact of the 1998 flood, indicating that the rural economy of the 1990s had higher resilience and more diversified sources of growth than that of the 1980s.

Fourth, the pace of poverty reduction was faster in urban areas than in rural areas in both the 1980s and 1990s. The pace of rural poverty reduction was slow in the 1980s but accelerated considerably in the 1990s. The pace of urban poverty reduction was slightly higher in the 1990s compared with the 1980s.

Nonincome Dimensions of Poverty

Bangladesh has achieved favorable human development conditions at a relatively low level of per capita income. Compared with the predicted values for a given level of such income, actual progress has been higher for the contraceptive prevalence rate, lower for population growth rate as well as for total fertility rate and crude birth rate, higher for life expectancy at birth and child immunization coverage, and lower for infant mortality rate (table 4.2). Bangladesh has achieved success in three areas with a direct bearing on the basic capabilities of the poor: population, basic health, and basic education.[5]

Table 4.2 *Social Development in Bangladesh: Predicted versus Actual Values*

Indicators	Predicted values	Actual values
Population growth rate (annual %)	2.45	1.59
Total fertility rate (births per women)	4.68	3.20
Contraceptive prevalence rate (% of women aged 15–49)	23.16	53.00
Crude birth rate	35.26	23.40
Crude death rate	11.49	8.40
Infant mortality rate (per 1,000 live births)	70.78	66.00
Life expectancy at birth, female (years)	59.50	60.8
Life expectancy at birth, male (years)	56.19	60.4

Sources: Government of Bangladesh 2003; World Bank 1999.

Note: Predicted value is a theoretical value for the present (benchmark) level of national income and is derived from the implied functional relationship between the indicators of interest (as given in the table) and the level of per capita national income; parameters of the relationship are estimated from cross-country data.

Bangladesh's population growth rate decreased from 2.9 percent per year in the mid-1970s to 1.5 percent in the late 1990s through an impressive decline in the total fertility rate (TFR), which dropped from 7 in 1975 to 3.2 in 1999/00, according to Demographic and Health Survey data. Remarkably, this decline was achieved not only at a low level of income but also at a low level of literacy. The onset of decline in TFR can be dated to the mid-1980s, that is, at a fairly early stage of development in terms of both per capita GDP and human development. Factors contributing to this decline include strong emphasis on family planning through public policy, women's empowerment, and interaction among community groups, especially self-help groups (Dev, James, and Sen 2002).

Three indicators capture broad trends in the area of basic health relevant to pro-poor growth: child mortality, child malnutrition, and maternal malnutrition. A very high level of infant mortality prevailed in the 1950s and 1960s. The infant mortality rate (IMR) began decreasing slowly in the mid-1970s; by 1985, it stood at 121, compared with 173 in 1973. Only after 1989 did the IMR begin a dramatic decrease, dropping to 51 in 2002 (figure 4.1). Some observers consider Bangladesh to be the "fastest reducer of infant mortality" in the 1990s (Stern 2002).[6]

In Bangladesh, the prevalence of child malnutrition—by anthropometric measures—has decreased substantially. The proportion of children (6 to 71 months) underweight dropped nationally from 72 percent in 1985/86 to

Figure 4.1 Long-Term Trends in Infant Mortality

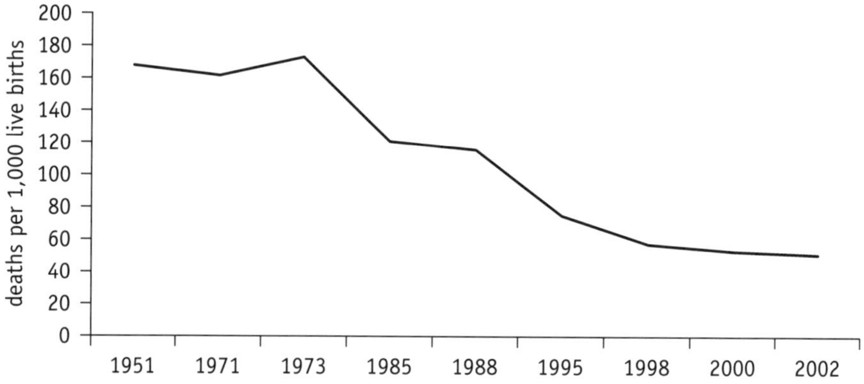

Sources: BBS 1975, 1992; Ministry of Health and Family Welfare 1993–2000.

51 percent in 2000.[7] Improvement in child malnutrition is closely linked to improvement in maternal malnutrition. The status of maternal nutrition has improved noticeably over the 1990s. The share of malnourished mothers was 52 percent in 1996/97 but 42 percent in 2000 (Sen and Ali 2005).

Bangladesh's achievements in education over the last two decades have been impressive, especially when compared with the performance of other countries in the region. Major successes include rapid expansion of primary education—gross primary enrollment increased from 72 percent in 1990 to 91 percent in 2000; lessening of the disparity between rural and urban primary enrollment; and closing of the gender gap, including the gender gap among the very poor.[8] Moreover, enrollment in secondary education expanded at an annual rate of 10 percent during the 1993–99 period. Gender and urban–rural parity in Bangladesh are comparable with that in Sri Lanka. Roughly 9 of every 10 children eventually enroll in primary school, and Bangladesh has achieved levels of primary and secondary gross enrollment similar to those in countries with higher per capita income, such as Indonesia, Thailand, and Vietnam (BIDS 2001; Government of Bangladesh 2003; World Bank 2003b).

Decadal GDP Growth

Impressive rates of poverty reduction in the 1990s were achieved through impressive GDP growth, as well as decreased volatility of that growth. The overall growth performance of the Bangladesh economy improved

Table 4.3 *Average Annual Economic Growth in Bangladesh at Constant 1995/96 Prices*

	Five-year average				Ten-year average		Recent years
	1981–85	1986–90	1991–95	1996–2000	1981–90	1991–2000	2001–03
GDP	3.7	3.7	4.4	5.2	3.7	4.8	5.0
Population	2.1	2.2	2.0	1.6	2.2	1.8	1.4
Per capita GDP	1.6	1.5	2.4	3.6	1.6	3.0	3.6

Source: Mujeri 2003.

considerably in the 1990s compared with earlier periods (table 4.3). In the 1980s, per capita GDP grew at a rate of only 1.6 percent per year; the growth rate nearly doubled to 3 percent during the 1990s. The acceleration in per capita income growth was due to a slowdown in the rate of population growth and an increase in the GDP growth rate. In relative terms, however, the economy's improved production performance played the dominant role in the acceleration of the per capita growth. It contributed nearly three quarters of the observed increase since the 1980s.

Historically, an important issue in Bangladesh's growth performance has been the volatility of economic growth, as reflected in considerable variations in yearly growth rates. These variations have been largely due to the economy's extreme vulnerability to natural disasters and other unforeseen events. A better growth record in the 1990s was due to the low volatility of growth itself.[9] From this perspective, a significant development in the 1990s was the diminishing severity of external events' effects on the economy's growth performance. The coefficient of variation of yearly GDP growth rate declined from a high of 29.5 percent in the 1980s to only 8 percent during the 1990s, indicating a substantial reduction in its yearly volatility. This reduction has been largely achieved through structural changes, such as improved capacity to mitigate natural disasters, agriculture's growing resilience, and the economy's increased diversification into nonagricultural sectors.

Strong growth performance should not be overplayed, however. First, Bangladesh's current GDP per capita is only $445 (in 2004/05), that is, way below the cutoff mark of $1,000 needed to graduate from LDC status. Second, gains are modest: current GDP per capita in purchasing power parity dollars is only 42 percent of the average estimated for all developing countries. Third, these gains need to be increased through "repeat games" in the coming decade, which is not an easy task given changing national and global circumstances.

Trends in Inequality

Although growth accelerated in the 1990s, leading to greater poverty reduction than in the 1980s, the pattern of growth became increasingly inequitable. Both consumption expenditure and income data point to this trend. According to surveys up to 1991/92, the level of consumption expenditure inequality did not vary much: the urban Gini ratio hovered around 0.30 to 0.32, while the rural Gini fluctuated in and around 0.25 to 0.26 (table 4.4). The situation has changed in a major way since the early 1990s. The increase in inequality—especially in urban areas—was sharp on a scale not seen before. Thus, the Gini coefficient for urban areas shot up from 0.32 in 1991/92 to 0.38 in 2000. Similarly, the rural Gini rose to 0.30, up from 0.26 during the same period.

Moreover, consumption data understate the degree of relative inequality prevailing in Bangladesh society. Distribution of income and wealth must also be considered. Analysis of current income distribution further confirms the increasing trend in relative inequality. The Gini ratio for rural income inequality rose sharply from 0.27 in 1991/92 to 0.31 in 1995/96 and to 0.36 in 2000. The corresponding rise in urban income inequality during the 1990s is

Table 4.4 *Trends in Inequality: Consumption Data (Tk/month/person)*

	Poverty line	Survey mean	Mean/poverty line (%)	Gini index
		Urban		
1983/84	301.72	396.53	131	29.8
1988/89	453.65	695.19	153	32.6
1991/92	534.99	817.12	153	31.9
2000	724.56	1430.12	197	37.9
		Rural		
1983/84	268.92	284.84	106	24.6
1988/89	379.08	435.39	115	26.5
1991/92	469.13	509.67	109	25.5
2000	634.48	820.20	129	29.7

Sources: Estimates for 1983/84 through 1991/92 are taken from Ravallion and Sen (1996); estimates for 2000 are authors' estimates.

even more striking, the urban Gini having increased from 0.33 in 1991/92 to 0.39 in 1995/96 and to 0.44 percent in 2000.[10]

More of the gains from the overall growth in the 1990s could have been translated into additional pro-poor growth effects but for this sharp rise in inequality (table 4.5 and figure 4.2). The distinction between overall and

Table 4.5 *Ordinary Growth and Pro-Poor Growth Rates in Bangladesh: 1990s versus 1980s*

Growth rates (% per year)	National 1983/84–1991/92	National 1991/92–2000
Ordinary growth rate	0.83	1.78
Rate of pro-poor growth	n.a.	0.71
Annual change in Gini index, rural (%)	0.45	1.94
Annual change in Gini index, urban (%)	0.88	2.21

Source: Estimated from the unit-record data of Household Income Expenditure Survey.

Note: The Bangladesh estimates are based on a national headcount index of 50 percent for 1983/84 and 1991/92, as there has been negligible change in headcount index of poverty during the 1980s (see table 4.1). Note that the rate of pro-poor growth has been calculated as the mean growth rate of the poor at the beginning of the period. Gini index for consumption expenditure is taken from table 4.4. Calculations are made on the basis of a national headcount index of 50 percent, urban head-count of 33 percent, and rural headcount of 53 percent in 1991/92.

Figure 4.2 *Bangladesh's Growth Incidence Curves, 1991/92–2000*

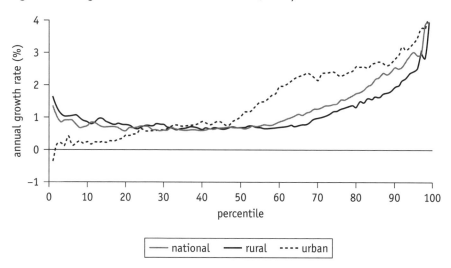

Source: Estimated from the unit-record data of Household Income Expenditure Survey 1991/92 and 2000 (Bangladesh Bureau of Statistics 1991/92 and 2000).

Table 4.6 Ordinary Growth and Pro-Poor Growth Rates in Bangladesh: Rural, Urban, and National, 1991/92–2000

Growth rates (% per year)	Rural	Urban	National
Ordinary growth rate	1.42	2.34	1.78
Rate of pro-poor growth	0.80	0.37	0.71
Distributional effect	0.56	0.16	0.40

Source: Estimated from the unit-record data of Household Income Expenditure Survey.
Note: Estimates are based on unit-record data. Calculations are made on the basis of national head-count index of 50 percent, urban head-count of 33 percent, and rural headcount of 53 percent in 1991/92.

pro-poor growth becomes clearer when the contrasting experience between the rural and urban areas during the 1990s is taken into consideration. Although per capita average consumption expenditure growth was 65 percent higher in urban areas, the reverse is true when it comes to the rate of pro-poor growth. *The latter is 116 percent higher in rural areas than in urban areas* (table 4.6). Given the prevailing distributive arrangements at the present stage of development, the acceleration of rural growth would have had greater poverty-reducing effects at the national level than an urban-biased growth strategy.[11]

How Did Bangladesh Achieve Pro-Poor Growth?

Explanations for pro-poor growth in Bangladesh can be rooted in a stable macroeconomic environment that created fiscal space for public expenditures favoring the poor. In addition, political commitments to social development have been reflected in policy consistency, cutting across regime types since independence. Successive governments emphasized the need for reducing population growth, the importance of investing in primary and girls' education, and the role of primary health care in the forms of child and maternal immunization and universal coverage of safe drinking water.

Macroeconomic policies, vulnerability management and agriculture policies, and changes in rural factor markets have affected participation of the poor in the growth process of the 1990s. These factors and the dynamics of the rapidly developing ready-made garments (RMG) sector in urban areas are explored below.

Macroeconomic Environment for Increased Pro-Poor Growth in the 1990s

Several macroeconomic policies help explain the higher rate of pro-poor growth in the 1990s. These policies are related to macroeconomic stability, openness, and fiscal space for poverty-reducing expenditures such as human development and rural infrastructures.[12]

MACROECONOMIC STABILITY. In the 1990s Bangladesh's macroeconomic policies achieved relatively low inflation, a stable exchange rate, a low current account deficit, and a low fiscal deficit. Fiscal, monetary, and exchange rate management improved appreciably from 1989/90 to 1992/93, providing a reasonably sound basis for higher growth during the next 10 years (table 4.7). The average inflation rate in the 1980s, which was still on the order of 10.3 percent (a vast improvement over nearly 20 percent in the 1970s), decreased to 5.6 percent in the 1990s. Since the mid-1980s, management of the

Table 4.7 *Relative Performance of Macroeconomic Indicators, 1975–2000*

	Period			
Indicators	*I (1975–82)*	*II (1983–89)*	*III (1990–93)*	*IV (1994–2000)*
Average yearly growth rate (%) at 1984/85 prices				
GDP	2.7	3.9	4.7	5.3
Agriculture	1.5	1.5	3.9	3.1
Industry	1.4	3.1	6.7	6.2
Services	4.0	5.7	4.7	6.3
Per capita GDP	0.1	1.8	2.3	3.6
As percentage of GDP				
Gross investment	11.6	12.8	12.7	17.3
Gross domestic savings	1.6	2.4	4.9	8.1
Gross national savings	6.8	10.1	11.9	14.9
Exports	5.7	7.5	9.8	15.3
Imports	15.8	17.9	17.4	22.8
Current account balance	−1.4	−2.8	−1.2	−1.0
Tax revenue	6.3	7.3	8.4	9.5
Overall budget balance	−6.9	−6.4	−5.3	−6.8
Inflation (%)	12.3	10.0	4.7	5.8

Source: Mujeri and Sen 2003.
Note: Because national accounts data for the new series are not available for the entire period since the 1970s, the old series of national accounts has been used to ensure comparability across all periods. In the country classification, gross national savings is roughly equal to gross domestic savings plus remittances.

exchange rate has been characterized by a remarkable stability in the real exchange rate. Indeed, the real exchange rate has moved within a fairly small band of about 10 percent around its trend. By avoiding significant real exchange rate appreciation, the country preserved the competitiveness of its export sector.[13] Growth in exports (currently averaging 13 percent of GDP compared with 5 percent in 1981/82), combined with increasing remittances (currently at 5 percent of GDP), more than offset the drop in aid flows (currently averaging 2.5 percent of GDP compared with 10 percent in 1981/82 and 5 percent in 1990/91) and was sufficient to balance increases in imports resulting from trade liberalization measures during the 1990s.[14] As a result, the current account deficit, which averaged 2.6 percent in the 1980s, fell to an average of 0.8 percent in the second half of the 1990s.

OPENNESS. Outward orientation is an important instrument for sustained economic growth. In low-income labor-abundant countries such as Bangladesh, the problem of economic growth is to gainfully employ unlimited labor supplies while raising their productivity, for which incentives for reproducible and human capital accumulation become necessary. These incentives are governed by the limited size of the domestic market—hence the causal role of international trade in expanding the size of the market, especially in the early stage of development.[15]

Bangladesh's inward orientation—restrictive trade and exchange rate practices (an economic ideology common to most of South Asia)—created distortions in product and factor markets. As a part of the reform process, the Bangladesh economy opened significantly during the 1990s. The external sector substantially liberalized in terms of external trade and foreign exchange regimes.[16] A rapid increase in Bangladesh's global economic integration has also taken place. An open trade regime was, on the whole, beneficial to growth acceleration. Bangladesh's exports grew at an average rate of 11 percent per year in the 1990s and generated substantial employment, especially in the RMG sector (World Bank 1999).[17]

Such rapid openness has created challenges and opportunities for the Bangladesh economy. In particular, the interfaces of trade liberalization and poverty have proven to be complex. These interfaces appear to have depended much on the nature of the channels through which the liberalization effects have been transmitted to the economy and to different household groups (see, for example, Mujeri 2003). With differing mesoenvironments, net impacts also varied for household groups. The ability of heterogeneous poor groups to respond to the opportunities offered by liberalization depended on their access to markets and participation in socioeconomic transitions. In the future Bangladesh must effectively manage the liberalization process so as to provide opportunities in a credible and equitable manner.

FISCAL SPACE FOR EXPENDITURES WITH INCREASED PRO-POOR EFFECTS. After successive years of high and unsustainable fiscal deficit in the 1980s, which culminated in the fiscal crisis of 1988/89, Bangladesh made an impressive effort to stay on course in balancing the budget. It pursued reasonably prudent fiscal policies in the 1990s in the face of a rapid fall in foreign aid and inadequate revenue-raising measures. The average fiscal deficit for the 1980s stood at 5.8 percent, which was already lower than the deficit of many low-income countries, including the neighboring countries of South Asia; it dropped further to an average of 4.8 percent in the 1990s. In general, the public expenditure–GDP ratio has been lower than international standards, even relative to countries with similar per capita income.[18] Greater fiscal realism was expressed not only in better aggregate fiscal management than that of many neighboring countries, but also in channeling of public resources into sectors likely to be supportive of poverty reduction, namely, rural infrastructure and human development.

RURAL INFRASTRUCTURE DEVELOPMENT. Government policies have traditionally emphasized development of the rural economy as a means to alleviate poverty and contain the impact of natural calamities. In the 1970s the focus was on direct market interventions and large capital spending on flood control, irrigation, and drainage projects (table 4.8). In the 1980s most

Table 4.8 *Percentage Distribution of Public Expenditure in Agricultural and Rural Development in Bangladesh, 1980–2001*

Area	1980/81	1984/85	1989/90	1994/95	2000/01
Agricultural research	2.95	4.73	4.14	3.57	3.84
Extension and training	5.31	4.02	9.65	6.03	5.00
Market and institutions development	21.27	17.33	27.52	6.75	5.75
Rural infrastructure (roads and electricity)	6.09	9.03	15.69	47.64	56.60
Flood control and irrigation	46.72	64.30	42.65	28.90	25.47
Mixed type	1.04	0.59	0.35	1.16	2.15
Miscellaneous	16.62	0.00	0.00	4.91	2.19
Total	100.00	100.00	100.00	100.00	100.00

Source: World Bank 2003a.

public expenditures focused on broad agricultural development; rural infrastructure received relatively little emphasis. In the 1990s development of physical infrastructure—including roads, bridges, culverts, and marketplaces—was identified as the major element of the new rural development strategy.[19]

The Local Government Engineering Department (LGED) initiated development of feeder roads, *upazila* (subdistrict) connecting roads, and nascent market/growth centers throughout the country. The road projects, connecting 1,400 of the 2,100 growth centers/markets, helped increase farm and nonfarm output, employment, and income, especially of the rural poor and women. Other positive effects of the rural infrastructure development policy included rapid growth of nonfarm sector employment, roadside shops, and petty trading (Mandal 2002). Large-scale microsurvey data suggest that the number of small- to medium-size market centers more than doubled between 1994 and 2000 in rural areas, indicating the growing vibrancy of the rural economy (Sen and Hulme 2004). The rural road network, however, has reached a level at which a shift to investment in the quality of preexisting roads and selective expansion to connect rural areas to urban growth centers would be appropriate.

BASIC EDUCATION. Three key public policies underscored successes in primary and, in recent years, secondary education in Bangladesh: sustained injections of public resources, effective partnership with nongovernment institutions for service delivery, and provision of "smart" subsidies to influence the demand for education in favor of the poor and girls. The greater emphasis on primary education, especially girls' education, has been a consistent feature of the successive regimes, more explicitly after the transition to democracy in 1991. Spending in education has been the largest single item in the revenue and development budgets and has become an important part of electoral competition. Thus the proportional allocation of education has continuously increased over the past two decades: the matched share actually doubled from 8 percent to 16 percent between the early 1980s and the late 1990s.

Most government expenditure on education is directed to basic education—primary and mass education and secondary education. However, during the past decade, the focus has shifted from primary to secondary education. Primary education's share of the recurrent education budget decreased from 48.5 percent to 39.5 percent over the course of 1990s, while secondary education's share increased from 36.8 percent to 48.5 percent. The new emphasis reflected not only pressure to accommodate increasing demand for continuing education from the cohort that finished primary school but also a policy shift to widen secondary education, particularly for girls. Public–private partnerships played a crucial role in the expansion of secondary education. A large part of the public spending on basic education supports substantial demand-side incentives to boost enrollment (food-for-education program, secondary school stipends, and so on). The country's extensive nongovernment institutions have also contributed to developing education services, especially at the primary level, through the expanding net of nonformal education.

However, enrollment expansion and gender parity have not been matched by improvements in the quality of education, which remains low because of the poor quality of educational inputs and learning processes, weak accountability and incentive mechanisms, and inadequate checks and balances for teachers and administrators (CAMPE 1999, 2000). Public education expenditures need to be directed to improving quality in basic education and providing access to the hard-to-reach poor.

Distribution of public educational spending at the *national level* presents a complex picture (according to the HIES 2000 data). Benefit incidence analysis suggests that the distribution of primary educational expenditures is pro-poor. Thus the share of the bottom quintile in total public primary education spending is 22 percent, compared with 14 percent for the top quintile (the corresponding share for the poor and the nonpoor is 56 percent and 44 percent, respectively). The picture is reversed for secondary education. The corresponding share of the bottom quintile drops to 6 percent, while that for the top quintile increases to 40 percent (the matched share for the poor and the nonpoor is 24 percent and 76 percent, respectively). The picture for tertiary education is even more skewed (see World Bank 2003b for these estimates). Bangladesh clearly needs to address the pro-rich bias of public expenditures at the postprimary level.[20]

PRIMARY AND PREVENTIVE HEALTH CARE. As noted above, Bangladesh has achieved impressive gains in life expectancy, child mortality, and reproductive health during the 1990s. Bangladesh appears to have lower child mortality, higher access to drinking water and sanitation, lower maternal mortality, and a higher contraceptive prevalence rate than some of its neighbors (see, for instance, Drèze 2004 for favorable comparison with India in some of these respects). Although considerable public health challenges remain, some instructive policy lessons underpin achievements to date.

The national health program has focused on provision of affordable rural primary health care (through *upazila* health complexes and union health and family welfare centers) and on developing partnerships with nongovernmental organizations (NGOS). NGOs have been an extremely important source of health successes in Bangladesh, especially in the area of family planning and immunization services. Historically, they have supplied most health promotion services.[21] The immunization program, implemented in a collaborative framework, expanded from less than 1 percent of the population in 1981 to over 90 percent in the early 1990s. More recently, NGOs have become recognized partners of development within a long-term collaborative framework with the government to provide primary and community-based health care and nutrition services.

Consistent with Bangladesh's emphasis on human resources development, public spending on health has been increasing in both nominal and real terms over the last three decades. Although this spending is much lower than recommended by the World Health Organization, it is higher than that of many developing countries.[22] The distribution of public health spending also has a favorable redistributional effect. According to benefit incidence analysis, the share of public health spending accruing to the bottom quintile is 16 percent, while the share of overall income (expenditure) accruing to this quintile is 8 percent (World Bank 2003b). However, disparity in the distribution of benefits across quintiles and by the level of health care is considerable. Public spending on child health appears to be pro-poor: the weight of the bottom quintile in this category is 23 percent compared with 18 percent for the top quintile. But with respect to limited curative care, the matched shares of bottom and top quintiles are 11 percent and 28 percent, respectively. Scope for improved targeting and coverage of the poor and the poorest, especially at the secondary and tertiary levels of services, is considerable.

The preceding discussion points to the substantive role of the state in promoting pro-poor public investment strategy by way of increased allocations to rural infrastructures and social sectors. Some of the benefits of this strategy, such as lower transactions costs associated with the availability of all-weather roads and reduced burden of demographic dependency and lower health costs associated with fertility and mortality reduction, are likely to be readily translated into pro-poor growth. The positive effects on such growth of other categories of public investment, such as expenditures on primary and secondary education, take a longer time (usually 5–10 years) to become discernible.

Supporting Policies for Pro-Poor Growth: Agriculture and Vulnerability Management

Public expenditure is but one channel through which sound policy choices can accelerate pro-poor growth. The Bangladesh case study highlights the importance of two supporting policies that increase poor households' resilience to external shocks and ability to generate income: vulnerability management and technological advances in agriculture.

COPING WITH NATURAL DISASTERS. As one of the largest, and most densely populated, active deltaic regions of the world, Bangladesh is vulnerable to natural disasters, which can adversely affect pro-poor growth in three ways. First, floods and droughts affect food grain production, causing abnormal increases in food grain prices and decreases in the availability of jobs, in turn creating transitional food security problems. Second, the frequent occurrence of floods breeds systematic risks and uncertainty. It discourages private capital formation and hence depresses long-term growth in the economy. Third, natural disasters often lead to the dislocation and displacement of population groups.

Bangladesh significantly changed its approach to disaster preparedness and mitigation between 1988 and 1998, as is evident from the effects of major floods in those years. The 1998 flood was far more severe than the 1988 flood in terms of intensity and geographical coverage. Nevertheless, the macroeconomic and social effects of the 1998 flood were much less severe than those of the 1988 flood. As a result of the 1988 flood, overall per capita GDP growth was negative in 1988/89. In contrast, the effect of the much longer flood of 1998 on per capita GDP growth was much smaller, on the order of 3 percent in 1998/99.

The difference in the two floods' GDP growth effects is due to the enhanced resilience of poor people in the informal subaltern economy. First, the regions normally affected by floods have substantially increased food grain production during the dry season. Consequently, farmers may not have to wait a whole year to recover losses.

Second, the rural nonfarm sector has emerged as an important source of rural income and employment (especially part-time employment). Many nonfarm activities are supported by the microfinance operations of NGOs. Because a large proportion of the landless and near landless are now employed in the nonfarm sector, they can more easily adjust to the loss of employment in food grain production during years in which floods occur.

Third, disaster-coping mechanisms at the microeconomic level have strengthened. Overall leakage in food distribution has decreased (del Ninno 1998). Private sector food grain imports through formal and informal border channels have helped stabilize market supply. Policy makers better understand regional variations in food insecurity and better target the food distribution now that the government and NGOs coordinate relief and rehabilitation efforts. Weather monitoring and early warning systems have been strengthened. The ability to evacuate people from disaster zones and to provide shelter has improved. A free press and active democratic opposition have highlighted deficiencies within public action.

GREEN REVOLUTION. Since independence, Bangladesh has more than doubled its cereal production with the same or a smaller amount of cultivated land. This feat helped the country sustain the food-population balance and contributed to a decline in real prices of rice that benefits the rural landless and the urban poor. Most of the incremental production can be attributed to diffusion of modern rice technology and improved farming practices. High-yielding variety seeds have spread to about 65 percent of rice-cropped areas and irrigation facilities have expanded to more than 40 percent of cultivated areas. Total fertilizer use increased 10 percent per year over the last three decades. The government deregulated and liberalized markets and distribution of key agricultural inputs such as fertilizer,[23] irrigation, and improved crop varieties. Policy aimed at reducing government interventions as well as subsidies have completely transformed the markets for these inputs (Hossain 1996). Available evidence suggests that the policy reforms, on the whole, had a positive impact on the crop sector. Reforms in the input market contributed to increased production; prices of irrigation equipment and other inputs, including fertilizer, declined with no clear evidence of adverse distributional consequences.

The success of Bangladesh's green revolution highlights the crucial role of "productive forces" in bringing about favorable changes in traditional "relations of production." Many scholars argued that the preponderance of small and marginal farmers and the widespread use of crop-sharing tenancy that characterized the Bangladesh agrarian structure would impede technological progress and constrain agricultural growth (Boyce 1987; Jannuzi and Peach 1980). But later studies have shown that farm size and tenurial status do not affect adoption of modern varieties and intensity of chemical fertilizer use if farmers have access to water (Hossain 1996; Hossain and others 1994). In fact, diffusion of new technology has led to institutional changes—crop sharing has given way to fixed-rent tenancy in the cultivation of modern varieties, and tightening of the labor market during busy agricultural seasons has led to a shift change from daily-wage to piece-rate contracts.

Two areas have not yet benefited from the modern technology: those where irrigation development is uneconomical at current input–output price configurations and those with poor drainage and saline soils for which scientists have yet to develop appropriate high-yielding rice varieties. Improved crop management practices could increase the yield of modern varieties in both wet and dry seasons, but exploitation of this potential would require a more effective education and extension system and a closer link between this system and research institutions (Zohir, Shahabuddin, and Hossain 2002).

Changing Market Conditions and Pro-Poor Rural Growth

Marked changes in rural input, labor, and tenancy markets have influenced both the rate of overall growth and the pro-poor pattern of growth in Bangladesh. Liberalization and deregulation affected input markets and thus improved farmers' access to irrigation and mechanization. Labor markets became increasingly diversified into nonfarm activities, improving rates of remuneration. Changes in the rural tenancy market were also beneficial to the poor; they decreased sharecropping in favor of fixed-rental agreements, which were more conducive to productive investments.

PRO-POOR CHANGES IN RURAL INPUT MARKETS. Operation of rural input markets has changed significantly over the past two decades. Take, for example, shifts in the irrigation water market. Rapid expansion of land under irrigation has largely dictated adoption of modern rice varieties and, therefore, growth in the crop sector. Removal of restrictions on standardizations and placement of tube wells in the early 1990s had a positive effect on private sector investment in tube wells for expansion of groundwater irrigation. The number of shallow (and private force-mode tube wells) increased from 183,000 in 1987/88 to 624,000 in 1995/96. This spectacular growth was undoubtedly caused by the increased availability of relatively cheap Chinese and Korean engines made available as a result of engine standardization and a reduction in import duties. The resulting competition among engines and eventual elimination of duties caused engine prices to fall (Abdullah and Shahabuddin 1997). A vibrant water market has developed in which the owners of shallow tube wells (mostly large and medium-size farmers) sell water to farmers operating land within the tube well's command area.

Table 4.9 Returns to Labor by Mode and Sector of Employment and by Poverty Status in Rural Areas, 1999/2000

| | Farm | | Nonfarm | | |
| | Self-employment | Casual wage labor | Casual wage labor | Self-employment | Salaried wage labor |
Poverty status					
Extremely poor	16.43	30.15	40.53	38.47	56.10
Moderately poor	25.76	35.93	49.93	65.60	71.38
Moderately nonpoor	36.07	35.70	57.16	85.75	85.85
Rich nonpoor	47.73	37.39	72.42	239.58	125.30
All poor	22.75	33.33	45.70	57.22	63.75
All nonpoor	40.51	36.71	61.10	157.68	107.28
All households	33.51	33.85	51.98	116.08	96.29

Source: Osmani and others 2003.
Note: Estimated from the unit records of Household Income and Expenditure Survey, 2000. The rural population is divided into the extremely poor (bottom two deciles), the moderately poor (next three deciles), and the rich nonpoor (top two deciles).

In fact, a market for transactions in irrigation water has developed and given small and marginal farmers access to irrigation.

PRO-POOR CHANGES IN THE RURAL LABOR MARKET. Differences in rewards for rural labor among employment categories have an important bearing on poverty in rural Bangladesh (table 4.9). First, for each income group, any mode of employment in the nonfarm sector is, on average, far more rewarding than any mode of employment in the farm sector. This difference in the relative returns to labor lies behind the labor force shift to the nonfarm sector. Second, for the poor and especially the extremely poor, salaried jobs are far superior to self-employment in the nonfarm sector. Even for the moderately nonpoor, salaried jobs are at least as good as self-employment. Only for the very rich is self-employment in the nonfarm sector decidedly more rewarding than salaried jobs. These findings suggest that when the poor shift from farm to nonfarm activities, they will on average benefit, but their gain will be considerably higher if they are able to enter into salaried employment rather than self-employment (Osmani and others 2003).[24]

The shift of the rural labor force from farming to nonfarming activities has important implications for the dynamics of poverty in rural Bangladesh. Table 4.10 indicates that a sizable proportion of rural labor has shifted from farming to nonfarming activities between 1983/84 and 1999/2000. In

Table 4.10 Percentage of Rural Labor Force in Nonfarm Sector, 1983–2000

Sex	1983/84	1984/85	1990/91	1995/96	1999/00
Both sexes	34.3	34.4	38.6	37.8	38.7
Male	28.5	29.4	35.1	35.0	38.6
Female	89.5	88.8	61.3	51.0	39.0

Source: Osmani and others 2003.
Note: Labor Force Survey, various years. Employment estimates are based on the "usual definition."

1983/84, about 34 percent of the rural labor force was engaged in nonfarm activities, but by 1999/2000 this figure had increased to about 39 percent. This enlargement in the relative size of the nonfarm sector is an outcome of the contrasting trends in male and female labor force participation. Male participation in the nonfarm sector has steadily increased (consistent with the growing importance of that sector in the overall economy), while female participation has dramatically declined. The explanation for these contrasting trends lies in the structural shift within women's activities. High female participation in the nonfarm sector during the 1980s (when overall female labor participation was very low) was mainly in the form of low-productivity self-employment. In the 1990s, as alternative income opportunities opened up, overall female labor force participation also rose (from 8 percent in the early 1980s to 22 percent in the late 1990s). This increase has been accompanied by a shift from low-productivity nonfarm self-employment activities to generally more productive farm and nonfarm self-employment and wage-employment activities.

Apart from this gender contrast, the most important contrast lies in the structure of the rural nonfarm sector. Although no systematic surveys of this sector exist, Osmani and others (2003) have pieced together different kinds of evidence (using both Labor Force Survey and HIES data) to show that it was characterized by low-earning self-employment in the 1980s. By the 1990s, large-scale enterprises were entering the sector. They employed wage labor and were more productive than self-employment activities, and their emergence helps explain accelerated pro-poor growth in the 1990s.

PRO-POOR CHANGES IN RURAL TENANCY MARKET. A comparison of information provided by the 1983/84 and the 1996 National Agricultural Census indicates significant changes in rural land tenure in Bangladesh (table 4.11). Although the ratio of owner-occupied and tenant farms remains almost unchanged at 60:40, the proportion of the area under tenancy increased from about 17 percent of the operated area in 1983/84 to about 22 percent in

Table 4.11 Changes in Land Tenure, 1983/84–1996

Indicators	1983–4	1996
Owner-occupied farms (thousands)	6,239	7,250
Average size of owner-occupied farm (hectares)	0.86	0.65
Tenant farms (thousands)	3,730	4,548
Average size of tenant holdings (hectares)	1.02	0.76
Land rented-in (thousands of hectares)	1,541	1,837
Percentage of operated holding under tenancy	16.8	21.6
Area rented-in under sharecropping arrangements (thousands of hectares)	1,140	1,093
Area rented-in under fixed rent and other arrangements (thousands of hectares)	400	672
Number of farm holdings (thousands)	9,969	11,797
Operated land area (thousands of hectares)	9,180	8,181

Source: Report of Agricultural Census, 1983/84 and 1996, Bangladesh Bureau of Statistics (www.bbsgov.org/).

1996.[25] This change may be due to an increase in the area under absentee landownership resulting from urbanization and to the abandonment of marginal landholdings in favor of employment in nonfarm occupations.

More significant is the dramatic change in the structure of tenurial arrangements. The exploitative sharecropping tenancy, which provides disincentives to agricultural investments and adoption of input-intensive new technologies, is giving way to different fixed-rent tenancy and medium-term leasing arrangements. The area under share tenancy declined from about 74 percent of tenanted area in 1983/84 to about 62 percent in 1996 (this share was 91 percent in 1960), while the area under fixed-rent and other arrangements increased from about 26 percent to 38 percent over the same period.

Fixed-rent arrangements are generally more profitable to poor tenants than sharecropping arrangements. When tenants grow input-intensive modern varieties, they use fixed-rent arrangements that allow them to reap the fruits of additional investments in agricultural inputs. When they grow rain-fed crops, they continue sharecropping arrangements to share the risks to crop cultivation from floods or droughts.

Urban Dynamics of Pro-Poor Growth: The Case of Ready-Made Garments

From its modest beginnings in the early 1980s, the ready-made garments industry has registered phenomenal growth to become the leading industry of Bangladesh. By the mid-1990s, it was contributing 20 to 25 percent of total value added and employing 40 to 50 percent of the total workforce engaged in medium- and large-scale manufacturing. Its share in total exports was barely 4 percent in 1983/84 but 75 percent by the end of the 1990s. In 1990/91, fewer than 1,000 RMG units were in operation, but by the end of the decade that number tripled. In 1988/89, its value added was less than Tk 10 billion, but by 1997/98 it had risen to Tk 35 billion. These figures suggest that the additional income generated by RMG in the 1990s could have significantly boosted demand for services and other nontradables. Because garment workers are some of the poorest manufacturing workers, their spending must have been skewed toward the inferior-quality goods and services produced in the informal nontradable sector than toward those produced in the formal tradable sector or imported (Osmani and others 2003).

Interactions between the RMG sector and small and medium-size enterprises (SMEs) demonstrate how fast growth in manufactured exports can generate spillover effects in nontradables and boost demand for production of related materials and accessories. Summarizing the findings of various studies, South Asia Enterprise Development Facility (2003) and Bangladesh Enterprise Institute (2004) have identified important positive changes taking place in SMEs in Bangladesh. First, SMEs have diversified their activities. Second, entry and exit into the sector have become easier. Third, the RMG industry has contributed significantly to SME development by providing orders for accessories and packaging materials.

How Could Bangladesh Achieve Pro-Poor Growth with Weak Governance?

Bangladesh achieved relatively strong economic performance in the 1990s in spite of a generally poor institutional environment. Though ratings for democratic accountability were strong, institutional indicators in the areas of corruption and the rule of law remained poor and even worsened between 1996 and 2004, according to the International Country Risk Guide (Political Risk Services Group 2005) and the World Bank Governance Matters indicators (Kaufmann, Kraay, and Mastruzzi 2005). Since it first appeared in Transparency International's Corruptions Perceptions Index in 2001, Bangladesh has consistently been ranked as the country with the most corrupt government (Barbone and others 2006).

Bangladesh's corruption indicators are certainly relevant to its economic development. However, a focus on corruption indexes as a proxy for all aspects of governance would belie the heterogeneity within Bangladesh's institutional profile. Since 1984 Bangladesh has scored consistently much better on investment climate than on corruption, according to Political Risk Services Group (2005) and the World Bank (Kaufmann, Kraay, and Mastruzzi 2005). The latest publication in the World Bank *Doing Business* series ranks Bangladesh well above India and above Sri Lanka for ease of doing business (World Bank 2005b).[26] Moreover, conventional institutional indicators, which focus on the urban environment, do not adequately capture the institutional context of rural Bangladesh, which is very different from the one currently associated with Bangladesh.

Creating Pockets of Excellence in a Poor Institutional Environment

The government has attempted to circumvent institutional weaknesses where they have impeded pro-poor growth. Three elements of the strategy are

- insulating strategic growth and human development areas from negative influences from areas plagued by misgovernance (so-called ring fencing);
- reducing a "capacity deficit" by deploying nongovernmental resources; and
- tapping the resilience and self-improvement capacity of the poor through social learning, community interaction, and promotion of positive attitude changes.

RING FENCING. In Bangladesh, policies integral to the welfare of the poor, including family planning, disaster management, access to drinking water, and expansion of primary education (especially for girls) have taken on the character of public goods. Successive governments, irrespective of their political leanings and degree of democracy, have shielded these policies from budgetary and political pressures. Treatment of the green revolution reflects this strategy.

After a devastating famine in 1974, the quest for self-sufficiency in rice production became a goal for successive governments. The goal was realized by the end of the 1990s through a multipronged approach: resources were given to research institutes to develop indigenous high-yield varieties; farmers were convinced to adopt these new varieties; and, as discussed above, the government created space for the private sector to play a vital role in the "shallow tube well revolution." A comparison of Bangladesh and West Bengal with respect to food production illustrates how, in the case of the former, the ring-fencing policies offered a viable alternative to more radical institutional reform. The trend of accelerated rice production was similar in the two Bengals during the period 1981–2000, although in the case of West Bengal it required a Left-front government to carry out land reform measures, while in the case of Bangladesh self-sufficiency was achieved through the adoption of high-yield varieties and the liberalization of input markets.

In addition to ring-fencing policies integral to pro-poor growth, the government has invested resources in creating "islands of excellence" in otherwise weak institutional environments. Consider the creation of the Local Government Engineering Department (a powerful body outside the direct day-to-day scrutiny of the Ministry of Local Government) that oversees speedy implementation of rural all-weather roads. The LGED should be viewed as a major institutional breakthrough, without which the rapid development of the countrywide rural road network would not have been possible.

Another island of excellence is the Palli Karma Sahayak Foundation (PKSF), an autonomous microcredit fund that is insulated from the weaknesses of the public finance bureaucracy. The traditional microcredit market in Bangladesh is highly concentrated (the four largest microfinance institutions control over 80 percent of the total credit disbursement) and tends not to reach the very poor. PKSF furnishes microfinance to medium-size and small NGOs, which in turn provide microcredit services to the poor, particularly those usually excluded from microfinancing programs.

STRATEGIC PARTNERSHIPS FOR DEVELOPMENT. The government has created civil space for NGOs to compensate for "capacity deficits" in the area of service delivery. NGOs have featured prominently as providers of microfinance, health, and nonformal education to the poor, particularly poor women. The Grameen model of microfinance, originally developed in Bangladesh during the mid-1970s, has inspired much of the self-help group movement in South Asia. The Bangladesh Rural Advancement Committee (BRAC), which also originated in the 1970s, has taken a multifaceted approach to poverty reduction by providing, among other services, microcredit, training, and nonformal primary education. Its successes in providing rural education are well documented: 90 percent of graduates from BRAC schools had moved on to formal schooling in 1995 (Mondal 2000). More than 400 NGOs are currently engaged in nonformal education programs nationwide (World Bank 2005a). Civil society also plays an important role in the delivery of health services, particularly family planning.

By the 1990s, Bangladesh had become the leading example of the use of NGOs as vehicles of development. Nearly 80 percent of villages are covered by some NGO program or project (World Bank 2005a). Even if the capacity of government agencies has decreased, the combined capacity of public agencies, NGOs, and the private sector has not.

ENCOURAGING COMMUNITY PARTICIPATION. The potential of communities to implement strategies that enhance their own welfare is enormous. Diffusion of new agricultural technologies and adoption of better health practices, as well as changing norms regarding women's education, health, and mobility, point to a dynamic independent of the contributions of governmental and nongovernmental initiatives. For example, levels of education and income provide a less robust explanation for declining birth rates than the diffusion of birth control practices through a social framework. The decline in fertility in Bangladesh has been explained in terms of a unique culture, history, and language that facilitate social learning (Basu and Amin 2000). Another important mechanism for diffusion is the role of self-help groups in which women are predominant. They encourage people to have smaller families and educate their children (Dev, James, and Sen 2002).

In summary, Bangladesh demonstrates that a weak institutional environment can be circumvented for a prolonged period to promote a pattern of growth and poverty reduction. But the government's reliance on NGOs as service providers, while a pragmatic and effective second-best solution, raises problems of accountability. Particularly at the local level, a long-term reliance on NGOs can impede development of effective governance institutions and lock beneficiaries in a charitable, rather than rights-based, relationship with service providers (Haque 2002; World Bank 2002). Moreover, weak accountability mechanisms can be linked with growing inequality levels: where the poor lack social and political capital they will be unable to tip economic institutions in their favor. As illustrated below, growing levels of inequality in urban areas might be redressed by a focus on institutions that enhance the urban poor's access to assets. While Bangladesh has overcome institutional impediments to growth and poverty reduction for more than a decade, the long-term sustainability of pro-poor growth will rest in part on institutional reforms.

Is Rising Inequality a Concern for Pro-Poor Growth?

Inequality has increased in Bangladesh in recent years. Theoretically, a case can always be made to show that distributionally neutral growth will yield higher poverty reduction, but the growth dynamics for a given country may not render such a choice feasible.[27]

Did Bangladesh have alternative options in terms of higher poverty reduction with lower income inequality during the 1990s? The answer is different for rural and urban areas. In both cases the sources of growth also contributed to deteriorations in the distribution of income. Although the government has responded with an appropriate institutional framework to equip the rural poor with sufficient assets to benefit from these sources of growth, the urban poor lack the necessary institutional mechanisms to similarly benefit.[28]

Was a Rise in Inequality Unavoidable in Rural Areas?

Table 4.12 presents information on the sources of income inequality in rural Bangladesh.[29] It shows that the three most important sources of income behind the deterioration in rural income equality or distribution are activities that are intensive in financial capital (such as trade and many nonfarm self-employment activities), income sources associated with human capital (such as salaried wage employment), and migration to foreign countries ("remittances from abroad"). The table also shows that the disequalizing tendencies of these three sources of rural income have magnified over the 1990s.

Could anything have been done to avert these developments in the 1990s? The answer is no for two reasons. First, the main sectors of rising income inequality in rural Bangladesh also represented the most growth-seeking sectors of the rural economy. Second, recognizing that gains from these sectors were not sufficiently benefiting the poor, the government designed an appropriate institutional response to enable the poor to participate in sources of growth in the future.

The three main disequalizing forces in the rural economy—nonfarm self-employment income, salaried wage employment, and remittances—have also represented key sources of growth. Although income from nonfarm self-employment was equalizing in the early 1990s, it had become highly disequalizing by the end of the decade: the concentration ratio rose from 0.22 to 0.48. At the same time, the share of nonfarm enterprise income in total rural income increased from 15 to 20 percent. As a result of the combined effect of these two tendencies, the contribution of this source of income to overall rural income inequality increased from 12 to 27 percent. Salaried wage employment and remittances from abroad have contributed 21 percent and 19 percent, respectively, to overall rural income inequality.

Table 4.12 *Rural Income Inequality and Its Sources, 1991–2000*

Sources of income	Share of total income (%)		Gini/concentration ratio		Contribution of income component to overall inequality	
	1991/92	2000	1991/92	2000	1991/92	2000
Farm income	41.48	20.92	0.33	0.35	49.90	20.45
Crop	n.a.	16.01	n.a.	0.35	n.a.	15.65
Livestock	n.a.	1.47	n.a.	0.24	n.a.	0.99
Fishery	n.a.	1.62	n.a.	0.40	n.a.	1.81
Forestry	n.a.	1.83	n.a.	0.37	n.a.	1.89
Wage income	21.42	31.17	0.10	0.21	7.90	18.28
Casual agriculture	10.86	10.29	−0.11	−0.15	−4.38	−4.31
Casual nonagriculture	4.23	7.33	0.14	0.07	2.17	1.43
Salaried nonagriculture	6.32	13.55	0.45	0.55	10.42	20.82
Nonfarm enterprise	15.33	20.24	0.22	0.48	12.40	27.14
Property income from land	0.89	3.41	0.55	0.56	1.80	5.33
Transfer and remittance	10.90	12.17	0.36	0.55	14.40	18.70
Transfer	n.a.	1.31	n.a.	0.06	n.a.	0.22
Informal	n.a.	1.07	n.a.	0.11	n.a.	0.33
Formal	n.a.	0.24	n.a.	−0.16	n.a.	−0.11
Remittance	n.a.	10.86	n.a.	0.61	n.a.	18.51
Within	n.a.	3.33	n.a.	0.39	n.a.	3.63
Abroad	n.a.	7.53	n.a.	0.71	n.a.	14.93
Rental value of housing	7.74	5.29	0.35	0.33	9.80	4.88
Misc. income	2.29	6.79	0.37	0.27	3.60	5.12
Grand total	100.00	100.00	0.276	0.358	100.00	100.00

Sources: 1991/92 estimates are from Khan and Sen (2001); 2000 figures are from Khan and Sen (2004).
Note: Column totals do not add up exactly to the amounts shown due to rounding.
n.a. = not available.

Because the three main sources of rising income inequality in rural Bangladesh also represented the most growth-seeking sources of the rural economy, the key policy challenge was enabling the poor to benefit from these sources. According to a process of evolutionary diffusion of new ideas and technologies—as historically typified in Bangladesh by the gradual "deepening" of the green revolution and population control—development opportunities are first accessed by the nonpoor, then percolate to the moderately poor and finally to the extremely poor.[30] This pattern of diffusion is not inevitable: extending development opportunities to the extremely poor is very difficult.

In the 1990s the nonpoor and, to a considerable extent, the moderately poor benefited most from new sources of rural growth, such as nonfarm self-enterprise income, salaried wage employment, and remittances. In contrast, participation of the extremely poor in these activities was either very limited or was restricted to the low-productivity end of these activities.[31] Thus, the extremely poor are twice disadvantaged: they are unable to fully access the activities that could raise them above the poverty line and, even when they do gain access to such activities, they are unable to earn as much as the moderately nonpoor. These disadvantages have a lot to do with the relative inability of the extremely poor to access salaried jobs in the nonfarm sector and to earn high rates of return from self-employment. The key factor in their relative backwardness is their comparatively limited access to capability-enhancing assets such as human capital, physical assets (both personal and collective), and support from social networks. The extremely poor are often excluded from the "progressive segment" of the market and face the most conservative terms of conditions and most exploitative relations of production.[32]

In the 1990s the government began providing institutional responses to the limited access of the extremely poor to capability-enhancing assets. These responses include microcredit programs and stipend schemes for attracting students from poor families. However, the benefits from these human capital development programs could not be readily translated into growth advantages, at least over the medium term. The positive effects of these programs are likely to show up in the next decade's income distribution dynamics.

In short, Bangladesh could not have avoided rising rural income inequality in the 1990s, given the evolutionary nature of the growth path. The 1990s was largely the decade of escape from poverty for the moderately poor in rural areas. The government's institutional responses to rural inequality are likely to increase gains for the extremely poor in the coming years.

Was Higher Pro-Poor Growth Possible in Urban Areas?

Table 4.13 presents the sources of rising inequality in urban areas in the 1990s. The role of nonfarm self-enterprise income, salaried wage employment, and remittances is highlighted in the case of urban distribution

Table 4.13 Urban Income Inequality and Its Sources, 1991–2000

Sources of income	Share of total income (%)		Gini/concentration ratio		Contribution of income component to overall inequality	
	1991/92	2000	1991/92	2000	1991/92	2000
Farm income	6.09	2.41	0.12	0.22	2.10	1.21
Crop	n.a.	1.75	n.a.	0.20	n.a.	0.80
Livestock	n.a.	0.23	n.a.	0.05	n.a.	0.03
Fishery	n.a.	0.20	n.a.	0.59	n.a.	0.27
Forestry	n.a.	0.23	n.a.	0.19	n.a.	0.10
Wage income	36.55	38.03	0.28	0.31	30.80	26.92
Casual agriculture	3.25	0.89	−0.03	−0.25	−0.30	−0.51
Casual nonagriculture	10.01	8.03	0.09	−0.18	2.76	−3.30
Salaried (nonagriculture)	23.29	29.11	0.40	0.46	28.40	30.57
Nonfarm enterprise	28.42	28.84	0.31	0.50	26.60	32.92
Property income from land	3.76	1.59	0.64	0.51	7.40	1.85
Transfer and remittance	9.27	10.10	0.43	0.62	12.10	14.30
Transfer	n.a.	4.27	n.a.	0.78	n.a.	7.60
Informal	n.a.	4.25	n.a.	0.78	n.a.	7.57
Formal	n.a.	0.02	n.a.	−0.32	n.a.	−1.46
Remittance	n.a.	5.83	n.a.	0.50	n.a.	6.66
Within	n.a.	1.93	n.a.	0.30	n.a.	1.32
Abroad	n.a.	3.90	n.a.	0.59	n.a.	5.25
Rental value of housing	9.19	12.77	0.43	0.58	12.20	16.91
Misc. income	6.72	6.26	0.42	0.42	8.70	6.00
Grand total	100.00	100.00	0.327	0.438	100.00	100.00

Sources: 1991/92 estimates are from Khan and Sen (2001); 2000 figures are from Khan and Sen (2004).
Note: Column totals do not add up exactly to the amounts shown due to rounding.
n.a. = not available.

dynamics, as it was in rural distribution dynamics (the additional contributing factor is rental value of housing). But the arguments applied to rural inequality trends cannot be applied to urban inequality, because human capital development programs have not been extended to the urban poor. Nearly all antipoverty programs (including human capital development programs such as stipend schemes and essential health service packages) have been targeted to rural areas only. As a result, initial disadvantages in the capabilities of moderately poor and extremely poor urban households have persisted.

As table 4.13 shows, activities such as casual nonagricultural jobs, in which most of the urban poor work, have equalizing effects on urban income distribution but exhibit no substantial growth prospects: indeed, their contribution to urban income actually dropped during the 1990s. Moreover, many of these activities (such as rickshaw pulling, brick breaking, or tannery) are not viable exit routes from urban poverty. They may pass as candidates for pro-poor growth because of their labor intensity, but they often represent long-term risks because of adverse health externalities.

The continuing absence of an institutional framework to enable the urban poor to gain from sources of growth suggests that this population's prospects for upward mobility will remain limited. The rapid rise, as measured by the Gini index, in urban income inequality from a level of 0.33 to 0.44 in a matter of a decade is a cause of concern in itself. This rise represents one of the fastest increases in inequality in the developing world and is a source of broader policy concern given the continued rise in urban population in Bangladesh—currently totaling 25 percent, up from just 12 percent two decades ago, and projected to reach 40 percent in 2018 (the metropolis of Dhaka will be the fourth largest city in the world in 2018). Clearly, more can be done in the areas of human development, sustainable job creation, access to basic social services, and improved urban governance. In short, the scope for improving the relative position of the urban poor in the urban growth process—not just for moderating the sharply rising trends of urban inequality, but also for accelerating the rate of rather modest pro-poor growth in urban areas—is considerable.

Conclusion

Bangladesh achieved impressive growth and poverty reduction in the 1990s through increased macroeconomic stability and trade openness, enhanced resilience to shocks and greater capacity for managing risks arising from vulnerability to natural disasters, and investments in rural infrastructure and agriculture. This strong pro-poor growth performance also reflected sustained political commitment to improving the welfare of the poor, as evidenced by improvements in human development indicators and a steady drop in fertility and population growth rates.

Future challenges relate to generating momentum for continued broad-based growth. Political attention must shift to ensuring that the gains from trade liberalization and structural transformation reach the extremely poor. Mechanisms to circumvent or fill gaps left by weak public institutions are at least in part responsible for a rise in urban inequality, which is particularly worrisome in the context of internal migration and urbanization. Institutional responses need to enhance the urban poor's access to capacity-enhancing assets.

A recent study has suggested that analysts need new cross-country databases—measuring the property rights of the poor and transaction costs for small-scale entrepreneurs, for instance—to better understand how institutions affect the poor (Barbone and others 2006). Future research might assess the extent to which current governance indicators accurately reflect elements of the institutional environment that are relevant to the poor in Bangladesh.

Notes

1. The estimated population of Bangladesh was about 130 million in 2000. The population density is about 880 persons per square kilometer—the highest in the world, excluding city states such as Singapore. The contrasting themes of "initial pessimism" and "subsequent success" of the 1990s reflect research on Bangladesh by Mujeri and Sen (2003), Government of Bangladesh (2003), World Bank (2003b), and Ahluwalia and Mahmud (2004).

2. Bangladesh is approaching self-sufficiency in production of rice, the staple food, through adoption of modern technologies. Increased disaster preparedness and expanded capacity to implement lean-season wage employment and transfer programs help ensure minimum food entitlements for the poorest in times of crisis.

3. The primary source of incomparability is different methods of food expenditure recording: memory was mainly used in surveys up to 1981/82, but the more reliable diary-keeping method was used in the later surveys (see Ravallion 1990; Hossain and Sen 1992). Thus the survey data between 1973/74 and 1981/82 are comparable, but *not* comparable to data from 1983/84 through 2000 (last year for which HIES is presently available). Within the later series, comparison between urban data of 1995/96 and 2000 is problematic: because of an overestimation of the average level of urban per capita expenditure, results yield average negative growth in real urban expenditure between 1995/96 and 2000 (see Government of Bangladesh 2003).

4. Assessment of the poverty level will vary depending on the poverty line used. On the basis of the 1991/92 poverty line (derived by the so-called upper poverty line method), World Bank (2002) found the level of poverty in 2000 to be 50 percent; on the basis of the 1983/84 poverty line (frequently used in the Bangladesh literature), it would be 40 percent. Although the level estimates vary between the two sources, the extent of poverty reduction is similar: about a 1 percentage point drop per year during the 1990s.

5. Notwithstanding expansion of primary and secondary education in the 1990s, the adult literacy rate reflects Bangladesh's enormous burden of illiteracy.

6. Demographic and Health Survey data confirm the trend with a different survey methodology and estimation procedures: the IMR has dropped from 101 in 1993/94 to 80 in 1999/00. DHS data also show considerable improvement in the under-five mortality rate, as the matched figure dropped from 150 to 110 between 1994 and 2000.

7. This refers to the child malnutrition data collected by the Bangladesh Bureau of Statistics. The DHS data also show that the proportion of children (0 to 59 months) underweight has dropped from 56 percent to 48 percent between 1996/97 and 1999/00.

8. The level of net enrollment rate is lower but shows impressive progress as well.

9. This low volatility of growth may be clearly seen within the framework of cross-country growth regressions. Adding volatility to the standard Barro-type cross-country regressions increases significantly the predictive power of the model, which was used to predict the long-terms growth of GDP per capita in Bangladesh (see World Bank 2003b).

10. The 1991/92 and 1995/96 figures are from Khan and Sen (2001); the 2000 estimates are from Khan and Sen (2004). The Bangladesh Bureau of Statistics (BSS) estimates differ from these estimates. Past BBS estimates of the income Gini index were based on the flawed "per household" income distribution rather than on the preferred "per capita" income distribution. Moreover, the BBS definition of income includes several kinds of nonincome revenues, which need to be reconsidered while computing the Gini index for relative income inequality. These items relate to capital receipts from the sale of assets, increases in financial assets, and receipts arising out of the repayment of loans. Excluding these items, Khan and Sen (2001) recomputed the Gini index for 1991/92 and 1995/96. The reworking gives lower figures for Gini in both rural and urban areas, though the underlying trend remains unaffected.

11. This is not to say that all the areas of urban growth have low poverty responsiveness. Ready-made garments, small- and medium-size industries, construction, transport, and informal service activities are likely to be poverty reducing. But, in the aggregate sectoral sense, urban growth in the 1990s emerged as a lesser poverty reducer than rural growth.

12. These policy factors also emerged as the key elements from the growth literature on Bangladesh and South Asia: Mujeri and Sen (2003); Osmani and others (2003); Tendulkar and Sen (2003); World Bank (2003b).

13. The strength of the taka since 1997 is due in part to the rapid growth of RMG exports and remittances. But given Bangladesh's narrow export base, appreciation of the real exchange rate during the 1990s was not a good outcome. This trend is being reversed, and Bangladesh adopted a flexible exchange rate regime in 2003.

14. From the perspective of pro-poor growth in rural areas, the relevance of remittances is best revealed by their use: land and agricultural input purchases,

children's education, and care for the sick. On average, temporary migrants remit 40 percent of their urban income and 45 percent of overseas income to their families in rural areas (Afsar and others 2000).

15. See Adam Smith's conjecture on dynamic gains from trade as described by Sachs (1998). The causal role of the lack of outward orientation in South Asia's long-term slowdown from 1950 to 1990 has been argued forcefully elsewhere. See Tendulkar and Sen (2003).

16. The unweighted mean tariff decreased from 94 percent in 1989 to 21 percent in 1998; it was 27 percent for the South Asia region in 1998.

17. Average total factor productivity (TFP) growth was estimated to be 6 percent annually between 1992/93 and 1996/97. TFP growth was considerably higher for import-competing firms than for export-oriented firms (11 percent versus 3.5 percent annually), reflecting the former's larger initial technology gap and scope for larger leaps in technological progress. Trade liberalization may have adversely affected some import-competing firms (in iron- and metalworks, engineering, rubber works, and cotton mills). However, many of the surveyed firms cited other factors, such as inadequate infrastructural services and the "high cost of doing business," as the key factors affecting their performance.

18. Public expenditure as a proportion of GDP was 1 percentage point higher in the 1990s than in the 1980s. Given low revenue mobilization and declining aid inflows this higher proportion was mainly achieved through increased domestic borrowing—a strategy that averted a potential demand contraction without creating excess demand (Osmani and others 2003). But this strategy cannot be viewed as sustainable, because interest payment on internal borrowing was already a significant item of budget spending. The tax-GDP ratio must rise to pay for the increasing envelope of public expenditures required to develop human resources and rural infrastructure.

19. Though rural electricity gained higher policy attention in this period, it was still a relatively neglected area by the end of the 1990s and therefore represents an important development challenge in accelerating pro-poor growth in the next decade.

20. Since 2000 the situation may have improved with respect to the pro-poor orientation of public secondary expenditures, especially with the introduction of the Female Secondary Education Stipend Scheme in rural areas. However, this scheme needs to be comprehensively evaluated.

21. NGOs can be credited with popularizing oral rehydration therapy for diarrhea and the use of contraceptives as well as providing nutrition, tuberculosis, and leprosy management services, mainly under contract from the government.

22. In comparing Bangladesh with India, Drèze (2004) attributes the former's somewhat superior performance on health indicators to a higher level of public spending on health as proportion of GDP.

23. Deregulation of fertilizer marketing was completed in 1992 when the Bangladesh Agricultural Development Corporation withdrew from wholesale trade, allowing the private sector to procure, import, and distribute fertilizers in

domestic markets. Privatization of the fertilizer market reduced the cost of marketing. The fertilizer crisis in 1995 partially reversed some gains realized through the reforms.

24. In this context the rural nonfarm sector can be considered a poverty-reducing force if the marginal income gained by the poor is higher in this sector than income gained in agriculture. Econometric analysis of 1990/91 HIES data (World Bank 1998) suggests that a shift from agriculture to nonfarm occupations entails a significant income gain for households with similar land ownership and other characteristics. The 1995/96 HIES data also provide strong evidence that people in nonfarm occupations are less likely to be poor (Rahman 2002).

25. Most of the tenants are owner-cum-tenants who own some land and rent more land for better use of farm resources (family workers, draft animals, farm equipment).

26. Bangladesh is ranked 65, India 116, and Sri Lanka 75.

27. It has been argued that had the observed rate of growth between 1991/92 and 2000 been distributionally neutral, the headcount index would have fallen by 17 percentage points or almost twice the actual rate of poverty reduction achieved during the period. See World Bank (2002).

28. This discussion of distribution dynamics is based on current income rather than current consumption expenditure data. Although a consumption expenditure measure of well-being gives a truer picture of poverty dynamics, it cannot be meaningfully used to shed light on the underlying structural/sectoral factors that drive distribution dynamics. That task requires current income data (however imperfect those data may be from the poverty measurement point of view). The methodological point here is the importance of collecting good income data, for only an effective combination of consumption expenditure data (for capturing changes in poverty) and income data (for understanding income distribution dynamics) can help analysts understand the determinants and dynamics of pro-poor growth.

29. If a component of income whose contribution to inequality (as represented by the last column in table 4.12) is higher than its percentage share of total income (as given in the second column), that particular source of income is "disequalizing": a rise in its share of total income increases the Gini ratio. In the reverse case, the source of income is "equalizing."

30. For a review of the literature on "diffusion" in the context of low-income countries, see Dev, James, and Sen (2002).

31. Osmani and others (2003) listed the activities that together account for 90 percent of the time devoted by the moderately nonpoor to productive activities. They found that the extremely poor are able to devote only half as much time to such activities and that their return from productive activities per unit of time is distinctly lower than the return to the moderately nonpoor.

32. Recent work on caste- and ethnicity-based discriminations also show that the extremely poor tend to have not only limited access to assets but also lower returns to their assets (World Bank 2004).

References

Abdullah, A., R. Afsar, A. Rahman, and B. Sen. 1991. *Modernization at Bay: Structure and Change in Bangladesh.* Dhaka, Bangladesh: University Press Ltd.

Abdullah, A., and Q. Shahabuddin. 1997. "Critical Issues in Agriculture: Policy Response and Unfinished Agenda." In *The Bangladesh Economy in Transition,* ed. M. G. Quibria, 28–76. Dhaka, Bangladesh: University Press Ltd.

Afsar, R., M. Yunus, and ABMS Islam. 2000. *Are Migrants Chasing after Perilous Illusion? A Study of Cost Benefit Analysis of Overseas Migration by the Bangladesh Labour.* Report prepared for the International Organization for Migration, Dhaka, Bangladesh.

Ahluwalia, I. J., and W. Mahmud, eds. 2004. "Bangladesh: Transformation and Development." *Economic and Political Weekly* 39 (36): September 4.

Alamgir, M. 1978. *Bangladesh: A Case of Below Poverty Level Equilibrium Trap.* Dhaka, Bangladesh: Bangladesh Institute of Development Studies.

BBS (Bangladesh Bureau of Statistics). 1975. *Statistical Yearbook of Bangladesh, 1975.* Dhaka, Bangladesh: Ministry of Planning, Government of the People's Republic of Bangladesh.

———. 1992. *Vital Registration Survey 1986–92.* Dhaka, Bangladesh: Ministry of Planning, Government of the People's Republic of Bangladesh.

———. 1991/92 and 2000. *Household Income Expenditure Survey.* Dhaka, Bangladesh: Ministry of Planning, Government of the People's Republic of Bangladesh.

Bangladesh Enterprise Institute. 2004. "Taking Stock and Charting a Path for SMEs in Bangladesh." Working paper, Dhaka, Bangladesh.

Barbone, L., L. Cord, C. Hull, and J. Sandefur. 2006. "Democracy, Institutions, and Poverty Reduction." Working paper, World Bank, Washington, DC.

Basu, A., and S. Amin. 2000. "Some Preconditions for Fertility Decline in Bengal: History, Language Identity, and an Openness to Innovations." Working Paper 142, Policy Research Division, Population Council, New York.

———. 2001. "Preliminary Report of Household Income and Expenditure Survey 2000." Bangladesh Bureau of Statistics, Dhaka, Bangladesh.

Boyce, J. K. 1987. *Agrarian Impasse in Bengal: Institutional Constraints to Technological Change.* New York: Oxford University Press.

CAMPE (Campaign for Popular Education). 1999. *Hope, Not Complacency: State of the Primary Education in Bangladesh.* Dhaka: University Press Ltd.

———. 2000. "Education Watch Report 2000: Quality of Primary Education in Bangladesh." Draft. CAMPE, Dhaka.

del Ninno, C. 1998. "Efficiency of Targeted Food Programs: A Preliminary Investigation of the VGD and the RD Programs." Draft report, Food Management and Research Support Project, International Food Policy Research Institute, Dhaka.

Dev, S. M., K. S. James, and B. Sen. 2002. "Causes of Fertility Decline in India and Bangladesh: The Role of Community." *Economic and Political Weekly* 37 (43): 4447–54.

Drèze, J. 2004. "Bangladesh Shows the Way." *The Hindu*, September 17.

Government of Bangladesh. 2003. "A National Strategy for Economic Growth, Poverty Reduction, and Social Development." Economic Relations Division, Ministry of Finance, Government of Bangladesh.

Haque, Shamsul. 2002. "The Changing Balance of Power between the Government and NGOs in Bangladesh." *International Political Science Review* 23 (4): 411–35.

Hossain, M. 1996. "Agricultural Policies in Bangladesh: Evolution and Impact on Crop Production in State, Market and Development." In *Essays in Honour of Rehman Sobhan*, ed. Abu Abdullah and Azizur Rahman Khan. Dhaka, Bangladesh: University Press Ltd.

Hossain, M., M. Quasem, M. Jabbar, and M. Akash. 1994. "Production Environments, Modern Variety Adoption and Income Distribution in Bangladesh." In *Modern Rice Technology and Income Distribution in Asia*, ed. C. C. David and K. Otsuka. Boulder, CO, and London: Lynne Reinner Publishers.

Jannuzi, F. T., and J. T. Peach. 1980. *The Agrarian Structure of Bangladesh: An Impediment to Development*. Boulder, CO: Westview Press.

Kaufmann, D., A. Kraay, and M. Mastruzzi. 2005. *Governance Matters IV: Governance Indicators for 1996–2004*. Washington, DC: World Bank.

Khan, A. A. 1996. *Discovery of Bangladesh: Explorations into the Dynamics of a Hidden Nation*. Dhaka, Bangladesh: University Press Ltd.

Khan, A. R. and B. Sen. 2006. "The Structure and Distribution of Personal Income and Poverty Reduction: A Case Study in Bangladesh during the 1990s." In *Human Development in the Era of Globalization. Essays in Honour of Keith Griffin*, ed., J. K. Boyce, Stephen Cullenberg, Prasanta K. Pattanaik, and Robert Pollin, 79–118. Northampton, MA: Edward Elgar.

Mandal, S. 2002. "Rural Development Policy in Bangladesh." In *Hands Not Land: How Livelihoods Are Changing in Rural Bangladesh*, ed. K. A. Toufique and C. Turton. Dhaka, Bangladesh: Bangladesh Institute of Development Studies.

Ministry of Health and Family Welfare. 1993–2000. *Bangladesh Demographic and Health Survey, 1993–2000*. Dhaka, Bangladesh: Government of the People's Republic of Bangladesh.

Mondal, A. 2000. "Social Capital Formation: The Role of NGO Rural Development Programs in Bangladesh." *Policy Sciences* 33 (3–4): 459–75.

Mujeri, M. K. 2003. *Economic Growth and Poverty Reduction in Bangladesh*. Dhaka, Bangladesh: Asian Development Bank and Embassy of Japan.

Mujeri, M., and B. Sen. 2003. *A Quiet Transition: Some Aspects of the History of Economic Growth in Bangladesh, 1970–2000*. Country paper prepared for the Global Growth Project, the Global Development Network, and Bangladesh Institute of Development Studies.

Osmani, S. R., W. Mahmud, H. Dagdeviren, and A. Seth. 2003. *The Macroeconomics of Poverty Reduction: The Case Study of Bangladesh.* Asia-Pacific Regional Programme on Macroeconomics of Poverty Reduction, United Nations Development Programme, Kathmandu, Nepal/Dhaka, Bangladesh.

Political Risk Services Group. 2005. *International Country Risk Guide.* New York: Political Risk Services Group.

Rahman, R. I. 2002. "Rural Poverty: Pattern, Processes, and Policies." In *Hands Not Land: How Livelihoods Are Changing in Rural Bangladesh,* ed. K. A. Toufique and C. Turton. Dhaka, Bangladesh: Bangladesh Institute of Development Studies.

Ravallion, M., and B. Sen. 1996. "When Method Matters: Monitoring Poverty in Bangladesh." *Economic Development and Cultural Change* 44 (4): 761–92.

Sachs, J. 1998. "International Economics: Unlocking the Mysteries of Globalization." *Foreign Policy* 110 (Spring): 97–111.

Sen, B., and Z. Ali. 2005. "Spatial Inequality in Social Progress in Bangladesh." Working Paper 7, Program for the Research on Chronic Poverty in Bangladesh, Bangladesh Institute of Development Studies, Dhaka, Bangladesh.

Sen B., and D. Hulme. 2004. "Chronic Poverty in Bangladesh: Tales of Ascent, Descent, Marginality and Persistence." Working paper, Bangladesh Institute of Development Studies, Chronic Poverty Research Center, Institute for Development Policy and Management, and University of Manchester.

Sobhan, R., ed. 1991. *The Decade of Stagnation: The State of the Bangladesh Economy in the 1980s,* Dhaka, Bangladesh: University Press Ltd.

South Asia Enterprise Development Facility. 2003. "The SME Sector: Taking Stock of the Present Situation." Working paper, South Asia Enterprise Development Facility, Dhaka, Bangladesh.

Stern, N. 2002. "The Investment Climate, Governance and Inclusion in Bangladesh." Public lecture given at the Bangladesh Economic Association, Dhaka, Bangladesh, January 8.

Tendulkar, S., and B. Sen. 2003. "Markets and Long-Term Economic Growth in South Asia 1950–97." In *The South Asian Experience with Growth,* ed. Isher Judge Ahluwalia and John Williamson, 146–218. New Delhi, India: Oxford University Press.

Transparency International. "Corruptions Perceptions Index." http://www.transparency.org.

World Bank. 1998. *From Counting the Poor to Making the Poor Count.* Washington, DC: World Bank.

———. 1999. "Bangladesh: Trade Liberalization. Its Pace and Impacts." Report 1591-BD, World Bank, Washington, DC.

———. 2002. *Taming Leviathan: Reforming Governance in Bangladesh, An Institutional Review.* Washington, DC: World Bank.

_____. 2003a. "Bangladesh: Public Expenditure Review 2003." World Bank, Washington, DC.

_____. 2003b. *Poverty in Bangladesh: Building on Progress.* Washington, DC: World Bank.

_____. 2004. "Tamil Nadu Poverty Assessment." Draft, World Bank, Washington, DC.

_____. 2005a. *Bangladesh: Attaining the Millennium Development Goals in Bangladesh.* Washington, DC: World Bank.

_____. 2005b. *Doing Business in 2006: Creating Jobs.* Washington, DC: World Bank.

Zohir, S., Q. Shahabuddin, and M. Hossain. 2002. "Determinants of Rice Supply and Demand in Bangladesh: Recent Trends and Projections." In *Developments in the Asian Rice Economy,* ed. M. Sombilla, M. Hossain, and B. Hardy, 127–52. Manila, Philippines: International Rice Research Institute.

5

Pro-Poor Growth in Vietnam: Miracle or Model?

Rainer Klump

In the 1990s Vietnam achieved rapid overall growth that proved remarkably effective in shrinking poverty without severely widening inequality. Average annual rates of per capita growth (5.7 percent) and of poverty reduction (7.8 percent) outpaced those of most developing countries. The poverty headcount—58.1 percent in the early 1990s and 28.9 percent 10 years later—dropped to under 25 percent by the end of 2004. If that rate of reduction is maintained, some expect that "abject poverty will soon be limited to ethnic minorities in remote areas."[1]

Vietnam's performance in the 1990s starkly contrasts with its performance a decade earlier, when the country was still suffering the repercussions of wars, political and economic isolation, famines, and hyperinflation. Against this background the country's remarkable successes of the 1990s might be regarded as a miracle in the form of beneficial external circumstances or the result of effective internal policy measures that could be regarded as a model for channeling high-growth dividends to the poor. An investigation of the successes suggests that the country made policy choices to take advantage of beneficial initial conditions for generating growth and reducing poverty. These choices were necessary not only to realize but also to sustain broad-based growth.

This chapter examines the way Vietnam tied rapid, overall economic growth to strong, sustained poverty reduction through a mix of economic, sectoral, and regional policies.[2] The country's rapid growth and poverty reduction owe to exogenous factors and to three types of policies: policies related to the quality and quantity of job creation, institutional and macro-economic policies that are particularly important for overall growth, and policies related to public expenditures that can provide public goods as well as targeted transfers to specific groups of households.[3]

Three factors significantly affected the quality and quantity of job creation in Vietnam. First, land reform, along with trade liberalization for coffee and rice and the boom in the world coffee market, benefited unskilled agricultural workers in rural areas. Second, the economy experienced a structural transformation as agriculture grew more productive and growth in nonagricultural sectors accelerated. By the end of the 1990s these sectors had begun to absorb labor released from agriculture. Third, economic and institutional reforms, and in particular a new legal framework for private enterprise, facilitated the emergence of a viable private sector and the movement of employment from informal to formal sector industry and services. Income growth and poverty reduction occurred in both urban and rural areas, as the latter increasingly became linked to the growth dynamics of urban centers.

The story of poverty-reducing growth in Vietnam is the story of the impact that the *doi moi* (renovation) reform process begun in 1986 has had on transforming the country's economy and, in the process, raising the incomes of millions of Vietnamese. The policy choices that unlocked Vietnam's potential for high growth and rapid poverty reduction deserve the closest study. If its past successes offer lessons to others, Vietnam itself may well need to learn from some of its efforts as it attempts to find new avenues to economic and social progress.

War, Economic Decline, Sociogeographic Diversity: The Setting for Reform

Vietnam's political, social, and economic conditions in 1986 appeared anything but conducive to economic growth and poverty reduction. Between independence from France in 1954 until the end of a devastating civil war in 1975, North and South Vietnam developed polar opposite economic and political regimes. Reunification put the capitalist South—an American client that had developed a base of light industry and services and had integrated into international markets—into a centrally planned state run on Communist principles. In the North, farmers and handicrafts had been collectivized and the private sector eliminated. Emphasizing heavy industry and large state-owned enterprises (SOEs), the Hanoi authorities imposed their system on the conquered South. Despite some misgivings even within the ruling

Communist Party, all land was collectivized, markets gradually abolished, and prices controlled. An orthodox, Soviet-model socialist economy was established nationwide.

That system was incapable of healing the deep economic wounds of division and war. At the end of the colonial period, Vietnam's development level was roughly similar to that of other Asian countries. In 1950, per capita income did not lag far behind most neighboring countries. It was even about 50 percent higher than in China, Vietnam's most important neighbor (table 5.1). But through the 1960s and 1970s, Vietnam's overall performance relative to other East Asian economies declined constantly, and, reversing the earlier pattern, the gap between Vietnam and China grew dramatically, as the latter's transition to a market economy got under way.

Political tension with China in these years also resulted in open military conflicts, such as the Vietnamese invasion of Cambodia in 1978 and skirmishes along the Chinese border in 1979. Political and economic tensions spurred a mass exodus of the ethnic Chinese who had been the backbone of South Vietnam's market economy. Around 1980, Vietnam found itself for the most part politically and economically isolated. Until 1993, U.S. veto power barred Vietnam's access to funds from the International Monetary Fund, the World Bank, or the Asian Development Bank. Only the Soviet Union lent political and financial support, both of which declined over the years.

Within reunified Vietnam, geographical contrasts added to the challenges of economic management. The big deltas of the Red River in the North and of the Mekong River in the South are known for their fertile soils. Along the eastern coast excellent natural ports and a relatively well-developed infrastructure have always fostered trade and urbanization. By contrast, along the western borders with Laos and Cambodia, settlement and economic development of the mountainous highlands have been

Table 5.1 *Vietnam's Per Capita Income (Percentage) Relative to Important Neighboring Countries, 1950–99*

	1950	*1960*	*1970*	*1975*	*1980*	*1990*	*1995*	*1998*	*1995*	*1999*
Thailand	80.5	74.1	43.4	36.2	29.7	22.4	21.1	27.0	22.5	30.1
Korea, Rep. of	85.5	72.3	37.6	22.5	18.4	11.9	11.8	13.8	11.2	13.2
Indonesia	78.3	78.4	61.6	47.2	40.5	41.3	42.1	54.6	41.8	55.5
China	149.9	118.7	93.9	81.2	71.0	56.0	52.9	52.8	54.0	57.3

Sources: Data for 1950–98 are taken from van Arkadie and Mallon (2003). Additional data for 1995 and 1999 are taken from the World Bank Pro-Poor Growth Database.

retarded by poor infrastructure and a historically high incidence of malaria (Hardy 2003). The starkest differences in development levels and speeds still separate the urban centers of the southeast and the sparsely populated areas of the northwest.

Demographic contrasts also added to the challenges of economic management. Vietnam is a multiethnic country. The ethnic Vietnamese, the Kinh, are the dominant group and are clustered especially in the delta areas and urban centers. In 2000, however, about 15 percent of Vietnam's roughly 80 million people belonged to one of the more than 50 ethnic minorities that predominantly inhabit rural and remote highland areas (Bhushan and others 2001). The strong Chinese minority is mainly concentrated in the urban areas of the South.

In this setting—diversity at multiple levels—central planning proved disastrous. By the beginning of the 1980s, Vietnamese political leaders recognized the need for fundamental internal economic reforms but lacked an approach for overcoming the country's inherited divisions. They began with somewhat isolated and gradual modifications of socialist planning mechanisms as applied at the microeconomic level in the agricultural sector. A contract system introduced in 1981 allowed farmers to use some plots of land independently of the cooperatives and thus to experiment in free market activity. In addition, some SOEs were allowed to become more market oriented.

These early experiments did not address key issues of pricing, property rights, fiscal discipline, and macroeconomic management. As a result, public and trade deficits increased at an alarming rate, as did inflation, which peaked at over 700 percent in 1986. Fluctuations in rice production in the mid-1980s led to famine in some rural provinces and made rice imports necessary, despite a lack of foreign-exchange reserves and a decline in external assistance. Estimates of national poverty at that time indicate a headcount index of about 75 percent (Dollar and Litvack 1998), a statistic defining Vietnam as one of the poorest countries in the world.

In this critical situation, the Sixth Congress of the Communist Party of Vietnam (CPV) approved in 1986 a comprehensive *doi moi* agenda. *Doi moi* recognized diversity to overcome the economic disaster facing the country. Reforms reintroduced private property without abolishing state property. Free-market exchange was allowed again, but sound macroeconomic management was also proclaimed necessary for sustained economic growth. Continuing along these lines, the rationing system for many commodities was abolished in 1987, and the formerly controlled prices of many commodities were liberalized. Starting in 1988, individual land use rights were granted. By 1990, nearly all commodity prices were determined by the market, macroeconomic stabilization had been implemented, and restructuring of the SOE sector had begun.

The move out of Cambodia in 1989 and the lifting of the U.S. embargo in 1993 paved the way for Vietnam's political and economic reintegration into the international community. Within 10 years, Vietnam managed to catch up with most of its more advanced neighbors and, most notably, to close the gap with China. Together with high growth and rapid poverty reduction, this reintegration became important for CPV leaders' ongoing political support of *doi moi*.

The new Vietnamese development strategy attempted to integrate, where possible, the heritage of opposing economic legacies: the South's market economy and the North's flexible and pragmatic economic system of central management during the war years. In addition, Vietnamese leaders gained various insights from the experiences of China and Asia's other surging economies: (1) sustainable growth in a market economy must be based on outward orientation, macroeconomic stability, and investment in people; (2) market economies can be compatible with authoritarian control of society—that is, the ruling elites can sell economic success as their own achievement; and (3) growth with equity is feasible—market economies do not necessarily result in the evils of mass poverty and exploitation (Leipziger and Thomas 1993).

Trends and Patterns of Pro-Poor Growth

Aggregate poverty reduction (table 5.2) brought the headcount index from a rate as high as 75 percent in the 1980s to less than 25 percent in just two decades. This spectacular decline, however, conceals sharp sociogeographic differences. Among the country's eight regions,[4] poverty levels differ most widely between the mainly rural northwest and the highly urbanized southeast. Poverty continues to dominate in rural areas and among ethnic minorities, of whom the northwest has the highest share. The southeast includes the country's main economic center, Ho Chi Minh City (HCMC)–Saigon.

This progress in aggregate poverty reduction is the result of the high average per capita growth rate of gross domestic product (GDP) of 5 percent during 1987–2001, along with the relatively stable income distribution (table 5.3). The tempo did slow in the late 1990s, but neither the Asian economic crises of the late 1990s nor the more recent SARS epidemic halted Vietnam's growth momentum. The steady improvement in human development indicators also confirms the progress made in reducing nonincome poverty.

Table 5.2 Dimensions of Poverty in Vietnam, 1993–2004

Poverty rates (headcount index, %)	1993	1998	2002	2004
National poverty rate	58.1	37.4	28.9	24.1
Regional dimension				
Northeast	86.1	65.2	38.0	31.7
Northwest	81.0	73.4	68.7	54.4
Red River Delta	62.7	34.2	22.6	21.1
North Central Coast	74.5	52.3	44.4	41.4
South Central Coast	47.2	41.8	25.2	21.3
Central Highlands	70.0	52.4	51.8	32.7
Southeast	37.0	13.1	10.7	6.7
Mekong River Delta	47.1	41.9	23.2	19.5
Spatial dimension				
Urban areas	25.1	9.2	6.6	10.8
Rural areas	66.4	45.5	35.6	27.5
Ethnic dimension				
Kinh and Chinese	53.9	31.1	23.1	n.a.
Ethnic minorities	86.4	75.2	69.3	n.a.

Source: Socialist Republic of Vietnam 2005.
n.a. = not available.

Table 5.3 Indicators of Growth and Inequality in Vietnam during the 1990s

Indicators of growth and development	1987–91	1992–97	1998–2001
GDP per capita growth (percent)	3.15	6.87	4.54
HDI (value)	0.603 (1990)	0.646 (1995)	0.688 (2000)
Income-based Gini coefficients (GSO)	0.35 (1994)	0.39 (1999)	0.42 (2002)
Expenditure-based Gini coefficients (WB/GSO)	0.34 (1993)	0.35 (1998)	0.37 (2002)
Ratio of richest/poorest expenditure quintile (WB/GSO)	4.97 (1993)	5.49 (1998)	6.03 (2002)

Sources: GSO 2003, World Bank Pro-Poor Growth Database, World Bank 2003, and UNDP 2001.
Note: HDI = Human Development Index.

As the growth incidence curve (figure 5.1) for 1993–2002 shows, all percentiles experienced expenditure growth. As a result of slightly increasing aggregate inequality, the national rate of growth for percentiles below the poverty line—as pro-poor growth is defined—over the two decades was

Figure 5.1 *Vietnam's Growth Incidence Curve, 1993–2002*

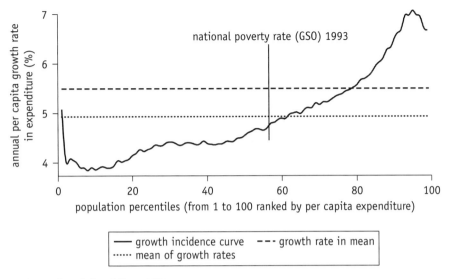

Source: Bonschab and Klump 2005.

as high as 4.1 percent. Although the relatively steady increase of the aggregate income-based Gini coefficients appears to indicate a continuous worsening of income distribution, aggregate inequality in Vietnam, as measured by expenditure-based Gini coefficients, did not actually increase much between 1993 and 1998. It has only recently begun to rise, a tendency also visible in the ratios of the richest-to-poorest quintiles. The expenditure-based urban and rural Gini coefficients remained relatively stable between 1993 and 2002 at values of 0.35 and 0.28, respectively, suggesting that most of the increase in inequality occurred between urban and rural areas.

A more detailed view (table 5.4) of the trends and patterns of growth among the poorest Vietnamese indicates that the rate of advance—nationwide and in urban and rural areas—slowed dramatically after 1998. The slackening pace resulted from declining growth rates in household incomes and signaled growing inequality for those below the poverty line, a trend not necessarily captured in the behavior of the aggregate Gini coefficients. In urban areas, income poverty had diminished to very low levels. Industrial restructuring, the high volatility of employment in the informal sector, and a continuous inflow of poor rural migrants created a new class of households vulnerable to changes, partially explaining the increase in urban poverty that occurred between 2002 and 2004. In the countryside,

Table 5.4 Rates of Pro-Poor Growth, 1993–2002

	1993–98	1998–2002	1993–2002
National	5.7	2.2	4.1
Urban	8.9	1.6	5.9
Rural	5.3	2.2	3.9
Northwest	4.5*	−1.64	n.a.
Northeast	4.5*	4.42	n.a.
Red River Delta	8.1	1.39	n.a.
North Central Coast	6.2	0.47	n.a.
South Central Coast	4.9	4.6	n.a.
Central Highlands	4.6	5.0	n.a.
Southeast	12.3	2.6	n.a.
Mekong River Delta	4.4	2.6	n.a.

Source: Bonschab and Klump 2005.
n.a. = not available.

where income growth rates were lower in both five-year periods, inequality rose more slowly. As a result, the rural rate of pro-poor growth dropped less, in absolute and relative terms, than the urban rate.

As with overall economic advance, growth rates among the poor from 1993 to 1998 differed sharply by region, ranging from 12.3 percent in the urbanized southeast to 4.4 percent in the mainly rural Mekong River Delta. In 1998–2002, however, the northwest recorded the lowest rate of any region (a 1.6 percent decline); the highest increase was 5 percent in the Central Highlands, where the introduction of coffee in 1995 paid off handsomely. Both are mainly rural regions with a high share of ethnic minorities, and the disparity between them, as well as other differences in rates of poverty reduction, undercuts simple explanations of the sources of pro-poor growth in Vietnam and requires a closer look at the various determinants of growth and poverty dynamics.

Policies and Initial Conditions for Pro-Poor Growth

When a laggard economy reverses course, as Vietnam did late in the 1980s, it can benefit—as Vietnam did for roughly a decade—from convergence, the process that endows certain investments with a disproportionate growth impact. A sickly house cat among Asia's tigers, Vietnam was in a position to derive high productivity from every unit of capital, human as well as financial, invested. Additionally, sectoral considerations—the dominance of agriculture and the relative unimportance of large industrial SOEs—created a high potential for restructuring to generate convergence effects. Finally, a threefold boost came from the almost three million Vietnamese living in more developed countries. Aside from providing considerable financial support and access to know-how and international business networks, many in the diaspora became agents of the knowledge and technology transfer that also feeds convergence.

Like a teenager's growth spurt, however, convergence does not last. Its effect diminishes the more the relative development gap is closed, as happened in Vietnam at the end of the 1990s. Growth continued, if at a slower pace, because the *doi moi* reforms had set forces in motion that profited from Vietnam's considerable growth potential. The reforms, while gaining momentum from convergence, tapped two other sources of high aggregate growth: the efficiency effects that stem from effective allocation of existing factor inputs and the high investment ratios that change the structure of factor inputs. Following the *doi moi* reforms, convergence, efficiency effects, and high investment ratios all contributed to growth, although with varying importance and in varying combinations.

A growth accounting exercise that seeks to measure the prime drivers of Vietnam's 1987–2002 growth shows that rising total factor productivity (TFP) led growth in the early *doi moi* years, indicating both convergence and initial efficiency effects (table 5.5). Until 1992 the growth contribution of

Table 5.5 Growth Accounting for Vietnam, 1987–2002

	1987–91	1992–97	1998–2002
Average annual GDP growth (percent)	5.05	8.77	6.04
Labor contribution to growth	34.6	15.9	20
Capital contribution to growth	5.1	69.3	57.5
TFP contribution to growth	60.3	14.8	22.5
Average investment ratio (percent)	n.a.	25.2	28.7
Average ICOR	n.a.	2.8	4.75
Human capital investment ratio (gross enrollment rate)	5.8 (1993)	9.3 (1998)	10.4 (2002)
Human capital investment ratio (net enrollment rate)	4.6 (1993)	7.5 (1998)	8.3 (2002)

Sources: Doanh and others 2002, and Nguyen 2003.
Note: The methodology of the growth accounting exercise is described in Bonschab and Klump (2005).
n.a. = not available.

labor is still higher than that of capital, but that relationship more than reverses in the five years before the Asian crisis, and TFP's contribution also drops sharply after 1992. This development reflects both the weakening of the convergence effect and growing investment ratios. The third phase (1998–2002) looks rather similar: growth contributions of capital and labor together account for almost 80 percent of the economic momentum and TFP for only about one-fifth. The increased investment ratio during this phase was not sufficiently strong to prevent a slowdown in growth rates and, consequently, a sharp increase in the incremental capita-output ratio. The final five-year period is also marked by an increased labor contribution to overall growth, resulting largely to the growing importance of Vietnam's skilled workforce.

Combining Factor Inputs to Shrink Poverty

The strategy that produced strong economic gains nationwide, significantly raising the incomes of the poor, included an effort to change the rural economic landscape. The 1990s produced a strong rural rate of pro-poor growth (3.9 percent). The rural poverty headcount dropped from 66.4 percent in the early years of the decade to 27.5 percent 10 years later, an annual rate of reduction of more than 4 percent. Poverty reduction was thus accomplished in those areas where the vast majority of poor Vietnamese live.

Vietnam mobilized both unskilled labor and farmland for vigorous pro-poor growth. Labor and land went naturally together, because throughout the 1990s more than 50 percent of the poor lived in rural areas and depended primarily on employment in agriculture. Estimates of the exact share of agricultural employment in total employment range between 50 percent and 60 percent (Glewwe, Gragnolati, and Zaman 2002).

Decollectivization of farmland was a pivotal step in the movement toward a market economy involving poverty-reducing growth. In 1988 land use rights were granted to individual households. Ravallion and van de Walle (2001) show that the land distribution proceeded in a remarkably egalitarian way. The 1993 Land Law instituted issuance of land use certificates to all rural households, enabling them to inherit, transfer, exchange, lease, and mortgage their rights. By 2000, nearly 11 million land titles had been issued, making Vietnam's one of the largest and swiftest titling programs in the developing world. The improvement of land-related property rights had strongly pro-poor effects, because it contributed to a higher diversification of rural incomes. Estimates by Do and Iyer (2003) show that in provinces where land use rights were most widely and effectively allocated, farmers invested more heavily in long-term, multiyear industrial and fruit crops and, thanks to higher productivity in farming, devoted more labor to nonfarm activities.

For poor Vietnamese as producers, consumers, or both, rice has traditionally been the dominant crop and staple food, a significance enhanced by the crucial *doi moi* shifts on rice policy (Haughton and others 2004). Extension of tenure security on land use, liberalization of rice exports, and relaxation of internal barriers to trade in rice led to an increase in the crop's real price. At the same time constraints to the import of fertilizers were reduced, so that prices for chemical fertilizers fell (Macours and Swinnen 2002). As a result of rising profitability, rice production in Vietnam has grown continuously since the late 1980s, averaging an annual output growth rate in the 1990s of 5.3 percent, as compared with 1.5 percent in Pacific Asia. Between 1992 and 1998, moreover, the average value of rice exports increased by 9.2 percent per year, and even after the Asian crisis Vietnam remained the second largest exporter of rice after Thailand (Macours and Swinnen 2002).

The progress that poor farm families made against poverty in the late 1980s and early 1990s soon encountered a natural barrier: limits on Vietnam's reserves of arable land. Rapid expansion of production in the early reform period has not only made areas suitable for cultivation scarcer, but also resulted in considerable erosion, particularly on the hillsides of central and northern Vietnam. In addition, pollution has risen to the point that the main rice-growing areas, the Red River and Mekong River deltas, face serious ecological constraints (Pingali and Xuan 1992).

Given the relative scarcity of land, broad-based growth in Vietnam had to rely in part on other complements to unskilled labor, specifically on investments in human capital. Their importance as a source of growth and a factor in poverty reduction emerges not only from the growth accounting exercise discussed above, but also from data (table 5.6) showing how investments in education,

Table 5.6 Net Enrollment Rates (%) in Vietnam, 1993–2002

	Primary			Lower secondary			Upper secondary		
	1993	1998	2002	1993	1998	2002	1993	1998	2002
Total country	86.7	91.4	90.1	30.1	61.7	72.1	7.2	28.6	41.8
Poorest quintile	72.0	81.9	84.5	12.0	33.6	53.8	1.1	4.5	17.1
Rural	84.8	90.6	89.2	26.3	57.9	69.9	4.7	22.6	37.7
Ethnic minorities	63.8	82.2	80.0	6.6	36.5	48.0	2.1	8.1	19.3

Source: World Bank 2003.

having aided growth, also paid high dividends for the poor. Vietnam inherited from the socialist era a high literacy rate by international standards. But in the lowest quintile, in which more than 70 percent of adults can read, illiteracy persisted as the more affluent were better positioned to exploit new opportunities for education. At the tertiary level, for example, very few students come from the poorest households, whereas enrollment of the upper quintiles increased (Bhushan and others 2001). Net enrollment rates at different levels of the school system, high by international standards, have steadily increased since the early 1990s as growing wealth appears to have fueled demand for education (Glewwe and Jacoby 2004).

Among the poor, who started from far behind, the advances in education during the 1990s are striking. Even though illiteracy actually increased among poor women, the poorest as a whole recorded a fourfold gain in lower-secondary school enrollment levels from 1993 to 2002. For rural Vietnamese the same levels rose about two and a half times and for ethnic minorities soared from 6.6 percent to 48 percent. Of course, the gains are relative. Enrollment rates of the poorest quintile and of ethnic minorities started from such low values that even with high growth rates they have not reached the national average.

Alongside education, health has a powerful impact on the human capital of the labor supply. One important component of Vietnam's growth and poverty reduction strategy was the decision to improve public health, an area in which Vietnam generally performs better than other countries at a similar development level.

From a poverty reduction standpoint, the most important early health care intervention was a family planning campaign that helped to decrease population growth from a yearly average of 2.2 percent in the early 1980s to 1.5 percent in the late 1990s. Along with increased mobility and the higher opportunity costs of having children as economic reforms took hold, introduction of family planning measures brought a significant slowdown of fertility (White, Djamba, and Anh 2001). In 1988 the Vietnamese government officially proclaimed the "two-child policy" and adopted a comprehensive family planning program (FPP), which financed specialized health centers at the commune or district level. Total public expenditure for the FPP, as a percentage of total public health costs, increased from 3.5 percent in 1992 to 10.2 percent in 1999. Despite these investments, large discrepancies in the health status of rich and poor are already noticeable; the most striking differences appear in the health condition of children (Wagstaff and Nguyen 2004).

Capital formation has thus far had the smallest impact on pro-poor growth. As table 5.7 shows, gross investment ratios in Vietnam doubled

Table 5.7 Ownership Structure of Total Investment in Vietnam, 1991–2000

Indicators of ownership (%)	1991	1996	2000
Share of total investment			
State	35.0	45.2	61.9
Nonstate domestic	50.0	26.2	19.5
Foreign	15.0	28.6	18.6
Total investment ratio (% of GDP)	15.0	28.1	29.5
Saving-investment gap (% of GDP)	−4.9	−10.9	−2.5

Source: Doanh and others 2002.

from 15 percent in 1991 to almost 30 percent in 2000. But this process resulted mainly from increasing state investment, which now accounts for more than 60 percent of the total. Foreign direct investment (FDI) peaked in the mid-1990s with a share of over 30 percent, leading to a high saving-investment gap and a resulting increase in the current account deficit. After the Asian crisis, FDI fell below 20 percent, the same level as domestic nonstate investment.

The formal private capital market is highly underdeveloped (Kovsted, Rand, and Tarp 2003). Reforms in this sector started in 1988: the socialist mono-banking system was replaced by a two-tier banking system in which the State Bank of Vietnam took over the function of a central bank, and four state-owned commercial banks were created. In addition, a multitude of joint-stock banks and a few foreign bank branches have been allowed to operate (Klump and Gottwald 2003). In July 2000 Vietnam established a new stock exchange in Ho Chi Minh City. Thus far only a few enterprises have been listed, and the trading floor remains fairly quiet.

Households—and in particular the poor—as well as private firms—mainly the informal ones—still must base their financing decisions on money mobilized through the informal financial sector. According to a 1993 survey, 73 percent of all households rely on informal credits; moreover, the emerging private sector uses the informal sector as its major source of capital financing (McMillan and Woodruff 1999). Average rates on loans from moneylenders, friends, or rotational saving and credit associations start at 4 percent per month and can reach as much as 10 percent, compared with rates of 0.5 to 1 percent from the Vietnamese Bank for Social Policy or the Vietnamese Bank for Agriculture and Rural Development. Reliance on informal credit restricts borrowers' growth potential (World Bank 2003) and works against higher pro-poor growth.

Growth's Progression: Farm to Factory to Services

Three phases of growth can be distinguished since the beginning of *doi moi*. The first phase (1986–91) was characterized by high exports of agricultural products and raw materials (mainly oil). As table 5.8 shows, the share of agriculture in GDP and in total employment diminished only slightly, whereas the underdeveloped service sector started to expand rapidly. As industry's share declined with the restructuring of inefficient SOEs, so did industrial employment. It did not rebound even as the export share of manufactured goods doubled in the second phase of high growth (1992–97). Starting in 1998, however, the pattern changed, and as industry expanded its share in GDP, it created more employment and significantly raised the share of manufacturing in total exports (Jenkins 2003).

Even though its role diminished in relative terms, agriculture—revivified by the *doi moi* reforms—was both the underpinning and the catalyst for structural changes that propelled millions of rural Vietnamese out of poverty. Between 1992 and 1997, as the strong increase in the economy's total productivity led to rising incomes, higher agricultural earnings accounted for more than 70 percent of total poverty reduction (Bernabè and Krstic 2005). Over the preceding five years, the employment elasticity of growth (table 5.9) was highest in agriculture, where productivity remained

Table 5.8 Growth and Structural Changes in the Vietnamese Economy, 1986–2001

	1986	1991	1996	2001
Average annual GDP growth (%)	4.9 (1980–86)	5.1 (1987–91)	8.8 (1992–97)	6.0 (1998–2002)
Sectoral structure of GDP (%)				
Agriculture	34.74	30.74	25.06	22.40
Industry	26.82	25.63	31.34	36.57
Services	38.44	43.64	43.60	41.03
Sectoral structure of total exports (%)				
Agriculture	n.a.	52.2	42.3	39.4
Mining industry	n.a.	37.4	28.7	23.5
Manufacturing	n.a.	14.4	29.0	37.1

Source: Bonschab and Klump 2005.
n.a. = not available.

Table 5.9 Sectoral Employment Elasticities and Labor Productivities, 1986–2001

Annual employment elasticity of growth (%)	1986–91	1992–97	1998–2001	1986–2001
Total economy	0.369	0.26	0.366	0.305
Agriculture	0.533	0.394	−0.177	0.374
Industry	−0.590	0.229	0.944	0.180
Manufacturing	n.a.	0.294	0.790	0.371
Services	0.820	0.5	1.910	0.710
Annual labor productivity growth (%)	1987–91	1992–97	1998–2001	1987–2001
Total economy	3.06	6.35	3.73	4.56
Agriculture	0.68	2.79	4.67	2.59
Industry	6.91	10.04	1.41	6.71
Services	1.73	3.98	−3.12	1.34

Source: Pham Lan Huong, Bui Quang Tuan, and Dinh Hien Minh 2003.
n.a. = not available.

low because agriculture provided fallback employment for jobless rural youth and for workers retrenched by SOE reform. In fact, aggregate agricultural productivity did not achieve its highest productivity growth before the end of the 1990s. In regions such as the Central Highlands, where farm job opportunities did expand in this period because of the growing coffee farms, rising agricultural employment and incomes led to high rates of pro-poor growth. The opposite, negative rates of pro-poor growth, occurred in the northwest region, where the increase in agricultural productivity led to a net drop in agricultural employment for which an expansion of nonfarm employment did not compensate.

The effect of early, vigorous agricultural growth on poverty reduction was greater in the South than in the North. Rural households in the South experienced an income growth of 95 percent between 1992 and 1998, compared with just 55 percent in the rural North. Benjamin and Brandt (2004) suggest three reasons for this development. First, the South commercialized the farm sector. In 1998, far more than half of all crop output was marketed in the South, compared with only one-third in the North. The South continued that commercialization until 2002; the North did not proceed much further with it (World Bank 2003). Second, southern regions producing surplus rice—particularly the south central coast, southeast, and Mekong River

Delta—tend to benefit from higher prices while rice-deficit regions lose. Third, higher rice prices had ambiguous effects on the poor: they raised income for producers while increasing the cost of the main food consumed by the poor. Net benefits were higher for the many households in the South that specialized in rice growing.

Even after many years of reform efforts, SOEs play an important role in Vietnam's industrial development. Restructuring of the more than 12,000 SOEs existing in 1991 sought to make these enterprises more efficient and competitive and, through mergers or liquidation, nearly halved their number to roughly 6,000 by mid-1994. Ten years later the total was roughly 4,700 (CIEM 2004). Especially in the early years, the downsizing of the public sector led to massive layoffs; by 1992 almost one-third of the 1988 SOE labor force, some 800,000 workers, had lost their jobs (Dollar and Litvack 1998). A distinct gender bias characterized these early layoffs: about 70 percent of the redundancies hit the female working population (Rama 2002). However, this gender disparity diminished over time, and further downsizing of SOEs is unlikely to hit women harder than men. In fact, female workers already dominate the sectors in which Vietnam's SOEs are comparatively competitive and receive the highest wages, such as footwear, leather, textile, and garments.

Industrial productivity increases brought only moderate job growth, because important subsectors were capital intensive, state owned, or import substituting. After the Asian crisis, private sector development began to increase employment in industry and services; the latter sector—though still small—absorbed some of the retrenched SOE workers. A massive increase in the informalization of employment in both industry and services contributed to high aggregate rates of pro-poor growth in the 1990s (Bernabè and Krstic 2005). In rural areas, nonfarm, informal wage employment created a safety net for both agricultural and former SOE workers. In 1998 almost 90 percent of manufacturing employment, supported by strong external demand for Vietnamese manufactured products, was informal. But growing wage differentials between informal and formal sectors led to a rise in inequality.

The most recent phase of growth has been marked by a dynamic private formal sector. After the first enterprise law was passed in 1991, new firms steadily appeared, at a rate of around 5,600 registrations per year. Significantly amended in 2000, a new enterprise law simplified registration processes and licensing rules. The result was striking; average yearly registrations tripled to nearly 19,000 between 2000 and 2002, an increase that led to a shift in the employment structure (Klump 2003). Private domestic firms created only 4 to 5 percent of jobs from 1995 to 1999 but 15 to 30 percent from 1999 to 2001. This growth appears to have shifted job creation away from household enterprises but to have little affected overall labor markets. Employment in private domestic enterprises currently amounts to only 2.8 percent of the total, and jobs are concentrated in a few industries and services, such as trade and retail. With productivity growth limited by low capital investment, the domestic private nonfarm sector has yet to become a major force for broad-based growth.

Regional Growth Poles and Migration

Industrial growth and private sector development in Vietnam have benefited from policy measures encouraging concentration of economic enterprise in three areas that serve as regional growth poles. The areas around Hanoi, Da Nang, and Ho Chi Minh City[5] have become central to Vietnam's recent development successes. Their share in GDP rose from 42.5 percent in 1990 to 46.6 percent in 1995 and 54 percent in 2002. Responsible for 60 percent of GDP growth in that year, they contributed 72 and 59 percent, respectively, to the growth of industrial production and the service sector. Moreover, 88.5 percent of domestic investment and 96 percent of FDI is concentrated in the three areas, which are also responsible for 80 percent of Vietnam's exports and 67 percent of its state income (Doanh 2004). The southern pole is responsible for the lion's share (33 percent) of GDP; the northern pole claims 23 percent and the central pole only 2.5 percent of total GDP. The government plans to increase these shares to 35 percent, 23.5 percent, and 4.6 percent, respectively, by 2010, which would mean almost a doubling of the importance of the central pole.

Hanoi and Ho Chi Minh City are natural candidates for growth magnets; they make up 25 percent of the wage labor market and allow for a wage premium of up to 80 percent over rural areas (Gallup 2004). But their role, along with that of Da Nang (historically one of Vietnam's most important ports), has been magnified by several directives issued since 1997. These directives call for the three growth poles to produce above-average economic growth and lead the entire economy in the processes of industrialization and modernization. In the northern zone the government invested in high-tech industrial parks around Hanoi's Noi Bai Airport and in modernization of the deepwater port of Cai Lan. In the poorer provinces of the central coast, the government expanded industrial development. In the central zone the government decided to establish Vietnam's only oil refinery in Dung Quat, south of Da Nang, at a yearly cost of some $130 million, and to upgrade and enlarge the road infrastructure, for which $250 million was set aside to build the longest road tunnel in Southeast Asia for Highway 1 through the Hai Van Pass, which separates the provinces of Da Nang and Hue (the city of Hue was capital of the Vietnamese empire for more than a century). Opened in 2006, the tunnel improves links between the coast and the hinterland and could make Da Nang the best natural port for Laos, northern Cambodia, northern Thailand, and even Myanmar.

The pace of poverty reduction provides one encouraging measure of the return on these public and private investments. The south central coast region around Da Nang recorded an average rate of pro-poor growth of 4.6 percent in the late 1990s. This rate was even higher than the regional growth rate of mean income (3.5 percent) in that period and higher than the rates of pro-poor growth on the national level (2.2 percent), in the Red River Delta (1.4 percent), and in the southeast (2.6 percent).

The power of the regional growth magnets, however, is proving limited. The magnets' growth does not appear to spread easily to poor rural areas in the form of significant investment flows that could capitalize on the differences in effective relative returns to capital.[6] The major obstacle to such development is the lack of infrastructure, including roads and telecommunication, and the underdevelopment of financial and other business-related services in poorer provinces. Informal finance alone has been unable to channel additional capital to poor areas. Moreover, differences in the way public administrations in rural provinces implemented the Land Law after 1993 and the new Enterprise Law since 2000 are pronounced (Malesky 2002). Finally, public investment in education increasingly differs from province to province. Provinces that handled the registration procedures for land titles or new firms most efficiently and that invested in their human capital—for example, through education—more easily attracted additional capital.

A strong, steady flow of internal migration is the main link between the three growth poles and the high-poverty rural areas. According to data collected by the 1999 Population and Housing Census (CCSC 2000), 4.5 million people—6.5 percent of the total 1999 population aged five years and older—moved residence between 1994 and 1999. The true numbers would presumably be much higher if nonregistered and temporary migrants had been taken into account.

Most migration in the 1990s was spontaneous, and some of it was made easier by reforms that enabled households to sell farmland and buy urban property. The movement came in response to gaps in employment opportunities and income levels; the majority of internal migrants were the young and the more highly educated. More than half (52 percent) of all migrants were under 25, and only 10.5 percent were older than 45, compared with 48 percent and 20 percent, respectively, for the nonmigrant population. Not surprisingly, ethnic minorities tend to migrate less and account for only 4 percent of all the recorded movement. The overwhelming majority, around 60 percent of the migrants, start to work in the private sector.

Migration generally helps widen preexisting spatial growth gaps by funneling cheap labor into the growth zones. But movement in the opposite direction has also occurred: the coffee boom of the late 1990s drew many migrants to Vietnam's rural Central Highlands region (Hardy 2003) and generated the highest regional rates of pro-poor growth in those years.

The tide of migrants has created new faces of poverty in urban areas. HCMC and Hanoi have been swamped by the large flow of migrants for whom the cities have been unable to provide sufficient infrastructure and other services (ILO, UNDP, and UNFPA 2003; World Bank 2003). Local governments' efforts to discourage additional migration by denying permanent registration or imposing other administrative barriers have encouraged more and more migrants to live and work in the informal sector where they not only are confined to unskilled, low-paid, and low-security jobs, but also are ineligible for public services and exemption from school fees, and lack access to housing with water and sanitation infrastructure (Anh, Tacoli, and Thanh; Oxfam 2003).

Nevertheless, strong positive effects on poverty reduction in poor rural areas stem from the remittances. Survey data for 1998 reveal that those payments constituted 60 to 70 percent of the total cash income of rural households (IOS 1998). Remittances often serve as the most important source of poor rural families' cash income and significantly reduce such families' vulnerability. The funds are usually used for consumption, like buying basic food, rather than for investment. From this perspective the flow of remittances can be understood as a highly pro-poor redistribution mechanism that builds on Vietnam's strong family ties and migrants' acceptance of hardships in crowded cities in return for improving the well-being of those left in rural villages (Oxfam 2003).

Remittances from abroad provide no such compensating balance. Counting only money moved through official channels, remittances from the roughly three million Vietnamese overseas—most of them in the United States, Canada, Australia, and France—increased from some $2.7 billion in 2002 and 2003 to between $3.2 billion and $3.5 billion in 2004, according to a forecast by the State Bank of Vietnam. Five percent of all Vietnamese households receive such remittances (Haughton 2004), but the great bulk of the funds flows into Vietnam's commercial centers—around 60 percent into HCMC alone—thus further contributing to the inequality between growth magnets and poor rural areas.

Macroeconomic and Administrative Reforms

Together with liberalization of markets and the reintroduction of private property rights, recognition that Vietnam needed to put its macroeconomic house in order was the foundation of the *doi moi* reforms. The comprehensive stabilization program adopted in 1989 included almost complete price liberalization, devaluation of the Vietnamese dong, reduction of SOE subsidies, harder budget constraints, restructuring of the tax base, and financial sector reform. The results were immediate. The inflation rate dropped to some 35 percent, and the growth rate climbed to 8 percent in the same year. Throughout the 1990s, inflation rates remained at 3.7 percent annually, and toward the end of the decade, inflation more or less ceased to be a problem (Hung 1999). The devaluation restored Vietnam's price competitiveness in world markets. About one-half of the rice export boom in the early 1990s can be attributed to this particular effect (Macours and Swinnen 2002). The overall growth-enhancing effects of macroeconomic stabilization aided the poor, but lower inflation rates, in particular, decreased the volatility of rice prices by one-fifth, reducing economic risks for producers and consumers (Goletti and Minot 2000).

In the late 1980s trade liberalization, which gained momentum after the end of the U.S. embargo in 1993, followed macroeconomic reforms to become a cornerstone of export-led growth. Over the years Vietnam became a member of the Association of Southeast Asian Nations Free Trade Agreement, and Asia-Pacific Economic Cooperation and signed various bilateral trade agreements. The country is currently negotiating accession to the World Trade Organization.

Vietnam's controlled integration into world markets has had far-reaching effects. First, it helped to increase the production not only of rice, but also of nonrice crops and other agricultural products between 1993 and 1998 (Niimi, Dutta, and Winters 2002). The largest production increases were those of coffee (almost 200 percent), annual industrial crops, and fruit crops. The 1995 introduction of coffee, in particular, was a deliberate response to a boom in the world price of coffee and the realization that Vietnam had a comparative advantage as a grower. Coffee exports grew at an annual rate of almost 60 percent between 1993 and 1998. In those years, according to an analysis of the dynamic effects of rice production and farm diversification (Litchfield and Justino 2002), rice-producing and coffee-growing rural households had a higher probability of moving out of poverty and a lower risk of falling back than other rural households. Second, trade liberalization successfully supported sectoral restructuring from agriculture to manufacturing (Jenkins 2003). Third, that liberalization is increasing returns, in particular to investment in human capital (World Bank 2003) that will be essential for future growth. Finally, the emphasis on exporting has induced comprehensive public sector institutional reforms aimed at meeting various regulations and standards of the international trading community.

Thorough administrative changes—in particular, efforts to decentralize the state administration—have also proved key to the success of the *doi moi* reforms. The public administration reform program (PAR), launched in 1995, aims at transferring some administrative, fiscal, and political responsibilities to local authorities so as to facilitate local implementation of the ambitious targets of Vietnam's poverty reduction programs. In 2002 the government introduced the Comprehensive Poverty Reduction and Growth Strategy and stressed that it be "rolled out to the provinces" (World Bank 2003).

Decentralization became a key element in Vietnam's public sector reform throughout the 1990s (Vasavakul 2002). Composed of fiscal, administrative, and political measures (Fforde 2003; Fritzen 2002), the broad policy change has emerged as Vietnam's most important strategic weapon for overcoming bureaucratic barriers and overcentralization under highly diverse natural, economic, and ethnic conditions. Fiscal decentralization deals with the reorganization of fiscal responsibilities and allows subnational levels to raise or share or to raise and share increasing amounts of state budget funds, whereas administrative decentralization involves the transfer of responsibilities to lower administrative levels. Under the terms of political decentralization, legally constituted local governments such as people's councils gain autonomous decision-making authority.

Fiscal decentralization is already comparatively advanced in Vietnam. Covering roughly 40 percent of all government expenditure and about 55 percent of social sector outlays, the share of the economy controlled by the central government is not exceptionally high and is in line with other fairly decentralized countries such as the United States (39 percent) and India (52 percent). Provincial governments, which gained more fiscal autonomy and more stable transfers from the central government under the 1996 Budget Law, acquired further power with the 2002 Budget Law. It extends provincial autonomy by (1) increasing the authority and jurisdiction of the National Assembly and people's councils, (2) allowing provinces a greater say in the allocation of budgets to districts and communes, (3) providing local government incentives for balanced household budgets, (4) granting local government units more discretionary power, and (5) calling for the local implementation of PAR (Fforde 2003).

Targeted Aid to the Poor

Recognizing that even strong poverty-reducing growth cannot assist the poorest citizens, Vietnam has long had policies to reach particular pockets of destitution. Such pro-poor policies include the Public Investment Programme (PIP), the special National Program for Hunger Eradication and Poverty Reduction (HEPR), Program 135 for commune-level investments, and special programs for ethnic minorities administered by the Commission for Ethnic Minorities and Mountain Areas (CEMMA).

The growth and poverty effects of Vietnam's Public Investment Programme between 1996 and 2000—more than 200 large-scale investment projects with a cumulative value calculated at $7 billion—have been notable for their added impact in Vietnam's poorer provinces. According to estimates, spending an additional 1 percent of GDP in public investment has been associated with a proportionate reduction in poverty on the order of 0.5 percent. But Larsen, Lan, and Rama (2004) found that the poverty-reducing impact of $50 million in PIP investments in the poorest one-fourth of the provinces ran 2.5 times as high as the impact in the richest fourth. Given the higher returns of PIP programs among the poor, a reallocation of public investment to the poorer provinces could help to reduce poverty.

Despite the provision of special funds for areas with a high share of ethnic minorities, the poverty rate among most of them remains high. For some, the rate is growing. Standard growth strategies do not appear to meet the particular needs of these groups of Vietnam's poorest. Special funds that CEMMA channels to minorities often do not reach the minorities but go instead to Kinh households living in the same area. As van de Walle and Gunewardena (2001) found, poor ethnic minorities and the Kinh majority work with fundamentally different models of income generation. If specially designed programs fail to take these differences into account, their effectiveness will remain weak. The problem is particularly acute in the northwest, where rates of pro-poor growth were negative during the 1998–2002 period.

In 1998 the National Program for Hunger Eradication and Poverty Reduction began to coordinate and integrate various social initiatives of the central government (MPI and MOLISA 2001). Some of these initiatives are targeted to poor households directly; others are targeted to poor communes. Examples of the first kind are provision of "poor household certificates" and "health insurance cards," both of which entitle recipients to free medical treatment in public hospitals. Other programs within HEPR provide partial or full exemption from school fees or access to subsidized loans from the Bank of the Poor, since renamed the Social Policy Bank.

The education-fee exemption program within HEPR has a particularly high coverage rate. It reaches almost one-seventh of all poor and one-fifth of the food-poor (World Bank 2003) and it has a statistically significant effect on school enrollment among the children of the beneficiaries. Commune representatives and village chiefs select the poor households, a highly decentralized arrangement that leads to a high degree of participation and social control.

Also dating to 1998, Program 135 is a national socioeconomic development program to assist poor communes technically and financially, especially in remote and mountainous areas. Its resources, used for irrigation, schools, construction of commune centers, and so on in settlements where 15 percent of the country's households live, reflect Vietnam's efforts at decentralization, particularly in rural public investment programs. Funded on an annual basis with resources transferred directly to the communes and districts, Program 135 grants finance small-scale infrastructure investments in poor and remote communes. Although it seems to have achieved pronounced coverage among the poor, problems with participation and control have led to reports of misuse.

Despite efforts at better targeting and coordination, a recent analysis of the static and dynamic incidence of pro-poor spending in Vietnam comes to a sceptical conclusion (van de Walle 2004). Given that relative development levels often dictate the availability of funds at the local level, social transfers do too little to enable poorer areas to catch up. More is spent in relative and absolute terms on the poor in the better-off communes. At the same time, the existing system of social transfers is ineffective in protecting households vulnerable to falling living standards. To make social transfers more efficient in reducing poverty would require not only better monitoring at the local level but also a higher level of risk pooling at the national level and redistribution through the central state budget.

Conclusion

Although it offers no simple model, Vietnam's spectacular success in achieving pro-poor growth over the 1990s provides some important lessons. It demonstrates that a poor country can be lifted out of extreme poverty within only two decades, if a strategy of internal and external liberalization successfully exploits the enormous growth potential of a latecomer. It also shows that the transition from a socialist to a market economy need not necessarily lead to a severe drop in growth rates and an increase in poverty. Finally, it underlines that a long-term sustainable strategy of pro-poor growth has to be based on high investment in human capital and public infrastructure.

Behind the aggregate numbers, however, lies a high diversity of results that recommends a considerable degree of caution to those who would try to teach (or transfer) the Vietnamese experience to other countries. Vietnam has taken advantage of its natural resources such as fertile soils in the two delta regions and the cheap and highly flexible labor force. But so far, despite ambitious pro-poor policies, it has not effectively fought the high and persistent poverty among some of its ethnic minorities. Inequality between the North and the South, between urban and rural areas, and between some particular growth poles and the rest of the country is also rising. Because strong political support for a comprehensive pro-poor growth strategy has been so remarkable in Vietnam since the *doi moi* reforms, widening gaps could, in the long run, put political obstacles in the path of further growth.

Further development of the domestic private sector is the key to keeping Vietnam on a pro-poor growth track. The private sector provides the most powerful potential for further employment creation, not only in the magnet zones but also in the poorer regions and provinces, which have thus far not been the main beneficiaries of Vietnam's extraordinary growth performance. Enforcement of the new Enterprise Law in 2000 constitutes a crucial step toward more private sector growth. In the years since the law's enactment, the number of average annual firm registrations has nearly tripled, and already a small shift in the employment structure can be observed. However, compared with the private sectors of other transition countries, the private sector in Vietnam is young and vulnerable. It not only encounters discrimination from local authorities and SOEs but also suffers from highly restricted access to sources of new capital.

Growth in the private sector could contribute to a more regionally balanced overall growth process and could work against the increasing gap between rural and urban income opportunities. New employment opportunities in small and medium-size enterprises emerging in rural areas could also serve to decrease the growing migration into large cities, where new facets of poverty have developed. Stronger political efforts will be required to encourage private sector growth throughout the country. Public investments in improved infrastructure and a cautious strategy of administrative decentralization that lends impetus to local government reform already point the way toward a new emphasis on private enterprise as an agent of sustained growth.

Notes

1. "Changing Gear," *Economist*, November 26, 2005, 49.

2. This chapter builds on the study by Bonschab and Klump (2005), which was part of the Operationalizing Pro-Poor Growth project.

3. See the conceptual framework for pro-poor growth analysis developed in Bonschab and Klump (2005) and refined in Klump and Miralles (2006).

4. Administratively, Vietnam is divided into 64 provinces and cities in eight regions: northeast, northwest, Red River Delta (including the capital city Hanoi and one of the major port cities Hai Phong), north central coast, south central coast (including the other major port city Da Nang), Central Highlands, southeast (including the main economic center, Ho Chi Minh City–Saigon), and Mekong River Delta.

5. The regional growth poles include the provinces around Hanoi in the Red River Delta (the "triangle" formed by Hanoi, Haiphong, and Quang Ninh, as well as Hung Yen, Hai Duong, Bac Ninh, Vinh Phuc, and Ha Tay), around Da Nang (Thua Thien Hue, Da Nang, Quang Nam, Quang Ngai), and around Ho Chi Minh City in the southeast (the "quadrangle" consisting of HCMC, Binh Duong, Baria-Vung Tau, and Dong Nai).

6. See the results of a study of interprovincial income convergence in Vietnam during the late 1990s by Klump and Nguyen Thi Tue Anh (2006).

References

Anh, D., C. Tacoli, and H. Thanh. 2003. "Migration in Vietnam: A Review of Information on Current Trends and Patterns and Their Policy Implications." Intergovernmental Panel on Forests, Hanoi, Vietnam.

Benjamin, D., and L. Brandt. 2004. "Agriculture and Income Distribution in Rural Vietnam under Economic Reforms: A Tale of Two Regions" In *Economic Growth, Poverty, and Household Welfare in Vietnam,* ed. P. Glewwe, D. Dollar, and N. Agrawal, 133–85. Washington, DC: World Bank.

Bernabè, S., and G. Krstic. 2005. "Labor Productivity and Market Access Matter for Pro-Poor Growth: The 1990s in Burkina Faso and Vietnam." Working draft.

Bhushan, I., E. Bloom, Ngyuen Hai Huu, and Nguyen Minh Thang. 2001. "Human Capital of the Poor in Vietnam." Asian Development Bank, Manila, the Philippines.

Bonschab, T., and R. Klump. 2005. "Operationalizing Pro-Poor Growth: Country Case Study Vietnam." Working paper, Deutsche Gesellschaft für Technische Zusammenarbeit, Eschborn, Germany.

CCSC (Central Census Steering Committee). 2000. "Population and Housing Census Vietnam, 1999." Sample Results. Hanoi, Vietnam.

CIEM (Central Institute for Economic Management). 2002. "Firm Level Survey." CIEM, Hanoi, Vietnam.

_____. 2004. *Vietnam's Economy in 2003, A Reference Book.* Hanoi, Vietnam: CIEM.

Do, Q. T., and L. Iyer. 2003. "Land Rights and Economic Development: Evidence from Vietnam." Policy Research Working Paper 3120, World Bank, Washington, DC.

Doanh, L. 2004. "Vietnam auf dem Weg der Wirtschaftlichen Reform und der Internationalen Integration." Draft, Hanoi, Vietnam.

Doanh, L., V. Thanh, T. Pham, H. Dinh, and N. Thang. 2002. "Explaining Growth in Vietnam." Global Development Network/Central Institute for Economic Management, Hanoi, Vietnam.

Dollar, D., and J. Litvack. 1998. "Vietnam's Renovation: A Unique Growth Path." World Bank, Washington, DC.

Fforde, Adam. 2003. "Decentralization in Vietnam: Working Effectively at Provincial and Local Government Level: A Comparative Analysis of Long An and Quang Ngai Provinces." Report prepared for the Australian Agency of International Development, Canberra, Australia.

Fritzen, S. 2002. "The 'Foundation of Public Administration': Decentralization and Its Discontents in Transitional Vietnam." Paper presented at the Asia Conference on Governance in Asia, City University of Hong Kong.

Gallup, J. L. 2004. "The Wage Labor Market and Inequality in Vietnam in 1990s." In *Economic Growth, Poverty, and Household Welfare in Vietnam,* ed. P. Glewwe, D. Dollar, and N. Agrawal, 53–94. Washington, DC: World Bank.

GSO (General Statistical Office). 2003. *Statistical Yearbook.* Washington, DC: GSO.

Glewwe, P., M. Gragnolati, and H. Zaman. 2002. "Who Gained from Vietnam's Boom in the 1990s." *Economic Development and Cultural Change* 50 (2002): 773–92.

Glewwe, P., and H. G. Jacoby. 2004. "Economic Growth and the Demand for Education: Is There a Wealth Effect?" *Journal of Development Economics* 74 (1): 33–51.

Goletti, F., and N. Minot. 2000. "Rice Market Liberalization and Poverty in Vietnam." International Food Policy Research Institute, Washington, DC.

Hardy, A. 2003. "Red Hills: Migrants and the State in the Highlands of Vietnam." Nordic Institute of Asian Studies, Copenhagen, Denmark.

Haughton, J. 2004. "Money Transfer." *Vietnam Business Journal.* http://www.fox.rollins.edu/~tlairson/intro/VIETNAM1.HTML.

Haughton, J., L. Duc, N. Binh, and J. Fetzer. 2004. "The Effects of Rice Policy on Food Self-Sufficiency and on Income Distribution in Vietnam." Draft, http://www.mail.beaconhill.org/~j_haughton/RiceArt3.pdf.

Hung, N. 1999. "The Inflation of Vietnam in Transition." Discussion Paper 22, Centre for ASEAN Studies, Ho Chi Minh City.

ILO, UNDP, UNFPA (International Labour Organization, United Nations Development Programme, United Nations Population Fund). 2003. "Internal Migration: Opportunities and Challenges for Development in Vietnam." Discussion paper, Hanoi, Vietnam.

IOS (Institute of Sociology). 1998. "Migration and Health Survey Vietnam 1997: Survey Report." IOS, Hanoi, Vietnam.

Jenkins, R. 2003. "Vietnam in the Global Economy: Trade, Employment and Poverty." *Journal of International Development* 16: 13–28.

Klump, R. 2003. "Was Growth Pro-Poor in Vietnam? Assessments and Policy Recommendations." Deutsche Gesellschaft für Technische Zusammenarbeit, Eschborn, Germany.

Klump, R., and K. Gottwald. 2003. "Financial Sector Reform in Vietnam." In *The International Handbook on Financial Reform*, ed. M. J. B. Hall. Cheltenham, UK: Edward Elgar.

Klump, R., and C. Miralles. 2006. "Pro-Poor Growth: Theory, Measurement and Policy Instruments." In *Pro-Poor Growth: Issues, Policies and Evidence*, ed. L. Menkhoff. Berlin: Duncker and Humblot.

Klump, R., and Nguyen Thi Tue Anh. 2006. "Patterns of Provincial Growth in Vietnam, 1995–2000: Empirical Analysis and Policy Recommendations." In *Wirtschaftliche Entwicklung und struktureller Wandel*, ed. T. Pfahler and P. Thuy, 69–79. Bern: Haupt.

Kovsted, J., J. Rand, and F. Tarp. 2003. "Financial Sector Reforms in Vietnam: Selected Issues and Problems." Discussion Paper 0301, Central Institute for Economic Management and Nordic Institute of Asian Studies, Hanoi, Vietnam.

Larsen, T., H. Lan, and M. Rama. 2004. "Vietnam's Public Investment Program and Its Impact on Poverty Reduction." Draft, World Bank, Washington, DC.

Leipziger, D., and V. Thomas. 1993. *The Lessons of East Asia: An Overview of Country Experiences*. Washington, DC: World Bank.

Litchfield, J., and P. Justino. 2002. "Poverty Reduction in Vietnam: What Do the Numbers Tell Us?" PRUS Working Paper 8, University of Sussex, Brighton, UK.

Macours, K., and J. Swinnen. 2002. "Patterns of Agrarian Transition." *Economic Development and Cultural Change* 50: 265–94.

Malesky, E. 2002. "At Provincial Gates: The Impact of FDI on Economic Transition." PhD diss., Duke University, Durham, NC.

McMillan, J., and G. Woodruff. 1999. "Interfirm Relationship and Informal Credit in Vietnam." *Quarterly Journal of Economics* 114 (4): 1285–1320.

MPI and MOLISA (Ministry of Planning and Investment and Ministry of Labour, Invalids, and Social Affairs). 2001. "National Target Programs." Hanoi.

Nguyen, Thi Tue Anh. 2003. "Wachstumspolitik und Sozialpolitik in der Transformation zur Martkwirtschaft am Beispiel Vietnam." PhD diss., University of Ulm.

Niimi, Y., P. Dutta, and A. Winters. 2002. "Trade Liberalisation and Poverty Dynamics in Vietnam." Working Paper 17, Poverty Research Unit, University of Sussex, Brighton, UK.

Oxfam. 2003. "Migration: A Viable Livelihoods Strategy of the Poor Men and Women in Rural Areas." Draft report, Oxfam, Hanoi, Vietnam.

Pham Lan Huong, Bui Quang Tuan, and Dinh Hien Minh. 2003. "Employment Poverty Linkages and Policies for Pro-Poor Growth in Vietnam." Issues in Employment and Poverty Discussion Paper, International Labour Organization, Geneva, Switzerland.

Pingali, P. L., and Vo-Tong Xuan. 1992. "Vietnam: Decollectivization and Rice Productivity Growth." *Economic Development and Cultural Change* 40 (4): 697–718.

Rama, M. 2002. "The Gender Implications of Public Sector Downsizing: The Reform Program of Vietnam." *World Bank Research Observer* 17 (2): 167–89.

Ravallion, M., and D. van de Walle. 2001. "Breaking up the Collective Farm: Welfare Outcomes of Vietnam's Massive Land Privatization." Policy Research Working Paper 2710, World Bank, Washington, DC.

Socialist Republic of Vietnam. 2005. "Viet Nam Achieving the Millennium Development Goals." Hanoi, Vietnam.

UNDP (United Nations Development Programme). 2001. "Human Development Report 2001: Making Technologies Work for Human Development." UNDP, New York.

van Arkadie, B., and R. Mallon. 2003. *Vietnam: A Transition Tiger?* Canberra: Asia Pacific Press.

van de Walle, D. 2004. "The Static and Dynamic Incidence of Vietnam's Public Safety Net." In *Economic Growth, Poverty, and Household Welfare in Vietnam,* ed. P. Glewwe, D. Dollar, and N. Agrawal, 189–228. Washington, DC: World Bank.

van de Walle, D., and D. Gunewardena. 2001. "Sources of Ethnic Inequality in Viet Nam." *Journal of Development Economics* 65: 177–207.

Vasavakul, T. 2002. "Rebuilding Authority Relations: Public Administration Reform in the Era of *Doi Moi.*" Asian Development Bank, Hanoi, Vietnam.

Wagstaff, A., and Nga Nguyet Nguyen. 2004. "Poverty and Survival Prospects of Vietnamese Children under *Doi Moi.*" In *Economic Growth, Poverty, and Household Welfare in Vietnam,* ed. P. Glewwe, D. Dollar, and N. Agrawal, 313–50. Washington, DC: World Bank.

White, M. J., Y. K. Djamba, and Dang Nguyen Anh. 2001. "Implications of Economic Reform and Spatial Mobility for Fertility in Vietnam." *Population Research and Policy Review* 20 (3): 207–28.

World Bank. 2003. "Vietnam Development Report 2004: Attacking Poverty." World Bank, Washington, DC.

6

Ghana: The Challenge of Translating Sustained Growth into Poverty Reduction

Ernest Aryeetey and Andrew McKay

Pro-poor growth is a particularly urgent issue in sub-Saharan Africa, given the lack of both growth and poverty reduction in the region over the past 25 years. Therefore analyzing the experience of the few countries in the region that have achieved growth and reduced poverty is critical. Ghana is one of these countries.

Though regarded as "the shining star" of the African continent on the eve of independence in 1957, Ghana's economic fortunes were marked by decline and volatility between 1965 and 1984. Weak economic performance over this period can be attributed to poor-quality economic policies and several policy reversals, which were exacerbated by frequent changes in power between predominantly military regimes. Decline was particularly severe in the late 1970s and early 1980s, when the country experienced widespread shortages.

In 1983 the government launched an economic reform program, with the support of the World Bank and International Monetary Fund (IMF), followed by a structural adjustment program from 1986 to 1991. Ghana has since become a recipient of significant international aid.

The country has achieved sustained economic growth (4.5 percent per year or 2 percent per capita) in the two decades since 1985. This growth was

The authors gratefully acknowledge comments by Gary Fields and volume editors Tim Besley and Louise Cord, as well as the editorial assistance of Catherine Hull.

accompanied by significant poverty reduction over the 1990s (the most recent period for which comprehensive information is available), and some evidence tentatively suggests that this trend may have continued in subsequent years. However, the pattern of growth has been highly uneven across economic sectors and population groups.

This chapter considers the factors driving growth in Ghana since the mid-1980s. It argues that growth over the last two decades has reflected important policy changes (including import liberalization), a relatively stable political environment, the rehabilitation of Ghana's traditional export sectors, and investment in human capital and infrastructure, along with increased aid inflows and falling fertility rates. But structural transformation of the economy has been limited, private sector investment has been minimal, little formal sector employment has been created, and growth in agriculture outside of export-oriented sectors has been slow. These trends have affected the pattern of poverty reduction: workers in (or able to move into) fast-growing sectors have benefited from increased income opportunities, while those in other sectors have experienced much slower poverty reduction. At the same time, increased levels of public spending have facilitated improvements in some geographically broad nonincome dimensions of poverty.

Growth, Inequality, and Poverty Reduction in Ghana

Moderate growth in the 1990s led to significant income poverty reduction, yet geographical and sectoral variations in the pace of growth contributed to rising inequality. In terms of nonincome dimensions of poverty, access to education increased, while data of health indicated less progress and in some cases deterioration.

Income Dimensions of Poverty Reduction

Poverty reduction in Ghana has been driven by steady growth, which has more than compensated for growing levels of inequality. Analysis of the distributional pattern of growth in Ghana, as well as of accompanying changes in poverty and inequality, is based on household consumption measures derived from household surveys (the Ghana Living Standards Surveys or GLSS) conducted in 1991/92 and 1998/99. These surveys provide the most recent such data. Over this period, the household consumption–based welfare measure[1] grew at an average annualized

Figure 6.1 *Ghana's Growth Incidence Curve, 1991–98*

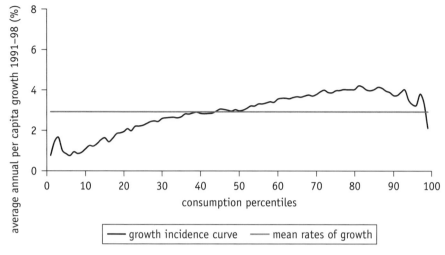

Source: Authors' computation based on Ghana Living Standards Surveys data.

rate of 3.1 percent.[2] An analysis of the distributional pattern of change in consumption using a growth incidence curve (figure 6.1) shows a fall in absolute poverty, along with a steady increase in consumption levels throughout the distribution. But the curve also shows an increasing slope: the growth rates in consumption were faster in higher percentile groups, and so inequality increased. Poorer households therefore experienced below-average growth rates of consumption.

Summary data on growth, poverty, and inequality in Ghana, based on the same data sets, are presented in table 6.1. The poverty headcount measure relative to a national poverty line[3] fell from 51.7 percent of the population to 39.5 percent, and the poverty severity index also fell; both of these changes are statistically significant. Growth has had a sizable impact on poverty, as indicated by the growth elasticity of poverty (0.98 at the poverty line), and the rate of pro-poor growth at the poverty line is 2.1 percent. As the shape of the growth incidence curve suggests, both of these figures are less at lower poverty lines (for example, the extreme poverty line at which expenditure covers only minimum food requirements). Estimates of the Gini coefficient also confirm the increase in inequality over this period, but the impact of this adverse redistribution effect on poverty is small compared with the large positive effect of growth (Aryeetey and McKay 2004).

Table 6.1 *Changes in Poverty and Inequality at the National Level,*
1991/92–1998/99

Indicators	1991/92	1998/99	Changes, 1991/92 to 1998/99
Average value of income standard of living measure (from survey; millions of cedis per person per year, constant prices)	1.44	1.78	3.1%
Change in real consumption per capita (national accounts)	—	—	2.9%
Gini coefficient	0.373	0.388	—
Poverty headcount index (%)	51.7	39.5	−12.2*
Poverty severity index	8.8	6.6	−2.2*
Annualized rate of pro-poor growth at poverty line	—	—	2.1%
Annualized rate of pro-poor growth at 20th percentile	—	—	1.3%
Growth elasticity of poverty headcount index	—	—	0.98
Net primary school enrollment rate: girls (%)	71.5	76.5	+5.0
Net primary school enrollment rate: boys (%)	81.9	84.9	+3.0
Ill/injured consulting health personnel (%)	49.3	43.8	−5.5
Households with access to potable water (%)	64.8	75.1	+10.3

Source: Authors' computations from GLSS survey data and national accounts data.
Note: *denotes a statistically significant change at the 1 percent level.
— = not applicable.

Nonincome Dimensions of Poverty Reduction

Studies of nonmonetary indicators suggest a mixed picture of poverty reduction in Ghana.[4] The first participatory poverty assessment carried out in 1993 and 1994 (Norton and others 1995) emphasized the negative impacts of vulnerability and livelihood insecurity. This study, and the later Voices of the Poor study (Kunfaa 1999), reported widely held perceptions that poverty levels had worsened in the 1990s. Interpretations of the contradiction between data indicating a reduction in the income dimensions of poverty and perceptions of rising poverty levels vary but include uneven improvements in access to public services and growing inequalities between regions and sectors (discussed below).

In terms of nonincome indicators, the evidence is mixed. Table 6.1 shows improvements in net enrollment rates in primary schools for boys and girls and in access to potable water between 1991/92 and 1998/99. But use of health care facilities declined over the same period. Demographic and Health Surveys (DHS) and Core Welfare Indicators Questionnaires (CWIQ) results corroborate rather gloomy health indicators. Life expectancy fell from 57.2 in 1990 to 57.0 in 2000, although the level is higher and rate of decline less than the sub-Saharan African average. Infant mortality fell from 74 in 1990 to 58 in 2000, but a DHS suggests an increase to 64 per 1,000 births in 2003. Moreover, the 2003 CWIQ results suggest an increase in under-five malnutrition rates between 1997 and 2003. The lack of progress in health indicators is of serious concern in its own right, and, if not arrested, is likely to have adverse implications for future growth performance.

Uneven Regional and Sectoral Patterns of Poverty Reduction

Aggregate figures for monetary poverty hide important variations by location and sector. Urban poverty reduction occurred mostly in Accra, the capital, and rural poverty reduction occurred mostly in the rural forest zone, where many of Ghana's key exports are produced. Other regions experienced much lower poverty reduction, or even slight increases. The same geographic pattern does not hold for nonmonetary indicators (table 6.1), many of which are influenced by patterns of public spending. In fact, education and drinking water indicators improved faster in slow-growing regions, in part because the indicators there were low to begin with in 1991/92.

Regional variations in poverty reduction reflect sectoral variations in growth rates, as demonstrated by changes in poverty according to the main activity in which a household is engaged (table 6.2). Although all but the nonworking households experienced poverty reduction, the largest proportionate reductions occurred among those working in the formal private sector, concentrated in Accra, and farmers producing export crops, concentrated in the rural forest zones.

Contributions of different household economic activities to poverty change are more clearly seen if decomposed into intragroup and migration effects using the Ravallion-Huppi decomposition (table 6.3). This operation shows that reductions in poverty among food crop farmers and the nonfarm self-employed make the largest contribution to the overall reduction in poverty, but this contribution reflects the number of households in these categories. The contribution of poverty reduction among export farmers is disproportionate to its size. In addition the migration effect, associated with some household movement to higher-return activities (away from food crop agriculture toward export crops and nonfarm self-employment), is positive. A similar decomposition for the poverty severity measure highlights the importance of poverty reduction among export crop farmers and identifies

Table 6.2 *Trends in Poverty Incidence by Main Economic Activity of Household, 1991/92 and 1998/99*

Main economic activity	Population share		Incidence of poverty, P_0 (standard errors in parentheses)	
	1991/92	*1998/99*	*1991/92*	*1998/99*
Public sector employment	13.5	10.7	34.7 *(3.0)*	22.7 *(3.1)**
Private formal employment	3.9	4.9	30.3 *(4.6)*	11.3 *(2.5)**
Private informal employment	3.1	2.9	38.6 *(5.2)*	25.2 *(4.5)***
Export farmers	6.3	7.0	64.0 *(3.5)*	38.7 *(3.5)**
Food crop farmers	43.6	38.6	68.1 *(1.7)*	59.4 *(3.0)**
Nonfarm self-employment	27.6	33.8	38.4 *(2.3)*	28.6 *(2.8)**
Nonworking	2.0	2.1	18.8 *(4.3)*	20.4 *(4.7)*
All	100.0	100.0	51.7 *(1.7)*	39.5 *(2.3)**

Source: Authors' calculation from the GLSS 1991/92 and 1998/99.
Note: *denotes changes in poverty between the two years that are statistically significant at the 1 percent level; ** denotes changes that are significant at the 5 percent level.

a still stronger migration effect. Both poverty reduction among export crop farmers and the migration effect appear to have aided some households far below the poverty line.

Factors Driving Growth in Ghana

The main factors underlying the uneven pattern of growth in Ghana over the past 20 years and the possible legacy of the previous decline are examined below.

Postindependence Legacy

Growth accounting analysis reveals the contribution of different productive factors to Ghana's growth performance since independence. Over the period 1960–97 Ghana's growth performance was worse than the sub-Saharan African average (table 6.4). This weak performance reflected low levels of physical and human capital accumulation, due in part to their very productivity, particularly over the 1965–69 and 1975–84 periods.

Table 6.3 Poverty Reduction by Main Economic Activity, Decomposed into Intragroup and Migration Effects (Percentage Contributions), 1991/92–1998/99

Effects	Contributions to reductions in poverty headcount measure, P_0	Contributions to reductions in poverty severity measure, P_2
Intragroup effects		
Public sector employment	13.2	16.8
Private formal employment	6.1	4.6
Private informal employment	3.3	1.9
Export farmers	13.0	23.7
Food crop farmers	30.6	21.2
Nonfarm self-employment	22.0	13.8
Nonworking	−0.2	−1.3
Total intragroup effect	88.0	80.7
Total migration effect	10.6	18.5
Residual (interaction)	1.4	0.8
Total	100.0	100.0

Source: Authors' calculation from the GLSS 1991/92 and 1998/99.

Table 6.4 Collins and Bosworth Growth Accounting-based Decomposition of Sources of Growth, Ghana versus Sub-Saharan Africa, 1960–97

Period	Growth in real GDP per worker	Physical capital per worker	Education per worker	Contribution of residual
1960–64	1.56 [1.26]	3.02 [0.86]	0.49 [0.14]	−1.96 [0.26]
1965–69	−0.28 [1.60]	0.94 [1.03]	0.78 [0.18]	−2.01 [0.39]
1970–74	2.41 [2.29]	0.40 [1.22]	0.20 [0.20]	1.81 [0.87]
1975–79	−4.22 [−0.10]	−0.13 [0.81]	0.23 [0.27]	−4.32 [−1.18]
1980–84	−3.94 [−1.28]	−0.93 [0.41]	0.66 [0.30]	−3.66 [−1.99]
1985–89	2.32 [0.64]	−0.40 [0.06]	0.72 [0.30]	2.01 [0.28]
1990–97	1.27 [−1.55]	0.75 [−0.14]	0.41 [0.18]	0.11 [−1.59]
Total: 1960–97	−0.12 [0.41]	0.52 [0.61]	0.50 [0.23]	−1.15 [−0.42]

Source: Aryeetey and Fosu 2003.
Note: Figures in parentheses report the sub-Saharan Africa average.

Low growth rates between 1965 and 1984 can be attributed to poor and inconsistent policies, political instability, and institutional weaknesses. The state sought to play a key role in the economy over most of this period (especially the 1970s) by pursuing an import substitution industrialization strategy (while seeking to increase manufacturing exports). But a strong antiexport bias in policy (including high taxes on cocoa, one of Ghana's key traditional exports), plus a highly overvalued exchange rate, decreased exports, especially cocoa exports, and led to major disinvestment in cocoa (Frimpong-Ansah 1991); many farmers switched to alternative crops or activities.

Government ambivalence and hostility toward the private sector, dating back to the immediate postindependence government of Kwame Nkrumah, also discouraged investment. On ideological grounds and to preserve his political power, Nkruma actively opposed development of an entrepreneurial class in Ghana. As a consequence the state played a major role in industrialization (to be funded in part by cocoa taxation), took measures to limit the size of private business, and preferred foreign capital over domestic private investment (Acemoglu, Johnson, and Robinson 2005; Frimpong-Ansah 1991; Killick 1978). Several subsequent governments, including the Acheampong regime in the 1970s, pursued similar policies. These policies were largely unsuccessful at promoting industrialization, not least because of their internal inconsistency, but they did lead to major adverse impacts on the cocoa sector and the maintenance of a large and complex public sector.

The state's stance on economic development before 1984 helps explain the factors driving growth and those constraining growth in more recent decades. Although the adverse impacts of the above-noted policies on exports have since been reversed, the ambivalent attitude to the private sector and the size and complexity of the state sector appear to have left an enduring legacy.

Factors Driving Growth

In the early 1980s the downward spiral caused by economic mismanagement and neglect of the private sector, as well as a major drought, prompted introduction of an economic reform program, with substantial support from the IMF and World Bank. Starting in 1986, a structural adjustment program was geared toward correcting structural imbalances in order to engender healthy economic growth. The economy responded positively to these liberal reform programs: in 1983 the growth rate was negative, but the next year it was 8 percent (Aryeetey and Kanbur forthcoming).

Improved policies and political stability have played a key role in the recovery of growth since 1984, though levels of factor accumulation remain low (table 6.4). Thus growth recovery, including increased total factor productivity, partly reflects a process of making up lost ground. But the fact that economic and political reforms came with substantial aid inflows (by far exceeding previously received sums; Hutchful 2002) makes individual contributions to Ghana's growth performance difficult to isolate. Christiansen, Demery, and Paternostro (2003) identify improved macroeconomic policy as a key factor in the recovery of growth between 1975–84 and 1985–97 in their cross-country analysis drawing on the African growth model of O'Connell and Ndulu (2000). In the analysis, they decompose changes in predicted per capita GDP as a function of country characteristics, institutional factors, climatic shocks, and macroeconomic policy variables.

Of the key macroeconomic variables, Christiansen, Demery, and Paternostro (2003) identify the reduced parallel exchange rate as of particular importance to Ghana's growth. Exchange rate devaluation—alongside reform of the marketing system—improved access to inputs, and gradual improvement in prices represented a conscious effort to stimulate exports, particularly in the cocoa sector. Significant numbers of poor farmers have benefited by growing (or replanting) some cocoa. Investment in mining ores—another key export—also increased since the mid-1980s. Nontraditional exports—mostly agricultural or processed agricultural products, including pineapples, yams, wood products, cocoa products, canned tuna, and oil palm products—have also contributed to a growing share of trade.[5]

Trade as a proportion of GDP increased from 33.2 percent in 1991 to 81.0 percent in 1998 and has continued to increase with rehabilitation of cocoa and gold production and growth of nontraditional exports. However, trade reforms have resulted in faster growth in imports compared with exports; many imports are consumer goods or food products. The faster growth of imports has adversely affected some local production, for example, rice growing, chicken rearing, and manufacturing. But import liberalization has also been an important stimulus to growth in wholesale and retail sectors.

Sharply increased aid inflows (Ghana received little aid during the 1970s and early 1980s) represent another key factor behind growth. Associated increased levels of demand have stimulated economic activity in the informal sector (especially wholesale and retail trade) and in construction; this effect is particularly evident in Accra (an observation confirmed by GLSS data; Coulombe and McKay 2003). Increased spending on public services, especially education and physical infrastructure (roads, electricity, water) has also had growth benefits. Some of these benefits, such as increased education spending (heavily supported by donors), have had positive impacts throughout the country. However, infrastructure investments, such as improved roads and electricity, have been more concentrated in export-producing or better-connected areas.

Finally, an increasing flow of international remittances, chiefly from the Ghanaian diaspora in Europe and North America, appears to be an important contributor to growth. The precise magnitude of this flow is unknown, because much of it may not go through the formal financial sector. Nonetheless, recorded inflows of remittances increased from around $15 million to over $30 million between 1991 and 1998; survey-based evidence suggests somewhat higher figures. Formal evidence of the uses of remittances is scanty, but the proportion financing physical capital accumulation (other than construction of dwellings) is believed to be quite low; on the other hand, significant amounts are used as payment for education.[6] However, evidence that international remittances frequently do not flow to poorer households suggests that their poverty-reducing impact may be limited.

This brief consideration of the sources of poverty reduction in Ghana also provides the key to understanding limits to pro-poor growth. Aryeetey and Tarp (2000) argue that external sources of cash through aid inflows have enabled increased use of capital without significant improvements in total factor productivity. Moreover, macroeconomic stability, though much improved relative to the 1965–84 period, remained precarious throughout the 1990s. Various factors, including fiscal profligacy, undermined the financial sector, inhibiting private sector growth. Perhaps most important, the lack of an overarching vision of development in support of a coherent program of structural transformation and reform threatens the sustainability of pro-poor growth to date (Aryeetey and Kanbur forthcoming).

Factors Constraining Participation of the Poor in Growth

Three major factors have influenced the ability of the poor to participate in growth in Ghana: agricultural performance; the operation of labor markets, in particular limits to employment creation; and the composition, effectiveness, and distributional pattern of public spending. Constraints to growth in these three areas stem from the absence of fundamental structural changes since colonial times: the domestic economy continues to depend largely on agriculture (which accounts for nearly 40 percent of GDP and 50 percent of all employment), and the industrial and manufacturing sectors remain underdeveloped. The examples below highlight the underlying policy environment, institutional framework, and considerations of political economy that have precluded structural reforms that would have further benefited the poor and led to a more diversified economy.

Agriculture

The importance of agriculture for poverty reduction in Ghana can be understood by even the briefest consideration of the evidence: while 66.8 percent of the population lived in rural areas in 1998/99, nearly 84 percent of the poor were rural dwellers; the latter proportion increases even more once the depth of poverty is taken into account or a lower poverty line is used. Agriculture is the main economic activity for the majority of the rural poor, and even for those primarily engaged in a nonfarm activities (who tend to be less poor on average), agriculture is often an important secondary activity.

The persistence of poverty in the agricultural sector is due to a basic lack of structural change in Ghana since colonial times. With the exception of cocoa, the key agricultural cash crop, the sector has remained largely untransformed; input use is limited (for example, only 16 percent of households engaged in agriculture in 1998 reported having purchased fertilizer). Thus, although the area under cultivation has increased, production processes have not become more intensive, and yields have largely stagnated below achievable levels (Nyanteng and Seini 2000). As a result, sectoral growth rates lagged behind other areas of the economy in most of the reform years (Aryeetey and Kanbur forthcoming).

Large export crop operations receive greater policy attention and infrastructure investments than small food crop operations. As described above, poverty reduction among households has depended heavily on the subsector of engagement (tables 6.2 and 6.3); poverty declined faster among the minority of export crop farmers than among food crop farmers. Many poor households in the forest area of the country do produce cocoa and have been able to benefit from export growth.[7] Smallholder households not producing export crops have experienced lower rates of participation in growth. Poverty reduction among this group has often been due to factors outside agriculture (receipts of remittances, greater engagement in nonfarm activities).

Though trade liberalization has benefited those producing export goods, the reduction of import protection has adversely affected local producers of products, such as rice, cotton, chicken, and tomato concentrate. Limited access to key inputs represents another major constraint on growth in food crops (especially since the removal of subsidies on inputs) and has kept levels of fertilization and mechanization low. Paltry budgetary allocations to irrigation over the past decade have exacerbated smallholders' vulnerability and limited their engagement in product markets. Access to credit, as well as extension services and other inputs, is especially difficult for women farmers, who make up the majority of the labor force in the food crop sector because they are less likely to grow crops that are marketed. Associated processing activities that are disproportionately undertaken by women suffer the same constraints. Moreover, poor roads and other infrastructure have limited the ability of food crop farmers to distribute their produce.

Complex and uncertain tenurial relations appear to hinder private investments in agriculture. Besley (1995) finds that the relationship between these investments and land rights is complex in Ghana. Further, judging the extent to which land rights issues affect the poor specifically is difficult. A study of the impact of land rights on investment and productivity in agriculture in Akwapim in eastern Ghana by Goldstein and Udry (2005) found that farmers who lacked local political power were not confident in maintaining their land rights over a long fallow period. As a consequence, they fallowed the land for much shorter durations and achieved lower output levels than politically powerful farmers. But this finding is not necessarily generalizable. First, land tenure arrangements vary widely across Ghana. Second, work at the Institute of Statistical, Social and Economic Research suggests that land tenure arrangements are undergoing considerable change, driven by new interests (including those of migrants/tenants) and market forces. Many conflicts and litigations arise from the way different groups perceive the changes. These conflicts and perceptions of future access (which may have little to do with local political power) are important to understanding productivity. The challenge for policy makers remains how to organize the imminent changes and ensure that they occur in a structured manner within a sound institutional framework.

The Medium-Term Agricultural Development Programme in 1990 took aim at food crop challenges that could be addressed more quickly: enhanced productivity through market liberalization, improved extension services, and additional support programs. The impact of these measures has been limited, and many other core issues such as infrastructure have not been addressed. Reform of land tenure systems governed by traditional power structures also represents a delicate issue and long-term challenge for government. As an area where substantial numbers of Ghanaians remain trapped in poverty, food crop agriculture calls for significant policy attention. The lack of policy focus on agriculture raises the question of the extent to which urban bias continues to affect policy making in Ghana.

The Labor Market and Generation of Private Sector Opportunities

The labor market should be a key channel through which the poor are able to participate in growth, assuming individuals can move into higher-return activities. In Ghana, households' net pattern of movement was from lower-return activities (such as food crop farming) to higher-return activities (such as export farming or nonfarm self-employment), and this movement has contributed to a net reduction in poverty (table 6.3). However, the benefits to be gained from such movement have been limited by the absence of substantial opportunities in the formal sector. Poor private sector development stems in part from the legacy of governmental hostility toward the private sector's role in the economy. Underdevelopment of the financial sector, itself partly caused by continued weaknesses in macroeconomic policy, remains the main factor discouraging private investment, even if macroeconomic stability has improved in the last few years.

Rather than being closely linked to open unemployment, poverty in Ghana is more readily associated with underemployment, work in agriculture, and, to some extent, in the informal sector. Participation rates in the Ghanaian labor market are high for both women and men, and open unemployment rates (with the exception of youth unemployment in urban areas) are still relatively low. According to the GLSS, more than three-quarters of Ghanaian households are self-employed in either agriculture or a variety of nonfarm activities.[8] Between 1992 and 1998, participation in nonfarm self-employment activities increased sharply, caused in part by a movement out of agriculture. Urban self-employment has been a significant channel through which many of the poor have escaped poverty: in Accra GLSS data suggest that returns to such activities increased significantly between 1991/92 and 1998/99. However, growth in the sector is limited by internal constraints, such as poor economies of scale and lack of access to technology or credit. Very few self-employment activities develop into more established companies that hire significant numbers of employees.

Wage employment, whether formal or informal, represents the primary economic activity in only about one-fifth of households, and this proportion declined marginally over the 1990s, mainly because of public sector retrenchment. Contraction of wage employment opportunities in Ghana over the period has deprived the poor of a potentially powerful mechanism for escaping poverty, as evidenced by economic development in East and Southeast Asia, where pro-poor growth was associated with an expansion of wage employment opportunities, especially for unskilled labor. In Ghana, neither the urban informal sector nor the rural economy has created substantial opportunities for employing hired labor. As a result, unskilled employees are relatively few. However, those that have obtained and retained jobs in the formal sector have generally experienced significant increases in their income levels.

One aspect of the paucity of wage employment opportunities in Ghana was low productivity in the manufacturing sector in the 1990s. Economic reforms' initial benefits to the manufacturing sector—the easing of supply constraints and price liberalization—were short-lived. Restructuring in the industrial sector in the following years was hampered by devaluation, erosion of liquidity, high interest rates, a lack of access to long-term credit, and increased competition from imported consumer goods as a result of trade liberalization. As a result, small firms and low capital-labor ratios dominate the private sector. Low productivity levels, hence high costs internationally, are associated with poor export performance (Teal 1999), thereby limiting the scope for growth.

Recovery of the manufacturing sector is an important priority for future employment creation and growth in Ghana, not least because of manufacturing's links to other sectors, including agriculture. However, the failure of employment creation has been an issue across all sectors, and this failure is intimately linked to low levels of private investment. The proportion of gross domestic investment in GDP increased from a low of 3.7 percent in 1983 to 16 percent in 1990, but largely as a result of increases in public investment. Private investment has remained consistently low. In turn, the weakness of the financial sector is a major constraint on private sector investment. Financial institutions, few in number, have preferred to hold treasury bills rather than lend to the private sector and reportedly have the highest interest rate margins in Africa (World Bank 2004).

Although financial sector reform, including improved supervision and regulation, is a sine qua non of private sector development, investor confidence is also highly contingent on macroeconomic stability. The continuing instability of the macroeconomic environment (even if much improved since 1983) has been a major factor accounting for lack of investment. Consequences include high and variable rates of inflation and persistent large fiscal deficits, in part the result of election-cycle spending patterns following the transition to democracy in 1992. Inconsistencies between monetary and fiscal policies reached their peak in 1997 with the government's decision to adopt a nominal exchange rate anchor without a prerequisite level of fiscal restraint. The result was a speculative assault and a real depreciation of 106 percent (174 percent nominal), which forced Ghana to seek relief under the Heavily Indebted Poor Country (HIPC) Initiative (Youngblood and Franklin 2005).

Since 2000 the new government has sought to create a "golden age" for business and has increased macroeconomic stability, while avoiding the large preelectoral spending boom that characterized the 1990s. But this performance has not yet led to a significant increase in investment. Generation of poverty reduction opportunities will be dependent on boosting wage employment in manufacturing through enhanced private sector investment. Labor market opportunities are hence closely linked to key policy choices of government, including the consistent pursuit of macroeconomic stability and financial sector reform.

Public Spending and Poverty Reduction

Public spending potentially plays a critical role in relation to the poor, notably through provision of key services, such as education and health, and investment in infrastructure, including roads, markets, and electricity, and extension services. In Ghana, the public sector has always been a highly significant employer. Although public spending has had poverty-reducing impacts in Ghana, it has benefited the poorest of the poor less than others because of its composition and distributional pattern.

A significant proportion of public spending is interest payments on debt, especially domestic debt, the legacy of past high fiscal deficits. In 2001 interest payments on debt were at 7.8 percent of GDP or 40 percent of total operational expenditures (World Bank 2004). Apart from these payments, spending on education and health has dominated the budget; these ministries account for nearly 70 percent of government employment in 2003 (World Bank 2004). Allocation to the social sectors, clearly important from a poverty perspective, has fallen as a share of total expenditures from 40 percent in the first reform decade to 28 percent in the second decade, but it has remained steady as a share of GDP in both the prereform and reform years at about 6 percent of GDP. Capital expenditures moved from being only 3.3 percent of GDP in the decade before the adoption of economic reforms to 5.1 percent in the first decade of reforms and then to an average of 12 percent in the second decade. Investment in infrastructure, particularly roads, has gained remarkably in importance since 1992. By contrast, expenditure on agriculture today accounts for less than 1.3 percent of expenditure (compared with 8.4 percent in 1991).

The extent to which the poor have benefited from public spending depends on the effectiveness of this spending. Public expenditure patterns appear to be driven largely by revenue flows and political expediency and reflect no particular commitments to policies and expected growth outcomes. Wetzel (2000) has questioned the effectiveness of public expenditures, basing her comments on public expenditure reviews undertaken in the 1990s that suggested a proliferation of relatively small-scale projects with a lack of clear prioritization. Projects have often been linked to the electoral cycle—as evidenced by the abandonment of rural development projects after the 1992 elections (Barbone and others 2005)—and have been of questionable effectiveness (ISSER 2004). For instance, all district capitals are now connected to the national electricity grid, but economic activity in them has increased little, and very few households try to get connected. Despite the construction of, on average, 50 new schools in each district over the past four years, DHS results show declining pupil performance, which is attributed to the lack of teachers in schools (ISSER and UNDP 2005). Ye and Canagarajah (2002) report that the efficiency of the health system in the 1990s was below the sub-Saharan African average and that the overall level of public expenditure on health was low by West African standards over that decade.

At the heart of the issue of the effectiveness of public spending is the size and character of the public sector. Most postindependence governments in Ghana, dating back to Nkrumah, were committed to a state-led strategy of industrialization, which involved the public sector in many spheres of economic activity that generated little economic return. The size and complexity of the Ghanaian public sector remains an issue despite reform measures since 1984, including some attempts at retrenchment. Booth and others (2004) characterize the Ghanaian state as having a neopatrimonial character that has deep historical roots, where "public resources tend to be captured and 'owned' by networks controlled by dominant patrons" (Booth and others 2004). The legacy of this character, they argue, helps explain why successive donor-supported attempts at public sector reform have had limited success. Moreover, the effect of democratization on public sector reforms has been mixed. The advent of multiparty elections in the early 1990s coincided with a perceived increase in patron-based politics. For instance, the 1990s saw significant levels of public spending in electoral cycles. In the run-up to the 1992 elections, the ruling National Democratic Congress Party announced an 80 percent increase in civil servant wages, reversing its earlier attempts to trim the public sector (Barbone and others 2005).

Continued public sector weaknesses are related to the effectiveness of public expenditure management; actual spending often deviates substantially from public spending. Killick (2004) has estimated that the deviations between budget estimates and actual expenditure in the education and health sectors are in the region of *plus or minus* 42 percent and *plus or minus*

68 percent, respectively. Furthermore, funds released from the center are often smaller on arrival at the point of service delivery (Killick 2004).

Spending on education illustrates how the distributional pattern of public spending affects the poor. A high proportion of the budget is spent on education (and of that 70 percent goes into basic education). Benefit incidence analysis suggests that the provision of primary education and basic health care is progressive in the sense that the poorest quintile benefits more than in proportion to its income share (Demery, Chao, Bernier, and Mehra 1995; World Bank 1995; Ye and Canagarajah 2002). Richer groups still get a greater share than poorer groups, however, because they make more use of these facilities (and typically have fewer children). Furthermore, the distributional impact of spending is likely to be less progressive once the quality of education is taken into account, as lower teacher to pupil ratios and the lack of basic classroom materials reflect poorer quality of education in rural areas (Ye and Canagarajah 2002). Although primary school enrollment, even in poorer areas, has increased significantly since 1990, enrollment at the secondary level has changed little (even if rates are high by regional standards), especially among poorer groups. Benefit incidence analysis confirms that spending at this level is much less progressive. The distribution of health care spending reflects a similar bias in distribution toward higher-level facilities, urban areas, and more affluent groups.

These concerns about the effectiveness and distributional pattern of public spending mean that the poor, and especially those in more remote or deprived regions, find it difficult to accumulate a key asset, human capital, severely limiting their opportunities to participate in growth. These problems in relation to education are compounded by limited access to health care, which impedes the ability of the poor to protect themselves effectively against health shocks.

Patterns of public spending by region pose another important, and politically sensitive, distributional issue. They are believed to be highly unequal, but no data are available to clarify the situation. The lack of geographically disaggregated public expenditure data in Ghana is significant in itself. Decentralization of some public spending was enshrined in the 1992 constitution and the subsequent Law on Local Government, which devolved development planning and administration to district assemblies and gave them control over a substantial portion of their revenues. Since 2000 HIPC relief funds have enabled district assemblies to finance many development projects in specific areas—education, health, water and sanitation, production, and gainful employment—all of which can contribute to poverty reduction. Although decentralization could in principle provide opportunities for public spending to become more effective across regions, obstacles remain at the national and local levels. As already noted, the government's intended expenditure in any particular region or district may be far different from what is actually spent, and political economy forces at the local level may act against a pro-poor allocation of funds (Bardhan and Mookherjee 2000).

Conclusions

Ghana managed an impressive economic turnaround after more than 20 years of serious decline. A combination of large external inflows and policy change from 1984 onward resulted in adoption of more consistent policies and helped achieve political stability. Ghana attained a sustained level of growth that is impressive by West African standards and that represents one of few growth success stories in sub-Saharan Africa. Moreover, this growth has been associated with significant progress in poverty reduction, both in income and nonincome terms.

Success has reflected political stability, abandonment of poor policies, greater openness of the economy, increased public spending (and concomitant improvements in educational outcomes), and large inflows of aid and remittances. However, poor households' participation in growth has varied according to geographic area and economic sector. Poverty reduction over the 1990s has been fastest in the export-producing rural forest region and in Accra, and inequality has increased. Poverty reduction among those engaged in the agricultural sector but not in production of key export crops has been limited, reflecting a lack of policy concern with agriculture, as demonstrated by a very low budget for the sector. In addition, growth has been associated with little creation of wage jobs and little growth in the productive formal sector; low-order self-employment activities have only a limited capacity to generate growth. This lack of employment creation reflects low levels of private investment (domestic or foreign) despite 20 years of growth. Even though macroeconomic management has much improved since 1984, continuing macroeconomic instability, along with the associated underdevelopment of the financial sector, appears to be a constraint to such investment.

A lack of basic structural change in the economy, limited employment creation, reliance on external inflows, continued low levels of total factor productivity, and increases in spatial inequality raise questions about the sustainability of Ghana's growth. Prolonging growth and expanding its benefits to the poorest households and those in more remote locations will require fundamental policy and institutional reforms.

Increasing productivity in the agricultural sector outside of traditional export crops is a priority. It will require dry-season cultivation, production of a greater range of crops (including nontraditional export crops), increased input use, and market participation. Increased agricultural productivity poses the long-term challenge of appropriate tenurial arrangements. Improvements in intersectoral links, including the provision of infrastructure to remote areas, could promote agroprocessing activities as a reliable source of demand for agriculture. Unexploited scope for Ghana to become a trading hub in the region is considerable but would require infrastructure investment.

The absence of fundamental structural change has been attributed to a lack of concerted effort (Aryeetey and McKay 2004) or political commitment (Killick 2000, 2004). But such change is on the horizon. The current government has articulated not only a strong commitment to macroeconomic stability but also the goal of implementing structural change through improved agricultural productivity and private sector development. Specific policy focuses include improvement of market access through better road networks, support for agro-industry, strengthened supervision and regulation of the financial sector, and privatization of state-owned banks (Government of Ghana 2003). To increase pro-poor growth, these policy measures must pay explicit attention to the needs of currently lagging regions with growth potential, as well to current growth poles.

Perhaps the greatest challenge for future pro-poor growth in Ghana is the full reversal of historical legacies, which have created sectoral and regional biases and led to an inflated, and often distorting, role for the state. Decentralization represents a potentially powerful mechanism for human development, but its success depends in part on tracking of expenditures to ensure that they reach their target and generate expected outputs. Ghana demonstrates that the relationship between democracy and economic governance is by no means straightforward, but there is hope that as democratic practices become institutionalized, mechanisms of transparency and accountability and the rule of law will facilitate the state's role in development.

Notes

1. This measure was computed as total household consumption expenditure per adult equivalent, adjusted for price differences over time and space. For further details see GSS (2000) or Coulombe and McKay (2003).

2. This figure is very similar to the national accounts estimate of the growth rate in real consumption per capita (2.9 percent per year).

3. For further details on the computation of the poverty line, see GSS (2000) and Coulombe and McKay (2003). This computation followed standard international procedures, as discussed by Ravallion and Bidani (1994).

4. Surveys include qualitative studies—for example, Norton and others (1995) and Kunfaa (1999)—and quantitative assessments—for example, Demographic and Health Surveys 1993, 1998, and 2003 and Core Welfare Indicators Questionnaires 1997 and 2003.

5. From 1989 to 1996 earnings from nontraditional exports increased from $23.8 million to $276.2 million. This trend has continued, and in 2003 the subsector brought in $588.9 million.

6. Although education is notionally free up to the junior secondary level, in practice payments are frequently required; moreover, an increasing number of Ghanaians are sending their children to private schools, even at primary level (Ye and Canagarajah 2002).

7. The extent to which the poor have benefited from the growth of nontraditional exports is not well understood, in part because this development is relatively recent. Some nontraditional export crops, such as yams, are already produced in significant quantities compared with horticultural products and other export crops requiring greater input use.

8. These summary figures do not take account of the diversity of livelihoods in which households are engaged (Coulombe and McKay 2003, tables 6.2 to 6.4), thus a greater proportion of households are engaged in informal labor markets as a secondary activity.

References

Acemoglu, Daron, Simon Johnson, and James Robinson. 2005. "Institutions as the Fundamental Cause of Long-Run Growth." In *Handbook of Economic Growth*, ed. Philippe Aghion and Steve Durlauf, 385–475. Amsterdam: Elsevier.

Aryeetey, Ernest, and Augustin Fosu. 2003. "Economic Growth in Ghana: 1960–2000." Draft, African Economic Research Consortium, Nairobi, Kenya.

Aryeetey, Ernest, and Ravi Kanbur. Forthcoming. "Ghana's Economy at Half Century: An Overview of Stability, Growth and Poverty." In *The Economy of Ghana: Analytical Perspectives on Stability, Growth and Poverty,* ed. E. Aryeetey and R. Kanbur. Oxford: James Currey.

Aryeetey, Ernest, and Andrew McKay. 2004. "Operationalising Pro-Poor Growth: Ghana Case Study." Available at http://www.dfid.gov.uk/pubs/files/oppgghana.pdf.

Aryeetey, Ernest, and Finn Tarp. 2000. "Structural Adjustment and After: Which Way Forward?" In *Economic Reforms in Ghana: The Miracle and Mirage,* ed. E. Aryeetey, J. J. Harrigan, and M. Nissanke, 345–65. Oxford: James Currey and Accra, Ghana: Woeli Publishers.

Barbone, Luca, L. Cord, C. Hull, and J. Sandefur. 2005. "Democracy, Institutions, and Poverty Reduction." Draft, World Bank, Washington, DC.

Bardhan, P., and D. Mookherjee. 2000. "Capture and Governance at Local and National Levels." *American Economic Review* 90 (2): 135–39.

Besley, T. 1995. "Property Rights and Investment Incentives: Theory and Evidence from Ghana." *Journal of Political Economy* 103 (5): 903–37.

Booth, David, Richard Crook, E. Gyimah-Boadi, Tony Killick, and Robin Luckham, with Nana Boateng. 2004. "Drivers of Change in Ghana: Overview Report." Final draft, Overseas Development Institute, London, and Centre for Democratic Development, Accra, Ghana.

Christiansen, Luc, Lionel Demery, and Stefano Paternostro. 2003. "Macro and Micro Perspectives of Growth and Poverty in Africa." *World Bank Economic Review* 17 (3): 317–47.

Coulombe, Harold, and Andrew McKay. 2003. "Selective Poverty Reduction in a Slow Growth Environment: Ghana in the 1990s." Paper presented at ISSER-Cornell International Conference on Ghana at the Half Century, Accra, Ghana, July.

Demery, L., S. Chao, R. Bernier, and K. Mehra. 1995. "The Incidence of Social Spending in Ghana." Discussion Paper 82, Poverty and Social Policy Department, World Bank, Washington, DC.

Frimpong-Ansah, Jonathan. 1991. *The Vampire State in Africa: The Political Economy of Decline in Ghana.* London: James Currey.

Goldstein, Markus, and Christopher Udry. 2005. "The Profits of Power: Land Rights and Agricultural Investment in Ghana." Working Paper 929, Economic Growth Center, Yale University, New Haven, CT.

Government of Ghana. 2003. *Ghana Poverty Reduction Strategy, 2003–2005: An Agenda for Growth and Prosperity,* vol. 1. Accra, Ghana: Ghana Publishing Corporation, Assembly Press.

GSS (Ghana Statistical Service). 2000. *Poverty Trends in Ghana in the 1990s.* Accra, Ghana: GSS.

Hutchful, Eboe. 2002. *Ghana's Adjustment Experience: The Paradox of Reform.* Oxford: James Currey, Accra: Woeli Publishers, and Portsmouth, NH: Heinemann for the United Nations Research Institute for Social Development.

ISSER (Institute of Statistical, Social and Economic Research). 2004. *State of the Ghanaian Economy Report, 2003.* Legon, Ghana: University of Ghana.

ISSER and UNDP (United Nations Development Programme). 2005. *Ghana Human Development Report 2004.* Accra, Ghana: ISSER, UNDP, and United Nations Population Fund.

Killick, Tony. 1978. *Development Economics in Action: A Study of Economic Policies in Ghana*. London: Heinemann.

———. 2000. "Fragile Still: The Structure of Ghana's Economy 1960–1994." In *Economic Reforms in Ghana: The Miracle and Mirage*, ed. E Aryeetey, J. J. Harrigan, and M. Nissanke. Oxford: James Currey, and Accra, Ghana: Woeli Publishers.

———. 2004. "What Drives Change in Ghana? A Political-Economy View of Economic Prospects." Draft, Institute of Statistical, Social and Economic Research, University of Ghana, Legon, Ghana.

Kunfaa, E. Y. 1999. "Consultations with the Poor: Ghana Country Synthesis Report." Centre for the Development of People, Kumasi.

Norton, Andrew, Ellen Bortei-Doku Aryeetey, David Korboe, and D. K. Tony Dogbe. 1995. "Poverty Assessment in Ghana Using Qualitative and Participatory Research Methods." Discussion Paper 83, Poverty and Social Policy Department, World Bank, Washington, DC.

Nyanteng, V., and A. W. Seini. 2000. "Agricultural Policy and the Impact on Growth and Productivity 1970–95." In *Economic Reforms in Ghana: The Miracle and the Mirage*, ed. E. Aryeetey, J. J. Harrigan, and M. Nissanke. Oxford: James Currey, and Accra, Ghana: Woeli Publishers.

O'Connell, S., and B. Ndulu. 2000. "Africa's Growth Experience: A Focus on the Sources of Growth." Draft, African Economic Research Consortium, Nairobi, Kenya.

Ravallion, Martin, and B. Bidani. 1994. "How Robust Is a Poverty Profile?" *World Bank Economic Review* 8 (1): 75–102.

Teal, Francis. 1999. "Why Can Mauritius Export Manufactures and Ghana Not?" *The World Economy* 22 (7): 981–93.

Wetzel, D. 2000. "Promises and Pitfalls in Public Expenditure." In *Economic Reforms in Ghana: The Miracle and the Mirage*, ed. E. Aryeetey, J. J. Harrigan, and M. Nissanke. Oxford: James Currey, and Accra, Ghana: Woeli Publishers.

World Bank. 1995. "Ghana: Poverty Past, Present, and Future." Report 14504-GH, World Bank, Washington, DC.

———. 2004. "Ghana: Public Policy, Growth, and Poverty: A Country Economic Memorandum." Report 27656-GH, World Bank, Washington, DC.

Ye, Xiao, and Sudharshan Canagarajah. 2002. "Public Health and Education Spending in Ghana in 1992–98: Issues of Equity and Efficiency." Policy Research Working Paper 2579, World Bank, Washington, DC.

Youngblood, Charles E., and David I. Franklin. 2005. "Persistent Public Sector Deficits and Macroeconomic Instability in Ghana." In *The Economy of Ghana: Analytical Perspectives on Stability, Growth and Poverty*, ed. E. Aryeetey and R. Kanbur. Oxford: James Currey.

7

Uganda's Experience with Operationalizing Pro-Poor Growth, 1992 to 2003

John A. Okidi, Sarah Ssewanyana, Lawrence Bategeka, and Fred Muhumuza

The development literature is rich with analytical results that demonstrate the critical role of growth in poverty reduction. But because different groups of countries manifest different poverty and distributional outcomes, country-specific poverty reduction strategies should be informed by in-depth investigations of the key drivers of poverty-reducing growth. This analysis of poverty-reducing growth in Uganda between 1992 and 2003 focuses on the factors that drove the growth process and influenced the distributional outcomes of growth.

The poverty, growth, and inequality outcomes of Uganda's development efforts between 1992 and 2003 can be divided into three periods. The 1992 to 1997 period was characterized by high annual macroeconomic growth rates that peaked at above 10 percent in 1994/95. The high rates of growth in this period were accompanied by significant poverty reduction and declining income inequality. During the 1997 to 2000 period, growth slowed to an average of about 5 percent per year. Although the growth generated was sufficient to maintain a downward trend in poverty, the distribution of the benefits of growth during this period were so skewed that income inequality rose significantly. From 2000 to 2003 growth tapered off. The continued slowdown in growth, coupled with a worsening of the skewed distribution of the benefits of growth, reversed the downward trend in poverty.

These poverty, growth, and inequality patterns are interesting manifestations of pro-poor growth, both in the absolute and relative sense. The underpinnings of these development outcomes are explored below in reference to several questions. What were the sources of growth in the initial period of Uganda's reforms? What institutional and economic factors explain the failure of the initial growth surge to spur sustainable opportunities for future growth and poverty reduction? In particular, how did households respond to the policy of liberalization and private sector–led growth strategy? In that policy context, what happened to the main tradable commodities (coffee and cotton) that traditionally formed the cash base of households? What was the contribution of factor market access for broad-based private sector participation in the growth process? By attempting to answer these questions in the light of faltering poverty reduction in the early 2000s, this chapter investigates the extent to which fundamental building blocks for sustainable poverty-reducing growth were established and institutionalized during the 1990s.

Before the 1990s, Uganda suffered political, social, and economic disorder. The economy contracted significantly due to destruction, the absence of saving, physical and human capital flight, and reduced productivity through disruption and diversion of public expenditure (Collier and Reinikka 2001). GDP declined by 40 percent from 1971 to 1986, which Collier and Reinikka estimate to have translated into a 1 percent annual decline of the economy. Annual inflation rose to three digits mainly because the government financed fiscal deficits through domestic borrowing. Restoration of relative political calm in the second half of the 1980s and the credible signaling of commitment to reforms paved the way for an economic recovery that largely took effect in the early 1990s. The government then pronounced a private sector–led and export-driven economic growth policy. It stipulated that the role of the state would be limited to guaranteeing macroeconomic stability and providing legal and institutional frameworks that would support a liberalized market economy.

Uganda's history of economic recovery through commitment to sound economic policies, with country-owned initiatives for poverty reduction, provides useful lessons for economies in transition from conflict and from a controlled economic system to a stable and liberalized policy environment. Uganda's more recent experience with the challenge of sustaining recovery-based and growth-led poverty reduction provides equally important lessons for other countries.

Trends in and patterns of Uganda's poverty, growth, and inequality from 1992 to 2003 are examined below to illustrate the extent to which the country's growth-led strategies were pro-poor. The chapter also examines the role of traditional and nontraditional growth drivers in enhancing the participation of poor people in the growth process.

Growth, Poverty, and Inequality Trends, 1992 to 2003

By the beginning of the 1990s, Uganda had restored relative political calm and demonstrated commitment to massive reform as a prerequisite for economic recovery. Consequently, the country attracted substantial donor support for economic reforms that aimed to correct macroeconomic imbalances, remove inefficiencies in production and distribution of goods and services, and spur private sector–led and export-oriented growth. An important aspect of the reform strategy was trade liberalization through extensive reduction of nontariff barriers, competitive tendering for government purchasing, and a switch from export taxation to import taxation (Collier and Reinikka 2001).

Although good policies (along with favorable external conditions) were necessary for jump-starting the economy in the early to mid-1990s, they were insufficient for deepening the poverty reduction and growth outcomes of the recovery. Market liberalization in the early 1990s coincided with favorable external factors that led to rapid poverty reduction and growth. However, once the external environment was no longer so favorable, good macroeconomic policies needed to be accompanied by improvements in sectoral policies, institutions for economic governance, and the provision of safety net mechanisms if the broad-based growth of the first part of the decade was to be sustained.

Poverty Outcomes of Uganda's Recovery and Policy Strategies

Analysis of consumption expenditures from national household survey data shows that the recovery and policy strategies of the 1990s yielded significant poverty reduction, although it was uneven across sectors and regions (Appleton and others 1999; Appleton and Ssewanyana 2003). Income-poverty headcount declined from 56 percent in 1992 to 34 percent in 2000, after which it rose to 38 percent in 2003 (table 7.1).[1] However, poverty in Uganda remains a rural phenomenon and most pronounced among crop farmers. The disproportionate contribution of rural areas to national poverty has remained unchanged at about 96 percent. Regional imbalances, especially between the north and the rest of the country, have persisted. Overall, poverty declined faster in the central and western regions, which already had the lowest rates of poverty in 1992. The northern region has the highest level of poverty and experienced the smallest decline in the 1990s, although between 2000 and 2003 poverty headcount in this region remained about the same, while it rose in all other regions.

Table 7.1 *Decomposing Poverty Trends in Uganda, 1992–2003*

	Poverty headcount				Poverty gap				Poverty gap squared			
	1992/93	1997	1999/2000	2002/03	1992/93	1997	1999/2000	2002/03	1992/93	1997	1999/2000	2002/03
National	55.7	45.0	33.8	37.7	20.3	14.0	10.0	11.3	9.9	6.0	4.3	4.8
Rural	59.7	49.2	37.4	41.7	22.0	15.4	11.2	12.6	10.8	6.7	4.8	5.4
Urban	27.8	16.7	9.6	12.2	8.3	4.3	2.1	3.0	3.5	1.7	0.7	1.1
Central	45.6	27.9	19.7	22.3	15.3	7.6	4.4	5.5	7.0	3.0	1.5	1.9
Eastern	58.8	54.3	35.0	46.0	22.0	18.3	9.3	14.1	10.9	8.2	3.6	6.0
Northern	72.2	60.9	63.6	63.3	28.6	21.4	24.6	23.4	14.6	10.0	12.3	11.6
Western	53.1	42.8	26.2	31.4	18.7	11.0	6.1	7.9	9.0	4.0	2.1	2.9
Crop agriculture	63.6	53.0	39.1	50.4	23.7	16.9	11.3	15.5	11.7	7.4	4.7	6.7
Noncrop agriculture	52.4	37.0	41.9	33.6	20.7	11.5	14.4	9.8	10.6	4.9	6.6	4.1
Mining/construction	36.5	25.3	25.7	23.0	11.2	5.3	8.9	4.6	4.5	1.8	4.3	1.5
Manufacturing	44.4	36.4	23.3	28.4	15.8	8.0	5.2	8.0	7.5	2.8	1.7	3.0
Trade	26.5	20.5	12.7	17.4	7.6	5.8	2.6	4.3	3.2	2.3	0.9	1.6
Transport/communication	34.5	28.0	13.8	18.3	12.4	7.6	2.6	3.7	5.9	2.8	0.7	1.0
Government services	36.8	22.0	15.4	12.6	10.5	6.1	3.9	3.4	4.5	2.3	1.5	1.4
Other services	29.5	30.8	16.4	24.1	9.9	9.0	5.3	6.4	4.4	3.7	2.6	2.6
Not working	65.6	51.6	42.4	38.9	25.0	17.5	16.8	14.7	12.1	7.4	9.1	7.5

Source: Authors' computation from Uganda National Household Survey data.

Although poverty reduction in the 1990s was broad based, its incidence, depth, and severity were greatest among rural, northern, and crop-farming Ugandans (table 7.1). Applying the sectoral decomposition method of Ravallion and Huppi (1991), one can estimate that over 98 percent of the change in poverty during the 1990s was due to changes in the proportion of the poor within the occupational subgroups identified in table 7.1. Because most Ugandans are engaged in crop agriculture, and given the high world coffee prices in the mid-1990s, this sector contributed about two-thirds of the poverty reduction between 1992 and 1997. Rising incomes among workers in trade and government services accounted for about 15 percent of the poverty reduction during this period.

Distributional Effects of Uganda's Recovery and Policy Strategies

In each of the three subperiods presented in table 7.1, growth in average income consistently induced poverty reduction. For the whole period of analysis, average consumption expenditure per adult equivalent grew at 3.8 percent per year. Because growth was robust across percentiles (figure 7.1), irrespective of the choice of a plausible absolute poverty line, a decline in poverty was bound to occur. Nevertheless, the growth incidence curve for the whole period was skewed toward the top; only the richest 10 percent of the population enjoyed higher-than-average growth. The skewing of welfare distribution resulted in the Gini index of inequality increasing from 0.36 in 1992 to 0.43 in 2003.

Figure 7.1 *Prior to 2000 Growth Was Robust and Pro-Poor in Absolute Terms*

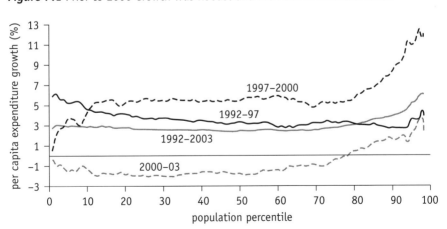

Source: Authors' construction from Natural Household Survey data.

Before 2000 growth was robust across percentiles and was, therefore, pro-poor in absolute terms (figure 7.1). From 1992 to 1997, when poverty headcount declined by 10.7 percentage points, about 96 percent of the decline was attributable to growth, and the rest was due to redistribution (table 7.2). As the growth incidence curves for 1992 and 1997 in figure 7.1 show, this period (which coincided with the coffee boom) was also the only period when welfare growth was disproportionately in favor of the lower end of the distribution. During this period, the rate of pro-poor growth was higher than the overall rate of growth. Irrespective of geographical or sectoral group, without growth Uganda would have not achieved the recorded high rate of poverty reduction, but growing inequality has dramatically weakened the poverty impact of growth since the late 1990s.

Of the three growth episodes considered, the highest growth in average consumption expenditure occurred during the period 1997 to 2000. The upward sloping growth incidence curve for this period illustrates that growth disproportionately favored the rich. Consequently, the Gini index of inequality rose from 0.35 to 0.40. Although the rate of pro-poor growth for the period was half the rate of growth in the overall average income, the poverty impact of the growth episode remained significant, given that a 10 percentage point drop in the headcount index was achieved.[2] In contrast, for the 2000 to 2003 period, the observed 0.7 percent growth in average consumption expenditure was driven by the top quintile, which was the only segment of the population that enjoyed positive growth in welfare. As shown in table 7.3 and explained below, the rate of pro-poor growth was negative during this period. The Gini index increased from 0.40 to 0.43, and the poverty headcount rose from 34 to 38 percent.

Uganda's Growth Experience

The growth literature identifies factor accumulation and productivity, geography, external environment, economic policies, and institutions as the main drivers of economic growth. During the period of analysis, Uganda could not have changed its geography. And being a small open economy, it could not have significantly influenced the external environment. It could only have taken advantage of global opportunities. But the country could have done something about the productivity and accumulation of its endogenous factors of production. Likewise, it could have changed its economic policies and established institutions for sustainable implementation of good policies.

Recovery of factor productivity and accumulation after widespread conflict was fundamental for growth and poverty reduction in the early 1990s. Strong growth performance was a product of restoration of relative political

Table 7.2 Contribution of Growth and Inequality to Poverty Reduction by Region and Category of Employment, 1992–2003

	1992–97		1997–2000		2000–03		1992–2003	
	Growth	Inequality	Growth	Inequality	Growth	Inequality	Growth	Inequality
National	−10.3	−0.4	−16.3	5.0	−1.4	5.3	−26.3	8.3
Rural	−10.9	0.4	−13.3	1.5	−0.4	4.7	−23.1	5.1
Urban	−5.6	−5.5	−14.7	7.6	−1.3	3.8	−22.8	7.2
Central	−13.7	−4.0	−14.1	5.8	−2.6	5.1	−31.1	7.7
Eastern	−6.7	2.2	−21.8	2.5	8.7	2.3	−18.7	5.9
Northern	−9.1	−2.2	2.6	0.2	−1.4	1.1	−8.6	−0.2
Western	−10.5	0.1	−20.9	4.3	−0.1	5.3	−27.9	6.2
Crop agriculture	−10.5	−0.2	−17.3	3.3	9.2	2.2	−18.1	4.8
Noncrop agriculture	−10.6	−4.8	−1.4	6.2	−10.6	2.3	−23.2	4.4
Mining/construction	−0.7	−10.5	−1.3	1.7	−2.3	−0.5	−5.5	−8.1
Manufacturing	−8.2	0.2	−22.3	9.2	8.4	−3.3	−18.1	2.2
Trade	−3.6	−2.4	−12.9	5.1	8.2	−3.4	−10.2	1.2
Transport/communication	−7.2	0.7	−15.3	1.1	0.6	4.0	−21.4	5.2
Government services	−12.2	−2.6	−15.2	8.6	−5.5	2.7	−32.0	7.8
Other services	−0.5	1.8	−20.2	5.7	0.9	6.8	−21.7	16.3
Not working	−16.1	2.1	−12.1	2.9	−2.1	−1.4	−34.1	7.5

Source: Authors' computation from National Household Survey data.

Table 7.3 Rates of Average Expenditure and Pro-Poor Growth, 1992–2003

	Growth in average expenditures	Rate of pro-poor growth
1992–2003		
National	3.77	2.66
Rural	3.09	2.57
Urban	5.25	3.45
1992–97		
National	3.02	3.94
Rural	3.03	3.83
Urban	2.50	5.07
1997–2000		
National	8.24	4.87
Rural	6.19	4.75
Urban	14.38	7.58
2000–03		
National	0.67	−1.67
Rural	0.19	−1.64
Urban	1.21	−4.16

Source: Authors' computation from National Household Survey data.

calm and policy incentives that mobilized idle human and physical capital for productive activities in pursuit of market opportunities for growth and poverty reduction. Specifically, strong growth from 1992 to 1997 was a result of rehabilitation and general postconflict recovery in most parts of the country (Bevan and others 2003). The early recovery efforts paid off in terms of high growth, leading to high rates of pro-poor growth. In addition, growth during the early to mid-1990s was broad-based, because it was accelerated by global opportunities in the form of high international prices of coffee, the production, storage, processing, and marketing of which involve over 13 million Ugandans. The case of coffee is typical of Uganda's taking full advantage of global opportunities.

Periods of the highest GDP growth rates were those with high growth rates in agriculture, the sector in which the bulk of the population is engaged (table 7.4). But the sustainability of the pro-poorness of growth appeared shaky and did not reflect a major structural shift to higher-value activities. After peaking in 1994/95, growth declined to the lowest level in 1997/98, after which it recovered modestly and remained well below the 7 percent target for achieving the ambitious national income-poverty headcount goal of less than 10 percent by 2017. Apart from deterioration of external terms of

Table 7.4 *Growth Rates by Industry Group, 1992–2003*

Industry group	1992/93	1993/94	1994/95	1995/96	1996/97	1997/98	1998/99	1999/2000	2000/01	2001/02	2002/03
Monetary agriculture	10.1	4.7	7.9	8.4	3.9	2.2	6.6	5.2	4.5	5.7	3.9
Cash crops	0.3	10.5	8.0	22.6	13.9	−2.8	9.3	7.0	−4.9	7.4	4.6
Food crops	17.3	5.3	11.7	4.4	−0.2	3.0	7.5	5.9	8.2	5.7	3.7
Livestock	3.5	2.8	−4.9	12.2	5.5	4.0	4.1	3.3	3.8	4.4	3.9
Fishing	4.1	−3.5	8.8	2.5	4.5	5.0	0.9	−0.1	4.0	3.5	3.2
Mining and quarrying	10.4	3.7	9.1	35.7	50.2	27.7	14.5	6.3	10.1	11.0	1.2
Manufacturing	1.9	15.4	11.6	29.5	14.2	4.4	14.1	3.6	8.9	4.3	4.5
Electricity and water	5.7	7.3	11.4	10.5	10.1	7.0	6.0	8.7	8.2	5.4	4.6
Construction	11.2	13.5	28.1	14.4	7.7	8.0	10.9	7.3	1.3	13.4	11.6
Trade	6.0	8.1	22.0	10.9	2.3	6.3	10.5	1.8	6.5	6.2	4.6
Hotels and restaurants	14.9	19.5	18.9	9.4	9.1	4.4	7.3	5.3	7.1	18.1	7.5
Transport/communication	7.3	10.0	13.4	10.6	10.8	9.6	7.0	7.3	9.6	12.4	16.8
Community services	7.4	6.0	7.0	6.0	6.3	5.8	4.5	8.6	2.4	7.0	2.7
Total GDP	8.0	5.4	10.0	8.3	4.8	4.4	7.4	5.8	5.0	6.4	4.7

Source: Uganda Bureau of Statistics.

Figure 7.2 Structural Transformation Tapered Off, 1992–2003

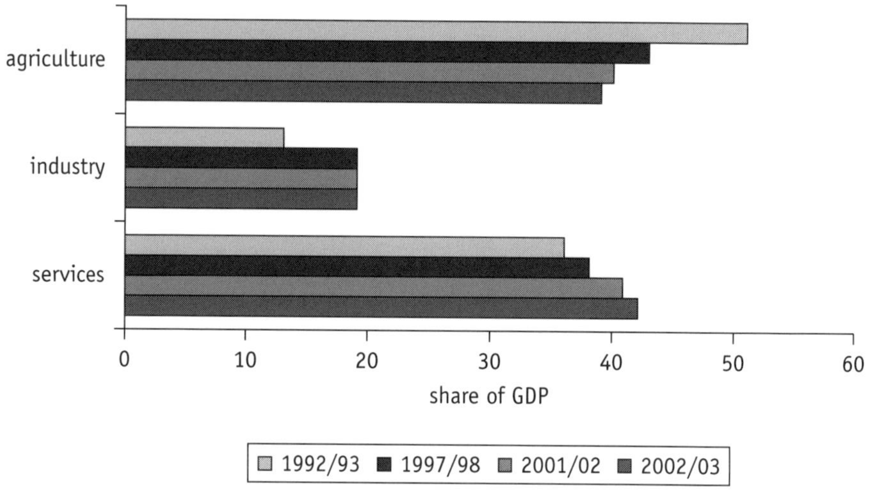

Source: Uganda Bureau of Statistics.

trade typified by rising oil prices and plummeting coffee prices after the boom of the mid-1990s, the slowdown in growth was a manifestation of the natural reality that the easiest efforts to engender postconflict growth had been undertaken by 1998/99. Although community services (education, health, and general government services) significantly increased, these trends mostly reflected growth in public expenditure in areas that would generate returns mainly in the long run. Moreover, Uganda's growth during the 1990s was not characterized by substantial structural transformation, especially between 1992 and 1997 (figure 7.2). Whereas services replaced agriculture as the largest contributor to GDP, the share of industry stagnated at about 19 percent, well below the 35 percent benchmark for countries to move from low- to middle-income status (Bevan and others 2003). Mining, construction, and manufacturing services did experience high rates of growth, but they remained insufficient to have a major impact on the economy.

Uganda's recent growth history reflects serious challenges of economic transition and calls for a new wave of reforms to build the fundamentals for longer-term economic growth. The daunting challenges can be illustrated by the fact that after 1999: structural transformation virtually stalled; investment rates reached a plateau well below the estimated 27 percent rate required for realizing the set national poverty goal; the exports-GDP ratio tapered off to about 12 percent; domestic revenue as a share of GDP stagnated well below the sub-Saharan African average of about 18 percent; and domestic savings remained abysmally low.

Explaining the Poverty Outcomes of Uganda's Growth Experience

Growth (rather than redistribution) has driven Uganda's poverty reduction process. During the 1990s policy stability, donor commitment, and external market environment were critical for broad-based access to the benefits of growth. But these favorable conditions were insufficient to sustain the downward trend of poverty. Inadequate institutions and a weak fiscal commitment to agriculture—the economic mainstay of the majority of Ugandans—reduced the impact of overall average growth on the incomes of the poor. The result was deepening welfare inequality.

The reforms of the early 1990s that corrected macroeconomic imbalances and removed distortions and inefficiencies in the economy through policy liberalization benefited households tremendously. Some of the greatest impacts of reforms occurred in the coffee sector following abolition of the coffee export tax and liberalization of coffee marketing in 1991/92. In particular, these developments resulted in a sharp increase in the share of farm-gate coffee prices in border prices from 30 percent to more than 80 percent (Collier and Reinikka 2001). Coupled with high international coffee prices in the mid-1990s and increased availability of high-yielding varieties, the coffee sector reform resulted in substantial income growth for the large number of Ugandans who participated in coffee production, processing, and marketing.

The massive inflows of foreign aid (at an average of 12 percent of GDP) that funded social sector and infrastructure development increased income growth opportunities and strengthened the government's capacity to deliver traditional pro-poor growth services. In addition, relative peace, respect for property rights, market liberalization, privatization, incentives for private sector–led growth, and the economic opportunities offered by high returns to investments in a politically unstable region attracted foreign direct investment and private remittances from Ugandans in the diaspora. This investment and remittances boosted physical and human capital accumulation and enhanced technology transfer that contributed to broad-based economic growth.

But the dividend from the recovery and the initial removal of distortions and improved economic efficiency was exhausted by 1999. Sustaining high recovery-related growth became a challenge, as illustrated by the structural stagnation of the economy. Because growth had been vital to poverty reduction in the 1990s, the slowdown in growth around the turn of the century negatively affected poverty reduction. Although growth was still positive from 2000 to 2003, the continuous rise in inequality since 1997 eventually outweighed the impact of growth on poverty. Had inequality not increased, poverty would have decreased an additional 8 percentage points for the whole period of analysis.

The reversal of the poverty trend after 1999 can also be explained by some sectoral patterns in the growth trend. Table 7.4 shows that the sectors that experienced the highest average growth rates are those from which relatively small proportions of the population earned a living. In general, these are industrial and service sectors, which were also the main destinations for foreign direct investment and official development assistance. Given that these sectors employ people with certain levels of human capital, most Ugandans could not have participated in their growth, because the average household was headed by someone with only four years of schooling at the beginning of the growth period.

As noted earlier, table 7.4 shows that periods of high overall growth coincided with strong growth performance in agriculture, the sector in which the bulk of the labor force is employed. But on the whole, growth performance of the agricultural sector has been lower than average. The share of agriculture in the national budget has also consistently been below 4 percent.[3] Inadequate direct funding of the agricultural sector has inhibited implementation of the Plan for Modernization of Agriculture, an innovative institutional framework for addressing supply-and-demand constraints facing the sector. One of the main supply-side challenges in agriculture is crop yield decrease due to declining soil fertility, low utilization of productivity-enhancing technologies, and poor land management practices (Nkonya and others 2004; Obwona and Ssewanyana 2004; Pender and others 2004). Food crop production may not have kept pace with population growth between 1999 and 2003,[4] given that consumption of home-produced food (in a largely subsistence society) fell by around 20 percent per capita (Appleton and Ssewanyana 2003).

On the cash crop side, the price of the main agricultural tradable, coffee, fell significantly after the boom of the mid-1990s, indicating that in the absence of diversification, good policies alone are not sufficient for predominantly agricultural households to ward off vulnerability to external shocks. The poor performance of the coffee sector in the second half of the 1990s prompted the government to promote other commodities such as fish, flowers, and vanilla for export. Although the fish and flower sectors have performed well and compensated foreign exchange losses due to plummeting coffee prices, they employ only a small fraction of the population, and thus their success has small direct poverty effects. In the case of vanilla, the international price dropped so drastically that during the 2000s farmers began neglecting the crop after having invested significantly in it.

In general, the poor performance of the agricultural sector between 1999 and 2003 is vividly reflected in the internal terms of trade between the sector on the one hand and industry and services on the other, which deteriorated against the former by 20 percent, severely affecting the purchasing power of the vast majority of Ugandans. This performance gap prompted a significant intersectoral shift, especially away from crop agriculture; households reporting it as their main economic activity decreased from 68 to 52 percent between 1999 and 2003. The shift was facilitated by improvements in infrastructure and market information, especially through mobile telephones. Most of the intersectoral shifts were into self-employment in trade and manufacturing, which do not appear to have offered opportunities for escaping poverty (see table 7.1).

The movement from agricultural to nonagricultural self-employment not only reflects low returns in agriculture but also indicates the failure of the wage employment sector to absorb the labor released from agriculture (Appleton and Ssewanyana 2003). Whatever labor was absorbed by the wage employment sector might have contributed to depressing wage rates, given that between 1999 and 2003 private sector real wages fell by about one-fifth. By contrast, government sector employment, which contracted during the 1990s, enjoyed a rise in real wages by about one-fifth, contributing to a decrease in the poverty headcount in the sector from 15 to 13 percent between 1999 and 2003. Because most of the poor are not employed in government but are self-employed or work in the private sector, the above highlighted wage declines and differentials must have contributed to the observed deepening of inequality and slippage into poverty between 1999 and 2003.

Poverty reduction in the 1990s occurred without major progress in job creation. The finding that the fastest-growing type of employment during this period was nonagricultural self-employment corroborates this argument; government sector employment (the largest sector in wage employment) dwindled over time (World Bank 2005). The limited job creation that accompanied Uganda's growth and poverty reduction is also evident in the observation that although about 45 percent of households are engaged in nonagricultural enterprises, only 15 percent of those owning such enterprises employ any labor at all because family labor is sufficient for their scale of operation (Deininger and Okidi 2003).

Other factors that have weakened the sustainability of poverty reduction include the accumulated effects of insecurity in northern Uganda and inaccessibility to credit financing. The disproportionate incidence of poverty in northern Uganda is largely attributed to the 20-year-old civil war, the cost of which has been estimated at 3 percent of GDP. Regarding credit, a regulatory framework has been established for development of financial institutions, but the cost of credit has remained high, at about 30 percent per year, undermining households' entrepreneurial efforts to diversify income sources. The high credit cost is a major problem in Uganda, where no risk-edging mechanisms are available to ward off the devastating welfare impacts of shocks such as those due to plummeting coffee prices in the 1990s and the sharp fall in the price of vanilla in the early 2000s.

Increasing the Participation of Poor People in Growth

Participation of the poor in the growth process can be examined from three perspectives: traditional drivers of economic growth, political economy and institutional factors that influenced growth and poverty reduction, and state actions aimed at enhancing participation of the poor in the growth process. Regarding traditional drivers of growth, the role of policy, factor accumulation and productivity, and external environment for pro-poor growth are important to consider. The discussion below links policy and external environments with accumulation and productive deployment of household assets such as land, labor, and human and physical capital. It also explores the impact of political economy and institutions on participation of the poor in the growth process. In particular, it analyzes barriers to participation arising from political and social relations, rules, regulations, and procedures.

During the 1990s, when Uganda's economy maintained relatively high average growth rates, growth momentum was generated from restoration of political and economic order. Participation in the growth process depended on households' capacity to take advantage of the stable macroeconomic environment. Government action programs intended to facilitate private human and physical capital accumulation and productivity affected this capacity. The extent of participation and the benefit of growth varied significantly across economic sectors and geographical areas according to ability to adjust to or capitalize on the new political economy and institutional structures of the 1990s. Because of the variability in participation in the growth process and the shortcomings of market-driven catch-up mechanisms, welfare inequality deepened.

Drivers of Growth and Participation of the Poor in Growth

As noted above, Uganda implemented far-reaching reforms that saw the economy grow at impressive average rates during the 1990s into the 2000s. The reforms were characterized by the "Washington Consensus" policy

Figure 7.3 *Ugandan Policy Makers Control Inflation to a Single Digit, 1991–2004*

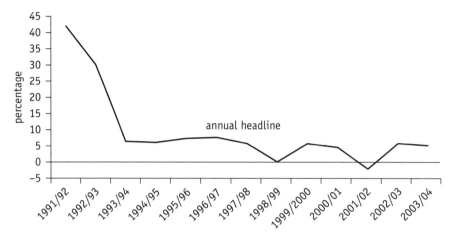

Source: Bank of Uganda.

package that included liberalization of commodity and financial markets, fiscal discipline, competitive currencies, privatization, and deregulation. The centerpiece of Uganda's commodity and financial market liberalization was stabilization of consumer prices, foreign exchange rates, and interest rates. Since 1992 inflation has been controlled to single digits (figure 7.3). Overvaluation of the shilling was corrected from an exchange rate of U Sh 966 per dollar in January 1992 to U Sh 1,940 in March 2003, and real interest rates (which were negative) turned positive in 1994.

The single-digit annual inflation rates that have been maintained since 1993/94 attest to the country's commitment to the control of inflation (figure 7.3). This commitment was based on an understanding that low inflation is good for investment planning and, therefore, necessary for economic growth. In relation to the poor, the control of inflation was justified as a means of protecting them from erosion of the value of their savings. Low inflation was seen as an important requirement for encouraging a saving culture and promoting participation of the poor in the growth process when they invested their meager savings.

Faced with tight monetary conditions and slow expansion of domestic revenue, Uganda had to rely on aid to support the country's growth and poverty reduction process. Aid led to significant expansion of money that the central bank mopped up using financial instruments to control inflation. The more the country relied on aid, the greater the need to mop up liquidity, leading to high interest rates that adversely affected credit financing of the productive sector of the economy.[5]

Nevertheless, correcting macroeconomic imbalances and opening the economy through removal of distortions and lowering of barriers to entrepreneurship promoted competitive and innovative deployment of factors of production as drivers of growth. Previously idle domestic human and physical capital began to be used for productive activities in the buoyant growth environment. Mobilization of foreign human, physical, and financial capital was accelerated by the 1991 investment code that created the Uganda Investment Authority, which contributed to refining policy incentives, in turn leading to reversal of capital flight (Collier and Reinikka 2001).

Foreign direct investment (FDI) contributed significantly to Uganda's structural transformation (to the extent that it occurred) and growth process. Liberalization policies, privatization of state enterprises, and the activity of the Uganda Investment Authority spurred the growth of FDI, which boosted the economic recovery process. The largest flows of FDI occurred in the manufacturing sector following the return of industries that had been confiscated from Ugandan Asians in the early 1970s, when the government "ugandanized" the economy (figure 7.4). Purchase of public companies by foreign entrepreneurs and blossoming opportunities in transport, telecommunication, financial, legal, and computing services attracted foreign investments in joint ventures and local subsidiaries in the emerging market economy (Obwona and Egesa 2004).

In spite of the significant role of net private inflows, the main source of external financing for Uganda's growth was foreign aid, which contributed

Figure 7.4 *Policy Liberalization Reverses Capital Flight and Attracts FDI to Industry and Services*

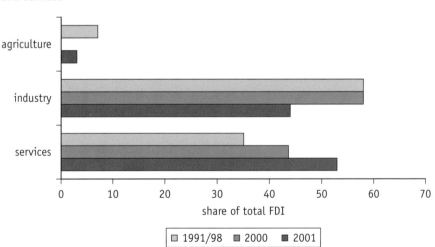

Sources: Bank of Uganda and Uganda Investment Authority.

31 percent of the country's growth and 29 percent of poverty reduction between 1992 and 1997 (Collier and Reinikka 2001). Donor leadership in financing Uganda's growth also attracted complementary external resources from international nongovernmental organizations. These inflows of financial capital combined with relative peace to further boost the productive employment of land, labor, and human and physical capital. The productivity outcome was a tripling of the contribution of total factor productivity (TFP) to economic growth during the 1992–97 period.

A major element of the liberalization policy was removal of export tariffs, which promoted trade and increased Uganda's export earnings. The coffee boom of 1994/95 and successful diversification into nontraditional export items such as flowers, fish, beans, and maize boosted the export sector, which was a significant driver of economic growth during the 1990s. A high average real GDP growth rate of about 6.4 percent per year was achieved between 1992 and 2003. The fastest rates of growth occurred in small sectors such as mining and quarrying, manufacturing, hotels and restaurants, and construction (table 7.4). Growth of the agricultural sector (the main economic sector for the majority of the population) was lower than the average GDP growth rate.

After achieving high growth rates of about 10 percent in the mid-1990s, the economy slowed significantly following exhaustion of the benefits of recovery, which coincided with a downward spiral of the world coffee price (figure 7.5). When the dividends of economic recovery end, as is typical,

Figure 7.5 *After the Boom of the Mid-1990s, Coffee Prices Plummeted*

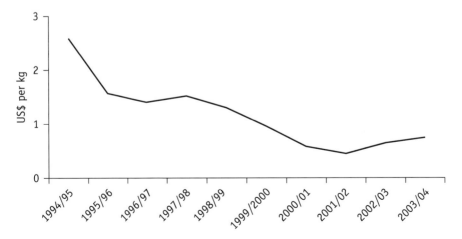

Source: International Coffee Organization.

countries must meet the challenge of sustaining normal growth through increased investment rates and continued export growth and diversification, which ought to be underpinned by increased efficiency in the employment of private and public capital (Bevan and others 2003; Collier and Reinikka 2001). In the long run, growth can be sustained if the return to capital does not diminish as economies develop (Lucas 1988; Rebelo 1991; Romer 1986). Maintaining positive returns to capital requires the economy to undergo structural transformation and to remain dynamic so that capital flows from low- to high-return activities.

The rate of growth of Uganda's agricultural sector has been slower than overall average growth, raising concern about the lack of political commitment to agriculture as the starting point for long-term development. Without this commitment, the sector may not serve as an engine for long-term structural transformation. Although GDP shares of monetary and nonmonetary agriculture declined during the 1990s, they did so not as a result of improved agricultural earnings' financing diversification into other sectors with higher returns to labor and human capital. The shares declined because of (1) structural transformation that saw the retreat of the state from active participation in the sector without corresponding advance of the private sector, (2) falling productivity caused by declining soil fertility, (3) limited use of fertilizers, and (4) lack of effective agricultural advisory services.

The agricultural sector's sluggish performance suggests that had political and fiscal commitment to agriculture been at the level given to social services during the 1990s, growth would have been higher and poverty reduction much greater. In brief, if policies and incentive structures do not cause fast growth in sectors that provide livelihoods to the majority of the people, overall growth is unlikely to have a sustained poverty-reducing impact, in which case its pro-poorness (both in absolute and relative terms) diminishes.

Because the majority of the population is engaged in agriculture, and most poor people hold their assets in the form of land (Deininger and Okidi 2003), security of land rights is fundamentally important for growing out of poverty. Although the poor have access to land, most of them hardly own the land they use. When they have a claim on land, they invariably have no registered interest in the land.

Uganda has a complex history of land tenure that features periodic disruptions in land market development. At independence, the colonial power gave both occupied and unoccupied land to a few notables, especially in the central and southern parts of the country (which came to be known as *mailo* land). Occupants of *mailo* land became squatters with use rights that depended primarily on the tenant-landlord relationship.

The 1998 Land Act (the prevailing land law) seeks to protect and enshrine rights of squatters, de facto tenants, refugees, absentee landowners, and women in the land law. The act gives bona fide tenancy rights to current occupants, making it easy for them to register the land in their names, hence making the land candidate collateral for bank loans. However, the act also requires that any transactions involving family land must have the consent of the spouse (or the rest of the communal members in the case of land registered under customary tenure). The transaction costs of enforcing this requirement has made land a less attractive form of collateral for loans.

The 1998 Land Act also creates land regulatory bodies such as district land boards, district land tribunals, and parish land committees. But because the Land Act in general has been viewed as too expensive to be fully operationalized, not all these bodies have been instituted. At the same time, existing mechanisms for land conflict resolution, such as courts of elders and village councils, were rendered illegal by the new law. Consequently, conflicts and complexities in land access and ownership have increased, counteracting the key objectives of the law to strengthen land rights, minimize conflicts, and increase land access for productive activities.

Regarding human capital, significant growth was registered. Between 1992 and 2003, the proportion of poor household heads and nonpoor household heads with no formal education declined from 34 to 27 percent and from 21 to 12 percent, respectively. The Universal Primary Education program, in place since 1997, is expected to maintain this trend. Nevertheless, the program has not achieved some objectives such as delivery of quality education for all and equity in access to public education resources. The shortfall in performance is due to problems with curriculum design, inadequate funding, insufficient supervision and inspection of schools, and inefficiency in the management of school grants.

Although the proportion of household heads without formal education continues to decline, about 55 percent of these individuals have not attained education above the primary level. Because human capital accumulation is critical for participation in long-run growth, its slow pace among the poor will, in turn, slow down the participation of the poor in future human-capital intensive growth opportunities. Notably, access to secondary education by the poor was on the decline throughout the 1990s and early 2000s. Because the impact of education on household income growth is nondecreasing (Deininger and Okidi 2003), inequality in access to higher education will certainly perpetuate welfare inequality and remain a major constraint to poor households' exploitation of market-driven opportunities for participation in future growth. Okidi and McKay (2003) illustrate this reality with evidence of poor households' intergenerational transmission of poverty through perpetually low levels of education.

As in the case of access to primary education, Uganda has removed user fees from government health units to improve poor people's health so that they can work and diversify their incomes. But the Uganda Participatory Poverty Assessment reveals that communities have noted a deterioration in quality. Household survey data show that the health status of Ugandans was quite poor during the period of analysis. Deininger and Okidi (2003) find that the number of days lost to illness in a month by the average house-hold increased from 8 to 12 between 1992 and 2000 and that 23 percent of households lost a family member in the 15-to-45 age group during the 1990s. The infant mortality rate increased from 81 to 88 per 1,000 live births between 1992 and 2000.

Although Uganda has decreased the spread of HIV/AIDS, it cannot boast of a similar level of progress with respect to malaria, which accounted for about 80 percent of all illnesses reported during the 1990s. The impor-tance of good health for participation in growth has been illustrated by Deininger and Okidi (2003), who estimate that the average income of a household affected by health problems in 1992 grew 1.8 percentage points less than the income of a household without such problems.

Even if access to basic education and health services is improved, the absence of financial resources may keep the poor from increasing the pro-ductivity of their most abundant factors of production, land and labor. The government implemented financial sector reforms with the objectives of strengthening the country's financial system and realizing substantial finan-cial depth. The reform regulations resulted in privatization of five banks and the main commercial bank owned by the government. The consequence was concentration of strong financial institutions in urban areas; rural areas were left grossly underbanked.

Microfinance institutions mushroomed in rural areas to fill the void in financial service delivery. But these institutions charge exorbitant lending interest rates because they do not take deposits and therefore have to bor-row money from the established commercial banks (at about a 16 percent rate of interest) for lending to their clients. The costs of transacting small credits to small and largely informal household enterprises and the risks associated with it dictate that microfinance institutions have to charge very high interest rates, at about 30 to 36 percent per year. Lack of credit financ-ing and the current structure of microfinance institutions have hindered the poor in seizing market opportunities for income growth.

Another factor constraining the participation of poor Ugandans in growth is lack of electricity. The disparity between rural and urban areas in access to electricity is stark: in 2003 more than 90 percent of urban households but only 13 percent of rural households lived in communities with electricity. How important is electricity to households' economic growth? During the 1990s, households with access to electricity experienced income growth 3.5 percentage points higher than that of households without such access (Deininger and Okidi 2003). Although the supply of educated workers is expanding, limited availability of electricity could severely constrain generation of better-paying jobs.

Irrespective of the availability of land, labor, and physical and human capital, participation in growth will be stifled unless people are guaranteed security of life and property. Panel data show that in the early 1990s civil strife in northern Uganda significantly curtailed income growth in subsequent periods by about 5 percentage points (Deininger and Okidi 2003). To address economic imbalances associated with the cost of the war, the government created a social fund for the region. But insurgency has undermined the fund's objective of enhancing the participation of the victims of war in the growth process. The most inhibiting factor in this regard has been the government's program to move people from their land to camps with the intention of reducing their vulnerability to rebel attacks. The displaced peasants cannot participate in the growth process, because they cannot access their most valuable resource, land.

Political Economy, Institutions, and Barriers to Participation

When the National Resistance Movement ascended to power through an arms struggle, its leadership shunned market liberalization and pronounced a mixed economic system as the new policy direction of Uganda. Barter trade arrangements were made, mainly with formerly Eastern Bloc countries to address foreign exchange shortages. But because the economy remained in the doldrums, the government eventually abandoned the socialist strategy in favor of programs supported by Bretton Woods institutions.

At the beginning of the 1990s, government institutions for formulation and implementation of the numerous policy reforms necessary for recovery programs were very weak. Priority was given to strengthening the Ministry of Finance, Planning and Economic Development because of its importance in designing, implementing, monitoring, and evaluating the recovery process. After capacity was built in the finance ministry, sectoral plans or programs necessary for implementing and sustaining various facets of economic reform programs could not be delegated to the respective line ministries, because they were considered weak. This situation led to creation of parallel program secretariats within the finance ministry—in some cases, at the displeasure of the line ministries that would traditionally discharge the responsibilities of the secretariat.

Concentration of key policy initiatives in the finance ministry appeared to facilitate coordination, monitoring, and evaluation in a sectorwide development context, but the concerns of other line ministries about the ownership of such program initiatives did not help the initiatives' countrywide implementation. The inability of the finance ministry to step in, outside of its traditional area of competence, compounded the challenge of implementing well-conceived policy programs in a sustainable fashion. The main policy programs housed in the finance ministry are the Plan for Modernization of Agriculture, which is aimed at transforming the peasant farming system into a commercially oriented system; the Medium-Term Competitiveness Strategy, which is aimed at identifying and alleviating constraints to private sector leadership in Uganda's growth; and the Strategic Exports Interventions Program, which originally identified specific traditional export commodities for aggressive promotion for value addition.

An institutional reform for facilitating broad-based policy program implementation was governance decentralization, which was primarily initiated to improve the efficiency and quality of social services delivery. Enactment of the Local Government Act in 1997 marked the beginning of devolution of political power to local governments and, with it, the power to manage the development process, including public finance at the local government level. But because of local governments' limited capacities to plan, implement, and monitor programs, decentralization fell short of expectations. Indeed, inefficiencies were decentralized and, therefore, replicated. Furthermore, decentralization and creation of new political districts did not bring services closer to people but became a means for job creation. From the mid-1990s to 2003 the number of districts grew from 35 to 56, tremendously increasing public administration costs and limiting the availability of resources for development activities.

To complement government's capacities and to pursue private sector–led development, the country embraced the principle of private–public partnership. But by the mid-1990s, it became apparent that the emerging private–public partnerships did not honor segregation of private actors and public actors. Government officials were the key domestic actors in the private sector. In the late 1990s various revelations of corruption at all levels of government started to surface. Nontraditional determinants of private sector growth, such as personal interest, personal favors, unfair regulations, and various forms of corruption, began to adversely affect implementation of policy programs, resulting in marginalization in the growth process and deepening of inequality.

Government interference with the free-market mechanism in determining allocation of opportunities and participation in the growth process has occurred in several forms, including the choosing of winners. A good example is the addition of the garment industry under the U.S. government initiative to promote trade with Africa: the African Growth Opportunity Act (AGOA). Because the garment industry was not part of Uganda's original exports interventions program, it had to be brought into the medium-term expenditure framework through ex post budget reallocation (Bevan and others 2003). Most important, the intervention was firm-specific to support the participation of a particular investor in the AGOA initiative. Such private bilateral arrangements are likely to induce or exacerbate a lobbying and rent-seeking culture, displacing or delaying emergence of a proper profit-seeking entrepreneurial culture (Bevan and others 2003). In brief, a transparent and systematic institutional mechanism and incentive structure for participation in growth opportunities, such as those introduced by the AGOA initiatives, are lacking. Where they exist, they are subject to individual or firm-specific policy reversal.

In the agricultural sector, aside from the government's investment in areas that support agriculture, the main agency for private-public partnership was National Agricultural Advisory Services. Under this program, private provision of extension services operates alongside related government services. In additional to limited budgetary provision for implementation, the program faces the challenge of inducing farmers' demand for advisory services. The assumption of government is that a communal spirit motivates farmers to form groups that demand certain services (from private providers) for government financing.

With regard to the traditional tradable crops, coffee and cotton, private–public partnerships had mixed results in translating policy liberalization into benefits to producers. The results were positive in the case of coffee. Coffee trees were largely in place and simply needed additional labor time to respond to revamped market opportunities. Most important, the coffee sector's liberalization coincided with the international price increases of the mid-1990s. Farmers were able to reap an increased fraction of the world market price of coffee, and rising international prices motivated middlemen. The private–public partnership enhanced the participation of coffee farmers in the growth surge of the 1990s.

In the case of cotton, a sufficient response to incentives for increasing cotton production would have necessitated reallocation of land away from some nontraditional cash crops that had replaced cotton. On the international market, the price of cotton was steady during the 1990s, meaning that farmers could be attracted by the extra farm-gate price margin due to liberalization but that middlemen had no global market surge of which to take advantage. Furthermore, the cotton sector generally did not respond well to policy reforms because of low incentives for private sector agents to supply seeds and to invest in revamping cotton-ginning facilities. The government not only withdrew from cotton input supply and produce marketing but also dismantled farmers' cooperatives that had functioned well during the 1960s and early 1970s. The cotton sector experience is a classic case of state withdrawal from productive activities without sufficient private sector advance into the activities.

In brief, liberalization increased farm-gate prices of commodities, but removal of subsidies and other forms of state support to agriculture and the collapse of cooperatives raised input prices and marketing costs. In a nutshell, the agricultural sector has not successfully adjusted to liberalization-related institutional restructuring. Incentives to invest in the sector have, therefore, remained low.

Lessons from Uganda's Pro-Poor Growth Experience

Uganda's pro-poor growth experience began with a period of high rates of pro-poor growth resulting from high average growth rates and declining income inequality. This was followed by a period of accelerated pro-poor growth rates and high average growth rates accompanied by rising inequality. Lastly, there was a period of significantly slowed average growth and large increases in inequality, leading to negative rates of pro-poor growth.

In a stable macroeconomic environment, accelerated pro-poor growth could result from (1) consistently and patiently investing in people and physical infrastructure, (2) strengthening institutions to increase the efficiency and effectiveness of public expenditure, (3) pursuing policies that ensure efficient links to international markets for commodities produced by the poor, (4) increasing access to key factors of production such as credit, and (5) investing in safeguarding the poor from the adverse effects of market liberalization.

Uganda's experience shows that despite the existence of good policies and programs, translation of these policies into desired outcomes can be undermined by practical political economy inconsistencies and institutional weaknesses, leading to economic slowdown. When this phenomenon occurred, welfare inequality deteriorated, and poverty eventually began to increase.

Structural transformation slowed as a result of an unimplemented agricultural modernization plan, weak institutions, the adverse impacts of liberalization on access to productive assets (especially credit), poor monitoring and evaluation of public sector interventions, corruption, and insufficient private sector investment in key areas from which the state disengaged.

Several policy messages can be drawn. On the macroeconomic front, the centrality of inflation targeting in Uganda's policy stances warrants a closer look. This examination is important in the context of the recent upswing in poverty, the huge gaps between Uganda's human development levels and the corresponding Millennium Development Goals, and the high rating of Uganda as a favored destination of development aid. Given that the economy is operating well below full employment, coupled with resource leakages resulting from high levels of corruption, policy makers could consider relaxing the country's inflation target. A high-corruption country should target a higher inflation than a low-corruption country, because doing so would raise social welfare more than a regime of mechanical inflation targeting (Huang and Wei 2003).

On the real sector front, throughout the 1990s into the 2000s, the contribution of TFP to growth has been extremely low. With capital accumulation accounting for about 85 percent of Uganda's real GDP growth (Pattillo, Gupta, and Carey 2005), the country cannot sustain growth, to which productivity, rather than the stock of capital, is crucial (Easterly and Levine 2001). Enhancing productivity will require institutions and policies that create incentives to generate and diffuse innovations within the country (Howitt 2004). Modernization of agriculture, the main real sector, will require political commitment, institutional strengthening, and substantial funding increases to deliver innovative ways of promoting productivity and output marketing. Glaring evidence of the weaknesses of the agricultural modernization plan is underscored by the fact that the constraints it set out to eradicate in 2001 still hold—and new ones, pertaining to land access and ownership rights and internal and external market volatility, have emerged (Oxford Policy Management 2005). Fixing supply-side constraints in agriculture should be the initial point of emphasis if the sector is to release labor to expanding sectors, in line with the pattern of structural transformation which some middle-income countries have experienced.

Regarding human capital development, access to secondary education for the poor should be enhanced through private–public partnership in financial assistance programs such as bursaries. In the short run, direct state financing for disadvantaged communities and households could be initiated. Such financing is hard to implement because of selection problems, but an effort should be made to build institutional capacity to implement it. Otherwise, the poor may not break the cycle of intergenerational transmission of human capital underdevelopment.

Another important element of human development is health care. Uganda's health sector strategic plan needs to be periodically reviewed to evaluate the impact of removal of user fees on access to quality care. Given that malaria is a major disruptor of economic activities, successful delivery of services under the Global Fund initiative is critical. Because the social sector development challenge is lack of resources, and given that Uganda is well beyond the Heavily Indebted Poor Countries debt sustainability level, concerns about Dutch Disease will have to be addressed through critical analytical work rather than through theoretically based intellectual articulations.[6]

A major issue in Uganda's growth process is the private–public partnership, which has suffered from a lack of comprehensive institutional direction. Where the private sector is weak and state action is required to energize the private sector response to global opportunities, an economy-wide policy should be instituted to encourage broad-based and competitive private-public partnerships instead of firm-specific interventions. Uganda's response to attractive international coffee prices shows what sectorwide interventions can achieve. In stark contrast, the firm-specific intervention that characterized Uganda's response to AGOA trade opportunities shows how narrow the benefits from such interventions can be. In that case, innovative structural incentives for creating backward links to Uganda's textile industry could have broadened participation.

In general, programs to remove obstacles to participation in growth opportunities should be transformable into longer-term policy programs. To this end, the programs require effective, transparent, and coordinated implementing institutions. Where capacities in a particular institution are weak, Uganda's experience suggests that the best recourse is to rebuild those capacities rather than to shift the policy responsibilities to other institutions.

Notes

1. Panel data evidence shows that between 1992 and 2000 a significant proportion of Ugandans (20 percent) experienced chronic poverty, 30 percent moved out of poverty, and about 10 percent fell into poverty (Lawson, McKay, and Okidi 2003).

2. Note that the rate of pro-poor growth accelerated between 1997 and 2000. Even if this was half the overall average rate of growth in this period, it was much higher than for the 1992 to 1997 period, when the rate of pro-poor growth was higher than the overall average rate of growth.

3. Policy makers argue that low direct public expenditure share in agriculture is compensated by spending in areas that support agriculture—the traditional

pro-poor spending areas such as education, health, water and sanitation, and roads and connectivity.

4. National accounts statistics show that Uganda's population increased from 22.2 million in 1999/2000 to 25 million in 2002/03. Uganda's annual population growth rate is one of the highest in the world, at 3.4 percent.

5. Uganda's debt-export ratio is well beyond the Heavily Indebted Poor Countries sustainability level.

6. In Uganda there is the concern that large aid inflows relative to GDP could drive up the real exchange rate, making the country's exports less competitive. In a discussion of Dutch Disease in the context of Uganda, Bevan and others (2003) downplay the problem and instead emphasize the importance of enhancing the country's capacity to absorb and utilize aid effectively.

References

Amsden, A., and R. van der Hoeven. 1996. "Manufacturing Output, Employment and Real Wages in the 1980s: Labor's Loss until Century's End." *Journal of Development Studies* 32 (4): 506–30.

Appleton, S. 1996. "Problems of Measuring Changes in Poverty over Time: The Case of Uganda, 1989–1992." *Institute of Development Studies* 27 (1): 43–55.

————. 2001. "Changes in Poverty and Inequality." In *Uganda's Recovery, the Role of Farms, Firms, and Government,* ed. Ritva Reinikka and Paul Collier, 83–121. Washington, DC: World Bank.

Appleton, S, T. Emwanu, J. Kagugube, and J. Muwonge. 1999. "Changes in Poverty in Uganda, 1992–1997." Working Paper, Center for the Study of African Economies, University of Oxford, Oxford.

Appleton, S., and S. Ssewanyana. 2003. "Poverty Analysis in Uganda, 2002/03." Draft, Economic Policy Research Centre, Kampala, Uganda.

Bank of Uganda. 2004. "Report on the 2003 Survey on Private Sector Investment and Investor Perceptions in Uganda." Joint survey with Uganda Bureau of Statistics and Uganda Investment Authority, Uganda.

Berry, A., S. Horton, and D. Mazumdar. 1997. "Globalization, Adjustment, Inequality and Poverty." Background paper for United Nations Development Programme Human Development Report. Prepared by Department of Economics, University of Toronto, Toronto, Canada.

Bevan, D., C. Adam, J. Okidi, and F. Muhumuza. 2003. "Economic Growth, Investment and Export Promotion." Paper prepared for Uganda's Poverty Eradication Action Plan Revision 2002/03.

Collier, Paul, and Ritva Reinikka. 2001. "Reconstruction and Liberalization: An Overview." In *Uganda's Recovery, the Role of Farms, Firms, and Government,* ed. Ritva Reinikka and Paul Collier, 15–48. Washington, DC: World Bank.

Datt, G., and Martin Ravallion. 1992. "Growth and Redistribution Components of Changes in Poverty: A Decomposition with Applications to Brazil and China in 1980s." *Journal of Development Economics* 38 (2): 275–95.

Deininger, K. 2001. "Determinants of Health Outcomes in Uganda, 1999/2000." World Bank, Washington, DC.

Deininger, Klaus, Gloria Kempaka, and Anja Crommelynck. 2005. "Impact of AIDS on Family Composition, Welfare, and Investment: Evidence from Uganda." *Review of Development of Economics* 9 (9): 303–24.

Deininger, Klaus, and John Okidi. 2003. "Growth and Poverty Reduction in Uganda, 1992–2000: Panel Data Evidence." *Development Policy Review* 21 (4): 481–509.

Dunn, D. 2002. "Economic Growth in Uganda: A Summary of the Post-Conflict Experience and Future Prospects." Draft, International Monetary Fund, Washington, DC.

Easterly, William, and Ross Levine. 2001. "It's Not Factor Accumulation: Stylized Facts and Growth Models." *World Bank Economic Review* 15 (2): 177–219.

Ekonya, E., D. Sserunkuuma, and J. Pender, eds. 2002. "Policies for Improved Land Management in Uganda: Second National Workshop." Environment and Production Technology Division, Workshop Summary Paper 12, International Food Policy Research Institute, Washington, DC.

Gauthier, B. 2001. "Productivity and Exports." In *Uganda's Recovery, the Role of Farms, Firms, and Government,* ed. Ritva Reinikka and Paul Collier. Washington, DC: World Bank.

Henstridge, Mark, and Louis Kasekende. 2001. "Exchange Reforms, Stabilization, and Fiscal Management." In *Uganda's Recovery, the Role of Farms, Firms, and Government,* ed. Ritva Reinikka and Paul Collier. Washington, DC: World Bank.

Howitt, Peter. 2004. "Endogenous Growth, Productivity, and Economic Policy: A Progress Report." *International Productivity Monitor* 8 (spring): 3–15.

Huang, H., and S. Wei. 2003. "Monetary Policies for Developing Countries: The Role of Corruption." Working Paper WP/03/183, International Monetary Fund, Washington, DC.

Kappel, R., L. Jann, and S. Steiner. 2003. The Missing Links—Uganda's Economic Reforms and Pro-Poor Growth. Study commissioned by the German Agency for Technical Cooperation, Eschborn, Germany.

Keefer, P. 2000. "Growth and Poverty Reduction in Uganda: The Role of Institutional Reform." Draft, World Bank, Washington, DC.

Klasen, S., and D. Lawson. 2004. "The Impact of Population Growth on Economic Growth and Poverty Reduction in Uganda." Paper prepared for the Ministry of Finance, Planning, and Economic Development, Kampala, Uganda.

Lawson, David, Andrew McKay, and John Okidi. 2003. "Poverty Persistence and Transitions in Uganda: A Combined Qualitative and Quantitative Analysis." Working Paper 38, Chronic Poverty Research Centre, University of Manchester, Manchester, UK.

Lopez, Humberto. 2004. "Pro-Growth, Pro-Poor: Is There a Trade-Off?" Draft, World Bank, Washington, DC.

Lucas, R. E. 1988. "On the Mechanism of Economic Development." *Journal of Monetary Economics* 22 (1): 3–42.

Mackinnon, John, and Ritva Reinikka. 2002. "How Research Can Assist Policy: The Case of Economic Reforms in Uganda." *World Bank Researcher Observer* 17 (2): 267–92.

Mijumbi, B. Peter. 2001. "Uganda's External Debt and the HIPC Initiative." *Canadian Journal of Development Studies* 22 (2): 494–523.

MoFPED (Ministry of Finance, Planning and Economic Development). 1996. "The Republic of Uganda, National Food Strategy: A Response to Overcome the Challenge of Poverty and Growth." Export Policy Analysis Unit, Kampala, Uganda.

_____. 2002. "Participatory Poverty Assessment Process: Deepening the Understanding of Poverty." Kampala, Uganda.

Nkonya, E., J. Pender, P. Jagger, D. Sserunkuuma, C. Kaizzi, and H. Ssali. 2004. "Strategies for Sustainable Land Management and Poverty Reduction in Uganda." Research Report 133, International Food Policy Research Institute, Washington, DC.

Obwona, M., and K. Egesa. 2004. "Foreign Direct Investment Flows to Sub-Saharan Africa: Uganda Case Study." Occasional Paper No. 25, Economic Policy Research Centre, Kampala.

Obwona, M., and S. Ssewanyana. 2004. "Rural Infrastructural Services and Agricultural Marketing and Food Security in Uganda." Draft.

Okidi, John. 2004. "Trends in Ugandan Household Assets during the 1990s." Draft, Economic Policy Research Centre, Kampala, Uganda.

Okidi, John, and Andrew McKay. 2003. "Poverty Dynamics in Uganda: 1992 to 2000." Working Paper 27, Chronic Poverty Research Centre, University of Manchester, Manchester.

OPPG (Operationalizing Pro-Poor Growth Research Program). 2005. "Pro-Poor Growth in the 1990s: Lessons and Insights from 14 Countries." World Bank. Washington, DC.

Owens, T., and A. Wood. 1997. "Export-Oriented Industrialization through Primary Processing." *World Development* 25 (May–September): 1453–70.

Oxford Policy Management. 2005. "Evaluation Report: The Plan for Modernization of Agriculture—Main Report." Prepared for the Plan for Modernization of Agriculture Secretariat, Kampala, Uganda.

Pattillo, C., S. Gupta, and K. Carey. 2005. "Sustaining Growth Acceleration and Pro-Poor Growth in Africa." Working Paper WP/05/195, International Monetary Fund, Washington, DC.

Pender, J., S. Ssewanyana, E. Nkonya, and K. Edward. 2004. "Linkages between Poverty and Land Management in Rural Uganda: Evidence from the Uganda

National Household Survey, 1999/00." Discussion Paper 122, International Food Policy Research Institute, Washington, DC.

Pieper, U. 1998. "Openness and Structural Dynamics of Productivity and Employment in Developing Countries: A Case of De-Industrialization." Employment and Training Papers 8, International Labour Organization, Geneva.

Ravallion, M. 2004. "Pro-Poor Growth: A Primer." Draft, World Bank, Washington, DC.

Ravallion, M., and S. Chen. 2003a. "Measuring Pro-Poor Growth." *Economics Letters* 78 (2003): 93–99.

————. 2003b. "What Can New Survey Data Tell Us about Recent Changes in Distribution and Poverty?" *World Bank Economic Review* 11 (2): 357–82.

Ravallion, Martin, and Monica Huppi. 1991. "Measuring Changes in Poverty: A Methodological Case Study of Indonesia during an Adjustment Period." *World Bank Economic Review* 5 (1): 57–82.

Rebelo, Sergio. 1991. "Long-Run Policy Analysis and Long-Run Growth." *Journal of Political Economy* 99 (3): 500–21.

Republic of Uganda. 2003. "Background to the Budget Financial Year 2003/04." MoFPED, Kampala.

————. 2004. "Background to the Budget, Financial Year 2004/05." MoFPED, Kampala, Uganda.

————. 2005. "National Budget Framework Paper for Financial Years 2005/06–2007/08." MoFPED, Kampala, Uganda.

Romer, Paul M. 1986. "Increasing Returns and Long-Run Growth." *Journal of Political Economy* 94 (October): 1002–37.

Solow, Robert M. 1956. "A Contribution to the Theory of Economic Growth." *Quarterly Journal of Economics* 70 (February): 65–94.

Svensson, J., and R. Reinikka. 1999. "How Inadequate Provision of Public Infrastructure and Services Affects Private Investment." Policy Research Paper No. 2262, World Bank, Washington, DC.

UBOS (Uganda Bureau of Statistics). 2003. "2003 Statistical Abstract." UBOS, Kampala, Uganda.

UNDP (United Nations Development Programme). 1997. "Human Development Report." UNDP, New York.

World Bank. 2003. *World Development Report 2003: Sustainable Development in a Dynamic World.* Washington, DC: World Bank.

————. 2005. "Republic of Uganda: Poverty Assessment Report." World Bank, Poverty Reduction Economic Management Unit Africa Region, Washington, DC.

8

The Success of Pro-Poor Growth in Rural and Urban Tunisia

Mohamed Hédi Lahouel

Tunisia has achieved relatively high growth and a sharp reduction in the incidence of poverty over more than four decades. Although poverty remains highly concentrated in rural areas and in some specific regions, particularly the center-west, growth has been consistently pro-poor, leading to steadily falling poverty rates. A favorable growth strategy, together with complementary social policies, has helped the poor contribute to and benefit from growth through asset accumulation and high labor market participation rates. This positive outcome can be explained by a growth strategy based essentially on the development of labor-intensive and export-oriented manufacturing without neglect of agriculture, active female participation in the labor market, and pro-poor social policies.

Underlying pro-poor growth has been strong political commitment. Fighting poverty has been one of the main objectives targeted by the regime in power since the early 1960s. The political leadership that led the struggle for independence came from the *petite bourgeoisie* and was free from the strong influence of local landlords or private industrialists. It developed deep roots in small towns and villages, which may explain why it prioritized, from the start, social and economic progress in villages and rural areas. Such political commitment makes a difference for poverty reduction: several other countries have equaled or outperformed Tunisia's

The author thanks the Agence Française de Développement for support; Ayadi Mohamed, Boulila Ghazi, and Montigny Philippe for their input on a draft report; Louise Cord for comments on this chapter; and Claudia Reitmaier for editorial assistance.

growth performance and yet have a much higher poverty incidence than Tunisia has today.

Because initial incomes were very low, any redistribution without growth would have made no dent in poverty reduction. Growth has been essential in providing job opportunities and higher incomes for the poor and the state, along with the resources needed to finance social spending. In addition to rural development, promotion of export-oriented labor-intensive light manufacturing and services, particularly tourism in coastal regions, has played an important role in accelerating growth and increasing the employment of low- to medium-skilled, mainly female, workers, many of whom migrated from neighboring rural areas. External migration also helped reduce poverty through two channels: remittances and lowered pressure on the local job market, in which the remaining active population, including the poor, could exploit employment opportunities.

This chapter assesses the extent to which poverty reduction in Tunisia has resulted from growth and reviews the drivers of growth with a focus on implications for poverty. In addition, the chapter identifies the channels through which low-income households were enabled to participate in and benefit from growth. Given the importance of social services, the role of social spending is explored.

Poverty, Growth, and Inequality Trends

At independence in 1956, Tunisia was a low-income country with widespread poverty and illiteracy. The political leadership that led the struggle against the French occupation had developed deep popular roots over more than two decades and drew wide support from the rural areas and villages. This historical background had a strong influence on the new political agenda, which stressed the importance of both economic and social development.

At the beginning of the 1960s, the Tunisian population was basically illiterate and had a very low standard of living. Average schooling was less than one year in 1960, which was very low even when compared with several developing countries. The lag was so huge that even 10 years later more than 72 percent of all adults and 85 percent of the female population were still illiterate. Poverty incidence was also high—33 percent in 1966/67, according to the first national Household Consumption Survey (HCS) conducted after independence—and had been much higher in previous years.

Agriculture was the dominant activity, but most of the fertile land was in the hands of French farmers until 1964. There was very little industry, and tourism, which later became an important activity, was almost nonexistent. Shortly after independence, most French civil servants returned to France, leaving a civil service vacuum that needed to be filled, which, given the scarcity of trained and experienced national civil servants, compounded the difficulties of running the country's affairs.

In the first years after independence, the priority of the new government was to rebuild the institutions and the civil service and to remedy the void left by the French civil servants. At that time, a new development strategy was drafted by the labor union, a full partner in the struggle for independence but later a quasi-opposition party. This strategy, which was finally endorsed by the government at the beginning of the 1960s, stressed the need for central planning and for the coexistence of the public, the cooperative, and the private sectors. It also emphasized major dimensions of human development: education, family planning and birth control, women's rights, and the eradication of poverty. In 1956 the country enacted a comprehensive law for women's rights, introducing major revolutionary reforms by Muslim countries' standards.

Poverty Trends in Tunisia, 1980–2000

Poverty steadily declined from the very high rates of the 1960s to very low rates by 2000. Absolute poverty declined roughly from about a third of the population in the mid-1960s to about 4 percent in 2000. More recent (and more comparable) trends show that poverty dropped dramatically after 1980. The overall headcount declined from 20.1 percent in 1980 to 4.1 percent in 2000 (table 8.1). This decrease is a major social achievement despite

Table 8.1 Incidence of Poverty in Tunisia: Headcount Ratios for the Lower and Upper Poverty Lines, 1980–2000

	Lower					Upper				
	1980	1985	1990	1995	2000	1980	1985	1990	1995	2000
Total	20.1	9.6	6.7	8.1	4.1	29.9	19.9	14.1	17.1	9.9
Urban	7.7	4.0	3.0	3.2	1.7	18.7	12.0	8.9	10.1	6.2
Rural	30.1	17.2	12.7	15.8	8.3	38.9	29.2	21.6	28.1	16.1

Sources: 1980, 1985, and 1990 estimates are based on survey microeconomic data; 1995 and 2000 estimates are based on World Bank (2003).

Note: Headcount ratios for 1995 and 2000 in this table are slightly different from those used in the decomposition of changes in the headcount in growth and inequality effects. The ratios used in this decomposition are calculated directly on the basis of survey data.

Table 8.2 *Poverty Incidence in Tunisia: Regional Headcount Ratios for the Lower Poverty Level, 1980–2000*

	1980	1985	1990	1995	2000
Greater Tunis	4.3	2.3	2.1	2.4	1.0
Northeast	15.6	8.9	5.9	6.3	3.5
Northwest	30.1	17.9	14.3	11.1	3.7
Center-west	33.8	18.0	12.5	20.0	10.8
Center-east	16.5	6.2	3.9	3.5	1.9
Southwest	13.0	6.7	8.8	8.2	6.4
Southeast	15.7	12.1	3.1	10.5	6.0
All Tunisia	20.1	9.6	6.7	8.1	4.1

Source: Household Consumption Survey.

the fact that rural poverty remains sensitive to fluctuations in agricultural production, such as the severe drought of 1990–95, when the poverty incidence remained stable in urban Tunisia but rose in rural areas. As elsewhere, the incidence of poverty has been higher in rural areas than in urban areas.[1] The rural share in the total poor population varied between 65 and 82 percent over the period 1980–2000 and is estimated at three-fourths in the latest survey of 2000.

Poverty remained also highly concentrated in two regions, the northwest and the center-west, although the last survey of the year 2000 shows a dramatic decline of poverty in the former. In 1980, the headcount was over 30 percent in the two regions, compared with 20 percent for the country as a whole (table 8.2). Since 2000, the incidence of poverty has declined in all regions; the drop in the northwest was steep, while the fall was more moderate in the center-west, the region that continues to have the highest level of poverty. This difference does not reflect more rapid economic growth in the northwest, because agriculture is the dominant activity in both regions,[2] but rather the northwest's more intensive migration and slower population growth. In the 1990s alone, the average annual population increase was 0.4 percent for the northwest but 1.5 percent for the center-west.

Sources and Drivers of Growth

Tunisia experienced relatively high GDP growth over the period 1960–2000. At an annual average of 5.3 percent, this growth places the country among the highest, if not the highest, growth performers in the Middle East and

Table 8.3 *Growth Performance, 1962–2000 (Annual Averages)*

Period	Growth of GDP	Growth of capital stock	Growth of employment	Total factor productivity growth	Growth in per capita GDP
1962–69	6.2	10.4	1.1	1.8	4.1
1970–80	7.0	7.7	2.6	2.8	4.8
1980–85	3.7	8.1	2.6	−0.8	1.1
1985–90	3.0	2.4	2.1	0.8	0.6
1990–95	3.9	3.1	2.5	1.2	2.0
1995–2000	5.6	3.1	2.6	2.9	4.2
1980–2000	4.1	4.2	2.4	1.0	2.0
1962–2000	5.3	6.3	2.2	1.7	3.2

Source: Author's estimates based on data from Institut d'Economie Quantitative, Ministry of Economic Development, and International Cooperation.

Table 8.4 *Growth Decomposition, 1962–2000 (in Percentage of Total GDP Growth)*

	Capital	Labor	TFP	Total
1962–69	59.0	11.4	29.6	100
1970–80	36.0	23.9	40.1	100
1980–85	76.2	45.5	−21.7	100
1985–90	28.5	45.8	25.7	100
1990–95	28.1	41.9	30.1	100
1995–2000	19.3	29.6	51.1	100
1980–2000	36.2	39.2	24.6	100
1962–2000	41.5	26.9	31.6	100

Source: Author's estimates based on Institut d'Economie Quantitative database.
Note: TFP = Total factor productivity.

North Africa. However, growth was unstable due to fluctuations in agriculture, domestic policy shifts, and international exogenous factors, which led to important fluctuations in productivity and the rate of capital investment (table 8.3). Overall, during the last four decades of the twentieth century, capital accumulation was the main driver of growth. Decomposition analysis shows that roughly 42 percent of growth came from capital accumulation, 27 percent from labor, and 32 percent from productivity gains (tables 8.3 and 8.4). However, while capital accumulation was by far the main source of growth in the 1960s (almost 60 percent), the contribution of capital steadily declined in later periods. Labor and productivity gains became more significant sources of growth in the 1980s and 1990s. These gains reflect structural reforms: streamlining of the public sector, trade and financial liberalization, realignment of the exchange rate, and fiscal discipline.

In the 1960s employment expanded at a very low rate, averaging 1.1 percent per year. Capital creation was relatively high during this period, but most of the investment went into capital-intensive public projects, such as a steel mill, an oil refinery, a paper plant, a couple of large textile factories, and an automobile assembly plant. Such projects absorbed a large share of investment resources but created few jobs. Even though the government had to be credited with a public policy favorable to education and to the development of infrastructure during this period, it did little to encourage private initiative. On the contrary, by imposing the cooperative system on agriculture and even on domestic commerce, it created uncertainty that discouraged private investment and job creation.

The government that came to power in 1970 abandoned the socialist policy of the 1960s and reversed the collectivization decisions hastily taken in 1968/69. While continuing to develop the public sector, it declared its intention to foster expansion of the private sector and to attract foreign direct investment. Industrial policy was reoriented toward light industries, and the private sector developed an increasing number of exports. The government developed finance mechanisms that facilitated the creation and growth of small- to medium-size enterprises, particularly in manufacturing, which grew by more than 10 percent annually. For exports, it established an offshore regime of generous fiscal incentives, easy access to European markets, and relatively light administrative burdens. This regime played an important role in the development of offshore clothing activity: imports by offshore firms were and still are duty free, and these firms have enjoyed exemptions from value-added tax and income taxes. These advantages not only directly raised returns to investment in offshore firms but also helped the firms avoid the heavy transaction costs faced by onshore firms.

As a result, starting in the 1970s, the private sector became the most important driver of growth and poverty reduction. Job creation in manufacturing was particularly impressive, growing by 5.6 percent per year on average throughout the 1970s. This growth was facilitated by tourism and windfalls from the two oil shocks of that decade, which the government used to build infrastructure and invest in human capital.

The economic situation changed in the early 1980s, as growth slowed despite large investments. The Tunisian economy experienced its lowest performance since independence. Economic mismanagement and political instability causal by political infighting were the main factors behind this poor performance. Starting in 1986, the government implemented a program of macroeconomic stabilization and structural reforms that turned out to be a success. Contrary to expectations, the short-run economic cost of these reforms was relatively small, and by the early 1990s growth rates recovered, although the strength of recovery was undermined by a succession of drought years and a sharp decline in agricultural output. By the late 1990s, strong export growth led to the highest growth in per capita GDP recorded since the 1970s.

Trends in Income Inequality

In the period of 1980–2000, for which data are available, income inequality varied little overall. The exception was the second half of the 1980s, when it declined by about 10 percent and remained thereafter more or less constant throughout the 1990s (table 8.5). The decline in the second half of the 1980s, a period of macroeconomic stabilization and structural adjustment, reflected strong agricultural growth and a rapid increase in labor-intensive manufacturing exports.

Table 8.5 *Trends in Income Inequality, 1980–2000 (Gini Coefficient)*

	1980	1985	1990	1995	2000
Total	0.455	0.453	0.401	0.417	0.409
Urban	0.418	0.432	0.374	0.389	0.391
Rural	0.412	0.379	0.354	0.353	0.358

Sources: 1980, 1985, and 1990 estimates are the author's; 1995 and 2000 estimates derive from World Bank (2003).

Distributional and Poverty Impact of Growth

Growth has generally gone hand in hand with poverty reduction since the early 1960s. Between 1980 and 2000, overall poverty levels dropped by 16 percentage points and by almost 22 percentage points in rural areas, while GDP per capita rose by almost 50 percent. The strong impact of growth is illustrated by Tunisia's growth incidence curve, which shows positive income growth across the distribution. Low-income households saw faster growth in consumption than other households, reflecting the decline in inequality that occurred mainly in the late 1980s (figure 8.1).

Figure 8.1 *Tunisia's Growth Incidence Curve, 1980–2000*

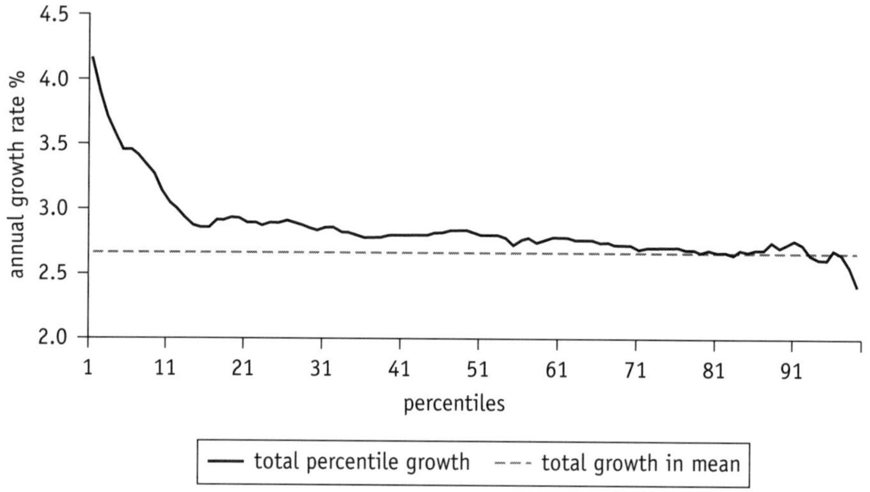

Source: Author's calculations.

Table 8.6 *Pro-Poor Growth Rates, 1980–2000*

	1980–85	*1985–90*	*1990–95*	*1990–2000*
All Tunisia	8.1	2.6	0.1	2.4
Urban	5.2	1.6	−0.8	3.9
Rural	7.2	2.3	0.1	1.9

Source: Estimates based on HCS data.
Note: Rates represent the average rate of income growth at the poverty line.

Table 8.6 shows countrywide, urban, and rural pro-poor growth rates. Seemingly puzzling is the sharp increase in the rate of pro-poor growth in 1980–85, a period of weak growth and stable inequality. The drop in poverty is, however, consistent with the rise in household consumption, which grew more than 5 percent annually during the period. Two factors account for this improvement: favorable agricultural conditions and foreign borrowing, which helped finance large increases in minimum wages, government salaries, and high levels of food subsidies.

Factors Affecting Participation of the Poor in Growth

Four sets of factors, mainly policy driven, played a particularly important role in enhancing the capacity of the poor to participate in growth and also led to attractive agricultural and nonagricultural opportunities that were generally accessible to low-income households. These four factors are macroeconomic stability and trade, agricultural policies, labor markets and migration, and public expenditures for social development.

Macroeconomic Stability and Trade Policies

The Tunisian government has been relatively successful in creating a stable macroeconomic environment conducive to growth and low levels of inflation. Macroeconomic stability is important for the poor, because their income, compared with that of nonpoor households, tends not to be adjusted for inflation and is less asset based and therefore less protected from the erosion of purchasing power (Easterly and Fischer 2001). Management of monetary and fiscal policy improved significantly after implementation of the stabilization and structural adjustment program in 1986–93. As a result, the budget deficit decreased from almost 5 percent in terms of GDP in the 1980s to 3.3 percent in the 1990s. In the early 1980s, large public investments and increases in salaries and food subsidies resulted in a sharp rise in inflation, a record budget deficit (exceeding 8 percent of GDP) in 1983, and a current account deficit close to 7 percent of GDP. As noted above, poverty dropped during that period of low growth but at the cost of a major macroeconomic disequilibria that had to be corrected. As the fiscal stance improved, inflation fell under 5 percent on average in the 1990s and decelerated to less than 4 percent during 1995–2000.

Trade policy strongly discouraged imports throughout the 1980s and the first half of the 1990s, but an active export policy helped to create jobs accessible to low-income households and contributed to macroeconomic stability. Since 1996, the government has gradually liberalized trade in manufacturing with the view of establishing a free trade agreement with the European Union. The offshore export sector has benefited since the 1970s from generous government incentives, particularly a special duty-free regime on imported inputs as well as a permanent corporate income tax holiday. Although protection of domestic industries may have hurt the poor by shielding capital-intensive activities from competition, export incentives have largely corrected this bias and fostered development of labor-intensive light manufacturing, a major source of growth and poverty reduction. Despite liberalization of the trading regime, the current account deficit decreased to less than 3 percent in terms of GDP during the second half of the 1990s, reflecting the strength of the export sector. Pursuit of an active exchange rate policy since 1986, which helped Tunisia avoid the real appreciation of domestic currency and quickly adjust any misalignments, has also contributed to the rapid growth of manufactured product exports and tourism services, as well as to macroeconomic stability.

Asset Holdings in Rural Areas and Agriculture

Poverty reduction in Tunisia is highly sensitive to agricultural growth, because most of the poor are concentrated in the rural sector. On the whole, this sector performed relatively well in spite of the predominance of rain-fed cropping. When it performed poorly, as in the first half of the 1990s, rural poverty increased, even if growth was positive elsewhere. Moreover, lack of access to land, uncertain title arrangements, and lack of irrigation equipment undermined the ability of poor households to raise their agricultural incomes and made them even more vulnerable to the frequent droughts of the 1990s. All these factors have made it difficult for poorer farmers to invest and achieve productivity gains. Nevertheless, agricultural price liberalization since the late 1980s and government incentives for livestock production have benefited the poor.

No major land redistribution has been implemented to benefit the poor, and land distribution remains highly unequal. Under the French protectorate, the most fertile land of the north of the country was in the hands of French landowners; Tunisian farmers were pushed onto marginal land. In 1964 the Tunisian government nationalized French farms. This land reform was supposed to be based on the cooperative system but in practice turned into collectivization. The failure of this reform has stymied any land reform since.

In 1991 more than two-thirds of the farmers owned about 10 percent of total land, while the 1.2 percent richest farmers held more than 22 percent. The state still holds large farms expropriated from the French. Some of these farms have been leased to private farmers on a long-term basis, but the poor have been excluded. Of the 400,000 hectares owned by the state, about half have been leased to private farmers. In addition to having little land, poor farmers generally have ill-defined property titles and therefore, difficulty accessing credit. Given these conditions, the sharp decline in rural poverty in Tunisia cannot be attributed to better access to land by or to increased investment opportunities for low-income rural households.

Climate conditions exacerbate income fluctuations and risk levels in rural Tunisia. Given the high volatility of farm production resulting from highly unstable rainfall, low-income rural households cannot rely exclusively on income from cultivating their own or others' land. In low-rainfall years, which are frequent and sometimes consecutive, production is so low that it cannot procure the minimum income required to avoid poverty. Irrigation has expanded over the past 20 years, but most low-income farmers do not have access to irrigation because they lacked capital and access to credit. They therefore seek additional income outside agriculture to secure a minimum income and to stabilize their consumption.

Removal of the antiagriculture bias of price policy at the beginning of the 1980s may have contributed to higher incomes for small farmers as well as to moderate increases in rural real wages. In the 1970s, the government maintained low prices for basic commodities, particularly for cereal-based products, to prevent wages from rising in the manufacturing sector. This policy was reversed in the early 1980s with sharp increases in the producer prices of cereals and later on with the granting of subsidies for dairy products. These incentives have benefited large- and medium-size farms more than small farms, but the latter have also been favorably affected by this shift in policy. Given the poor soil and climate conditions, small farms would probably not survive if trade in agriculture were liberalized and the domestic prices of field crops were aligned with international prices.

One of the most important activities from which the low-income rural population has benefited is livestock. Production of meat and milk has increased at more than 7 percent per year on average since the late 1980s because of a policy of self-sufficiency. This policy included high import duties, exceeding 100 percent on meat and dairy products, subsidies on milk collection from farmers, and creation of many milk collection centers. Development of the livestock sector, and particularly of the dairy subsector, also benefited from heavy government investments in the rural road network.

Labor Markets and Migration

Extensive job creation in manufacturing has led to structural transformation of Tunisia's economy, creating employment opportunities mainly for low-skilled workers. Migration (to urban areas and to other countries) has brought in remittances, boosting incomes in poor areas.

RURAL LABOR MARKET. The poor connect to growth significantly through the labor market. Rural labor productivity has increased, leading to very slow growth in agricultural employment and significant out-migration. Driven by the development of irrigation, more intensive use of fertilizers and other chemicals, and increased mechanization, agricultural labor productivity increased at more than 4 percent a year between 1960 and 2000.

This rising productivity spurred agricultural growth and released labor that was absorbed in the expanding manufacturing and construction sectors. As a result, agriculture has created an increase in jobs of no more than 5 percent over four decades.

The rise in agricultural labor productivity did not lead to significantly higher rural wages over the 1980–2000 period as a whole. The daily minimum real wage in agriculture increased at an annual average rate of 0.5 percent in 1980–2000, or roughly 10 percent over the whole period, which may account for only part of the decline in poverty. In 1980–83 real minimum wages in agriculture increased by 25 percent, which contributed to the sharp decline in the incidence of poverty during the first half of the 1980s. In contrast, in the first half of the 1990s rural wages declined at a time when the incidence of poverty increased in rural areas. In spite of competition for labor by other sectors in both rural and urban areas, the significant increase in mechanization, which was driven by important financial incentives, reduced the demand for labor in agriculture and prevented upward pressure on real wages.

Rural-urban migration and remittances alleviated pressure on the rural labor market, helped maintain rural wages at relatively high rates, and increased rural income through transfers from urban Tunisia and from abroad. Some internal migration between urban and rural areas has swung between work in the construction sector and tourism in urban areas and farming or unemployment in rural areas.

Remittances from abroad have been an important source of revenue, accounting for 4.2 percent of GDP over the period 1980–2000, which is equivalent to 70 percent of the total value added of the textile, clothing, and leather sector. In 1999 the Tunisian population living abroad, estimated at 550,000, accounted for about 7 percent of the population.

Remittances have benefited all regions, accounting for 8.5 percent of total expenditures nationwide, 8 percent in the northwest, and over 7 percent in the center-west. Solidarity between emigrants and relatives staying in Tunisia appears to be strong.

URBAN LABOR MARKET. Changes in the sectoral composition of employment in the last four decades of the twentieth century underscore the structural transformation experienced by Tunisia during that period. The share of agriculture decreased from almost 46 percent of total employment in the 1960s to 23 percent in the second half of the 1990s. Meanwhile, the share of manufacturing rose from about 14 to 24 percent. Currently, textiles, clothing, and leather account for about half of total manufacturing employment.

Most of the 300,000 workers employed by that sector are low-skilled women of low-income households. Within nongovernment services, tourism has been an important activity, not only as a source of foreign exchange but also increasingly as an employment generator. Its share rose from an insignificant level in the 1960s to almost 3 percent of total employment in the second half of the 1990s. In the same period, the nonmanufacturing industry, of which construction accounts for about 80 percent of employment, lost about one percentage point in total employment, from about 11 to 10 percent.

Underlying the structural transformation and the growth of nonagricultural sectors have been a well-focused manufacturing export strategy and preferential access to European markets. The industrial strategy established in the early 1970s has provided export-based incentives, mainly fiscal, that boosted manufacturing exports and employment. At the same time, the European Economic Community granted Tunisia duty-free access to its market for textile and clothing on the basis of quotas that were rarely binding. The fiscal incentives on the Tunisian side and the duty-free access on the European side attracted European foreign direct investment and later national investment to this sector.

As noted above, textile and clothing account for almost half of manufacturing employment. The growth of manufacturing was supported by the increasing presence of women in the workforce in the 1980s and 1990s. Manufacturing employs low-skilled, little-educated, and mainly young female workers. In the 1990s about 72 percent of the textile and clothing labor force, compared with 63 percent of the entire labor force, had no or only primary education. In 2000, women made up three-quarters of the textile labor force, compared with only one-third of the private sector labor force and one-quarter of the government sector labor force. Development of the textile and clothing sector had a significant impact on poverty, because the sector's workers came generally from low-income households, and many were migrants from rural areas. Salaries in this sector have therefore been an important additional source of income for these households.

Although construction and manufacturing were the main contributors to growth in nonagricultural employment between 1980 and 2000, their capacity to sustain job creation, particularly if growth slows in other sectors, is of concern. Because the textile and clothing sector is labor-intensive, with a capital-labor ratio estimated in 2000 at only 30 percent of the average capital-labor ratio in the whole economy, it has created many jobs with little capital, mainly foreign. The drawback of such investment is that it tends to be less stable than investments in other sectors and more sensitive to changes in location incentives, such as those resulting from dismantling of the Multi-Fiber Agreement (MFA). In that respect, Tunisia is expected to be one of the losers from liberalization of trade in textile and clothing; many low-income households could be hurt.

Many of the poor work in construction, where job stability is lacking though daily wages are about the same as minimum wages. Expansion of this sector, which has accompanied the good growth performance of the Tunisian economy, has helped improve living conditions of low-income households and contributed to poverty alleviation. Nonetheless, high flexibility in the construction labor market and lack of social protection for workers in this sector are such that any slowdown in construction may have severe adverse effects on workers' income and therefore on poverty.

Extensive job creation in manufacturing in general and in the garment industry in particular has occurred without forgoing labor rights.[3] Labor legislation is still too protective in Tunisia, considering its level of development, and may have contributed to the relatively high unemployment rate of around 15 percent of the active labor force over the past 20 years. Labor relations are regulated by a labor code that in the 1990s introduced greater flexibility in hiring and set limits on severance compensation. But layoffs for economic reasons remain highly regulated, and the labor law provides greater protection for Tunisian workers compared with workers in several other developing countries. Social security charges are also relatively high, amounting to 24 percent of the wage bill, distributed between employers (16 percent) and workers (8 percent). Firms pay an additional 12 percent on the wage bill for various other social charges.

Pro-Poor Public Spending

High rates of economic growth and a strong implicit social contract to help share the gains of growth through greater access to social services have led to significant public expenditures in education, infrastructure, a variety of safety nets, and food subsidies. Spending levels on these programs increased significantly in the 1990s and, with the exception of the food subsidies and to a lesser extent education (especially secondary and beyond), have been targeted to poorer households.

EDUCATION AND THE POOR. The government has been committed to free public education since independence. Private education has not been very important at any level, although it has developed in recent years at the primary level and to some extent in higher education for those students who cannot make it to public universities. Given the strong commitment of the government to education and the marginal role played by the private sector, education accounts for a large share of the state budget, exceeding 30 percent on the average.

Access to primary and secondary education for both girls and boys is fairly widespread across regions, although rural areas continue to be disadvantaged compared with urban areas. By 1990, gross primary enrollment rates exceeded 100 percent for both girls and boys.[4] Between 1990 and 2000, access to secondary school increased dramatically; gross enrollment rates rose from 50 to 76 percent for boys and from 40 to 80 percent for girls. Although school achievement is greater in the coastal regions, the improvements are widely shared among the population, including in the center-west, where poverty is concentrated. The rise in enrollment in rural areas has been significant for the 6 to 18 age bracket, rising from 60 percent in 1990, to almost 70 percent in 2000, with households in the first decile catching up with the rest of the rural population.

Secondary, rather than primary, education appears to have made the most difference for poverty reduction. A level of learning higher than primary education is needed to increase one's income comfortably above the poverty level. Not surprisingly, children from poorer households tend to have less access to secondary education than nonpoor children. In 2000, primary enrollment rates were almost the same for the first decile as for the whole population; by contrast, the difference in secondary education is fourfold. In private sector employment, the return on incomplete primary education is almost zero and reaches a moderate 9 percent on completed primary schooling. In contrast, the return on secondary education exceeds 26 percent. In the textile and clothing sector, which employs many low-skilled workers, the return to primary education is estimated at 2 percent, compared with 15 percent to secondary education (World Bank 2004).[5]

SOCIAL PROTECTION PROGRAMS. The main social assistance program is the National Program of Assistance to Needy Families, which was established in 1986 as a safety net accompanying structural adjustment. Eligible households are those falling below the poverty line with no other support. The main beneficiaries are the elderly poor, poor widows, and the handicapped. In 2001 this program covered about 114,000 households, a significantly large portion of poor households, and spent about $43 million, which corresponds to an average of $375 per beneficiary. On the basis of 3.7 persons per household, this transfer represents about 40 percent of the poverty line, which probably has helped many beneficiaries escape or nearly escape poverty. The allocation of this fund clearly favors regions with a high poverty concentration, particularly the center-west and the northwest.

Employment creation and productive capacity-building objectives are embodied in the government's assistance strategy. This strategy focuses on employment in public works, which has recently accounted for about 44 percent of program expenditures; assistance to productive employment and self-employment, accounting for almost 50 percent of expenditures; and training within firms for first-time job seekers. The total amount spent on the three categories rose from less than $80 million in 1993 to an average of $190 million in the years 2000–02 (UNDP 2004). This increase is due to the creation of a new employment mechanism in 2000 that provides assistance to the self-employed. In 1997 the state created a microcredit bank, the Solidarity Bank, targeting low-income households and unemployed youth, for which the banking system has remained inaccessible. The volume of loans has increased at a rapid pace, but the bank has encountered serious reimbursement problems.

INFRASTRUCTURE SPENDING. Government programs have sought to improve living conditions in poor areas with investments in housing and infrastructure. The poor benefit from the general state budget, but specific instruments focus on the poor. From 1993 to 2003 the National Solidarity Fund has benefited 220,000 households or close to 1 million inhabitants by spending about $575 million, mainly on infrastructure. Roads account for 30 percent of the outlays, followed by housing (21 percent), electrification (20 percent), and potable water (14 percent). Rural roads have played a particularly important role in helping the rural poor connect to urban goods and labor markets and to urban services, to cut their transaction costs, and to improve their living conditions. Returns to this infrastructure have not been estimated but are presumed to be high. The housing component of the fund has not only improved the living conditions of the poor but also freed up income and savings that would have been spent on housing.

FOOD SUBSIDIES. Food subsidies are controversial and can entail significant opportunity costs when they are not targeted, but in Tunisia they have most likely had very positive effects on poverty alleviation, particularly among low-income urban households. In the early 1980s, the subsidies reached alarming proportions, accounting for close to 4 percent of GDP in some years. They took more government resources than any other social spending program, with the exception of education (Tuck and Lindert 1996). In 1990 food subsidies to the first quintile accounted for almost

9 percent of households' total expenditures. Since the mid-1990s subsidies have become more targeted to products consumed by the poor (wheat-based products and cooking oil), and thus their relative burden decreased to less than 2 percent in terms of GDP. The resources allocated to the subsidies could have been put to other uses for the benefit of the poor or channeled into broad-based growth, but the administrative capacity needed to help the poor in a more direct way is lacking.

FAMILY PLANNING AND WOMEN'S EMPOWERMENT. Tunisia, atypically for a Muslim country, embarked as early as the 1960s on family planning and birth control programs. The slowdown in population growth has probably contributed in a significant way to the decline in poverty. The average

Table 8.7 *Population Growth and Poverty*

	Total population	*Urban*	*Rural*
Annual growth rate (%)			
1961–70	2.0	4.2	0.6
1971–80	2.2	3.7	0.9
1980–85	2.6	3.5	1.6
1986–90	2.3	3.8	0.5
1991–95	1.9	2.5	1.0
1996–2000	1.3	1.7	0.6
1980–2000	2.0	2.8	1.0
Dependency ratios[a]			
1990			
First decile	4.7		
Second decile	5.4		
All population	2.8		
2000			
First decile	3.2		
Second decile	2.5		
All population	2.0		

Sources: Population growth rates are from the Institut National de la Statistique; dependency ratios reflect calculations based on figures on size of households and number of active members per household from HCS 1990 and 2000.

a. Measured by the ratio of inactive members to active members of households.

population growth rate of 2.3 percent annually in the second half of the 1980s dropped to 1.3 percent in the second half of the 1990s (table 8.7), making Tunisia the country with the lowest population growth in the Middle East and North Africa. Growth of the urban population, which depends on natural growth, expansion of urbanization, and inflows of rural immigrants, outpaced that of the rural population, which has remained very low in recent decades. The main forces that have affected recent population trends are the rise in living standards, modernization of Tunisian society, high rates of urbanization, promotion of women's rights, introduction of birth control and family planning, and expansion of education, particularly among women.

The slowdown in population growth and the reduction in household size were associated with a decline in the incidence of poverty. The effect of falling fertility rates on poverty can be inferred from changes in dependency ratios across consumption deciles (table 8.7). Dependency ratios declined between 1990 and 2000 for all deciles, but the decrease was particularly marked for households in the second decile. Dependency ratios dropped by more than 50 percent in this decile, compared with about 30 percent for all households, and were a contributing factor to high poverty reduction rates in this decile. Indeed, households in the second decile were most likely to experience movement out of poverty between 1990 and 2000.

Conclusion

Tunisia's development strategy shows that good growth performance and significant poverty reduction can be achieved and maintained with limited initial resources and poor natural endowments. By providing jobs and resources for the public treasury to spend on lagging regions and poor households, growth has sharply reduced poverty.

Tunisia's growth strategy, not just the pace of growth, was crucial for reducing poverty. The government invested heavily in education, health, and birth control programs that increased the quality of human capital in rural and urban areas. Rising educational levels, falling fertility rates, and increased female participation in labor markets facilitated the contribution of women to growth and poverty reduction. The government implemented development programs that gave rural areas the infrastructure they needed to develop agriculture and to interact with urban areas. A strategy based on comparative advantage and the intensive use of labor also made a difference. The government stimulated development of labor-using industries and services, providing the poor with attractive job opportunities and income and easing pressure on the rural labor market.

Tunisia continues to experience strong growth and improvements in social indicators, along with increased infrastructure access. But some uncertainties raise questions about the future sustainability of Tunisia's pro-poor growth experience. These uncertainties are underscored by declining private investment.

Three of the most important challenges that Tunisia will need to address to sustain its strong pro-poor growth record include redressing high unemployment rates, improving the quality of the institutional environment, and adapting to changes in the world trading environment, particularly at the European Union (EU). High unemployment (15 percent) persists despite relatively high growth. Low poverty cannot be maintained unless job creation, particularly for youth just reaching the job market, is accelerated. The quality of public institutions in Tunisia has declined since the late 1990s: Tunisia's ranking on regulatory quality declined from the 67th percentile in 1998 to 44th percentile in 2004, and the country's voice and accountability indicators continue to remain significantly below those of other lower-middle-income countries.[6] Changes in the international trading environment offer both opportunities and challenges for growth and poverty reduction in Tunisia. Tunisia has benefited from geographical proximity to large developed countries, such as the EU countries, through access to their labor markets and remittances. Deeper integration with the European Union through liberalization of services and internal reforms could lead to faster growth and poverty alleviation.

Major challenges lie ahead. Because Tunisia's manufacturing is largely concentrated in textiles and garments, the dismantling of the MFA presents a big challenge in terms of both growth and poverty alleviation. In addition, liberalization of trade in agriculture may hurt poor farmers and should therefore be accompanied by compensatory measures and appropriate policies to facilitate the ensuing redeployment of productive resources.

Notes

1. The extent of poverty and its regional concentration depend on the definition of the poverty line for rural and urban areas. The Tunisian national statistical office (INS) estimates the urban poverty line to be almost twice as high as the rural line. Consequently, three-fourths of the country's poor appear to be in urban areas. World Bank experts (World Bank 1995) think that the INS has largely overestimated the difference between the two poverty lines and that removal of the bias will show that poverty is largely a rural phenomenon. The present analysis adopts the World Bank approach mainly for the reason that it assesses the unit value of food consumption

by reference to a household group with a level of expenditures around the poverty line rather than to the whole first quintile, which is the INS approach.

2. This conclusion is based on data from the Tunisian Institut d'Economie Quantitative. On the basis of employment surveys, a World Bank report (2004) argues that agriculture accounts for a large share of job creation in the 1997–2001 period. The surveys show that about one-quarter of new jobs were created in agriculture in that period, even though production decreased due to drought.

3. One additional feature of the Tunisian labor market, which has helped establish stable relations between employers and employees in the organized sector since 1990, is a system of collective bargaining through which wages are negotiated once every three years. This system, which can work only when inflation remains low and predictable, has probably reduced work disruptions and negotiation costs compared with a system of annual collective bargaining. Such costs would have been borne, at least partly, by workers in general and by low-skilled workers in particular.

4. Because enrollment data include out-of-age-group children, this rate may exceed 100 percent.

5. These estimates are derived from an econometric wage equation based on the 2001 Employment Survey of over 26,000 individuals.

6. See http://info.worldbank.org/governance/kkz2004/sc_chart.asp.

References

Easterly, W., and S. Fischer. 2001. "Inflation and the Poor." *Journal of Money, Credit and Banking* 33 (2): 160–78.

Institut National de la Statistique (Republic of Tunisia). Various years. "Enquête nationale sur le budget et la consommation des ménages." Tunisia.

UNDP (United Nations Development Programme). 2004. "Stratégie de réduction de la pauvreté, Etude du phénomène de la pauvreté en Tunisie." UNDP, Tunis.

Tuck, L., and K. Lindert. 1996. "From Universal Food Subsidies to a Self-Targeted Program: A Case Study in Tunisian Reform." World Bank Discussion Paper No. 351, World Bank, Washington, DC.

World Bank. 1995. "Poverty Alleviation: Preserving Progress while Preparing for the Future." Report 13 993-TUN, Middle East and North Africa Region, World Bank, Washington, DC.

_____. 2003. "Republic of Tunisia: Poverty Update." Middle East and North Africa Region, World Bank, Washington, DC.

_____. 2004. "Republic of Tunisia: Employment Strategy." Middle East and North Africa Region, Human Development Sector, World Bank, Washington, DC.

9

Human Capital, Inequality, and Pro-Poor Growth in Brazil

Naércio Menezes-Filho and Lígia Vasconcellos[1]

How does growth affect poverty reduction in environments with extreme income inequality? What are the main factors driving the relationship among growth, inequality, and poverty reduction? To answer these questions, this chapter examines the case of pro-poor growth in Brazil, one of the largest and least equitable economies in the developing world.

Understanding inequality and the role it plays in affecting the impact of growth on poverty and other social outcomes is key to understanding Brazil's relatively high rate of poverty. Inequality in Brazil is high relative to other countries and has been persistent. As a result, despite having a relatively high GDP per capita, poverty rates in Brazil are quite high compared with those of other countries in the same stage of development. Calculations based on household surveys reveal that the top 1 percent of the population appropriates about 15 percent of all income generated in Brazil, and the top 10 percent earn about half of all income. This pattern of high inequality persisted from the late 1970s through the late 1990s, contributing to the view that the stability of inequality in Brazil is "unacceptable" (Barros, Mendoça, and Henriques 2000).

What are the main determinants of inequality in Brazil? Ferreira, Leite, and Litchfield (2005) found that education accounted for more than one-third of total income inequality from 1981 to 2004 (table 9.1). Differences in mean wages across education groups accounted for 38 percent of total inequality (measured by the Theil-L index) in 1981, 34 percent in 1993, and 35 percent in 2004. By contrast, race, family type (stage in life cycle), region,

Table 9.1 *Inequality Decompositions in Brazil (%)*

Variable	1981	1993	2004
Age	1	1	3
Education	38	34	35
Gender	0	0	0
Race	n.a.	13	12
Family type	6	6	10
Region	13	9	10
Urban/rural	17	9	7

Source: Ferreira, Leite, and Litchfield 2005.
n.a. = not available.

and urban/rural location each contribute less than 15 percent of inequality. The share of inequality for which urban/rural differences account has declined by 50 percent since 1981, but the decline in inequality due to falling education differences was only 10 percent. Education drives inequality in Brazil, because it is very unequally distributed and because returns to schooling are very high (Menezes-Filho 2001). Understanding education's impact on growth and on the effectiveness of growth in reducing poverty in Brazil is therefore critical.

Growth and Poverty Trends

From the late 1970s to 2000, economic development and poverty reduction in Brazil were highly unstable, reflecting the faltering macroeconomy. This instability led to an uneven pattern of poverty reduction across time periods and regions, and the characteristics of the poor became increasingly heterogeneous.

In the 1960s and 1970s, Brazil was a fast-growing economy. During this period, total factor productivity rose substantially, driving high growth rates (Pessoa, Gomes, and Veloso 2003). From 1960 to 1980 per capita GDP jumped from $2,000 to about $6,000. A decade of stagnation and high inflation rates followed in the 1980s. Per capita income in 1990 was no higher than it was in 1980. The macroeconomic instability of the 1980s, and in particular hyperinflation, contributed to rising inequality. As Neri (1995) notes, large depositors had access to stores of wealth (such as overnight deposits) that could protect them from inflation, but the poor had few assets to hedge against inflation.

Moreover, labor markets were better at preserving real salary values for highly skilled workers than for unskilled workers (Neri 1995). In 1994, a plan to stabilize the *real* (implemented along with programs of privatization, deregulation, and trade liberalization) reduced inflation, but brought about only modest growth rates, which persisted into the early 2000s.

From 1950 to 2000, population growth, rising labor force participation, and increased capital intensity were the main drivers of growth. Although the role played by human capital is relatively small for the entire period, its relative contribution to growth tripled in the last two decades of the twentieth century, underscoring the growing importance of education. Pessoa, Gomes, and Veloso (2003) decompose Brazilian growth into its several sources, using a growth-accounting methodology. Over the period as a whole, the economy grew at a rate of 5.1 percent per year. Population growth accounted for about 46 percent of this growth, while labor force participation accounted for another 16 percent. Total factor productivity was responsible for 10 percent of overall growth, while capital intensity explained about 17 percent. Finally, human capital accounted for about 8 percent of growth, but its share rose to 25 percent in the last two decades.

Reflecting the high growth rates of the 1970s, the incidence of extreme poverty in Brazil almost halved in the 1970s, from 68 percent to 35 percent of the population. However, poverty trends varied greatly among regions and between urban and rural areas between 1970 and 1980. In the northeast, Brazil's poorest region, poverty declined from 87 percent in 1970 to about 60 percent in 1980, while in the metropolitan regions it declined from 52 percent to about 27 percent (figure 9.1). The percentage of poor in rural areas dropped from 79 percent to about 46 percent, so that, while in 1970 more than 50 percent of all the poor were living in rural Brazil, by 1980 this share had dropped to about 42 percent. At the same time, the share of the population living in rural areas declined from 51 percent to about 23 percent; outmigration of potentially poor people could explain the sharp drop in poverty that occurred in these areas.

Since 1981 poverty has declined at a considerably slower pace in Brazil. In the 1980s poverty rates actually rose, reflecting stagnant growth and rising inequality, before falling in the 1990s. Overall, poverty affected 26 percent of the population in 2001, compared with 32 percent in 1981; most of the decline occurred in the mid-1990s.

In the early 1980s poverty was relatively easy to associate with observable characteristics, such as region, education, and labor market status. In the late 1990s, probably because of improvements in education and infrastructure and to unemployment benefits, pensions, and other social

Figure 9.1 *Poverty Reduction in the 1970s*

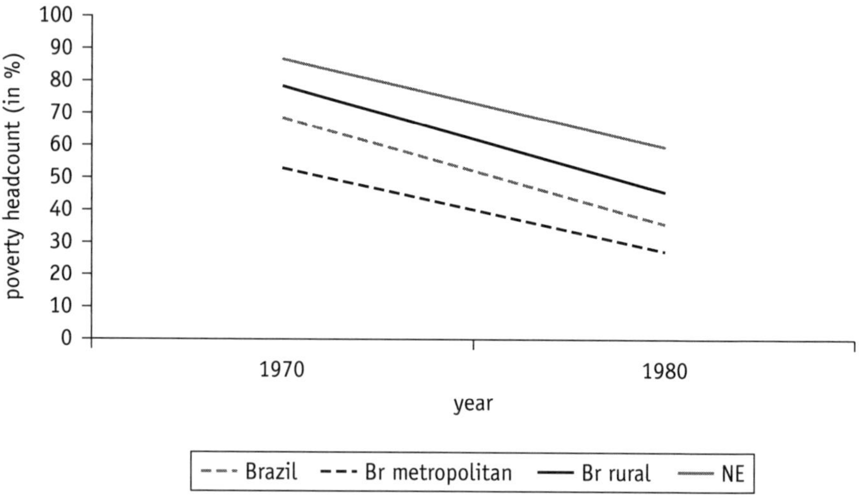

Source: Rocha 2003.

programs among the poor, poverty became less intensively associated with these characteristics. However, most of the correlations are still statistically significant, indicating that much work remains in terms of improving conditions that contribute to escape from poverty.

The fact that the poor in Brazil are no longer closely identified with traditional correlates of poverty—low levels of education, poor access to infrastructure, residence in rural areas, old age, and ethnicity—suggests that poverty has become more pervasive and that other, nonobservable characteristics make it difficult for certain households to expand income growth. Residence in urban areas became a positive predictor of poverty in 2001, whereas it had been a negative predictor in 1982. Between 1982 and 2001, households with older people became even less likely to be poor because of expanded pension schemes in the early 1990s (see next paragraph). In terms of ethnicity, whites are much less likely to be poor than nonwhites, a phenomenon that is becoming relatively less important over time. Education was one of the most important predictors of poverty, both in 1982 and 2001, but its effect lost importance over time, as did the effect of infrastructure. In terms of the labor market, head-of-household unemployment was the single most important determinant of poverty in 1982, but a marked drop in its coefficient occurred between 1982 and 2001, meaning that poverty

Table 9.2 *Effect of Pensions on Extreme Poverty*

Poverty rate	Income with pensions			Income without pensions		
	Overall	Urban	Rural	Overall	Urban	Rural
1981	0.328	0.239	0.626	0.381	0.299	0.659
1990	0.358	0.271	0.651	0.408	0.329	0.677
2001	0.257	0.215	0.503	0.364	0.318	0.633
Poverty change						
1981–1990	0.030	0.032	0.025	0.027	0.030	0.018
1990–2001	−0.101	−0.056	−0.148	−0.044	−0.011	−0.044

Source: Authors.

became more common among the employed as well. Those living in a household whose head is inactive are less likely to be in poverty than those living with an active head of household. With regard to sector of activity, those in agriculture are more likely to be poor than those in manufacturing and services, and informal employment is associated with poverty more so than formal employment; no qualitative change occurred in these effects over time. Finally, in terms of position in occupation, both the self-employed and employers are less likely to be poor than those working for an employer, but this effect also became less important over time.

Generalization of the pension system in rural areas appears to have lowered rural poverty rates. Starting in 1992, all rural residents over age 60 who had worked in agriculture (though they did not have to prove so) could claim a monthly pension equivalent to the minimum wage, even if they had not previously contributed to the system. Computation of poverty rates using a measure of household income that alternatively includes and excludes pensions reveals that poverty declined between 1991 and 2001 in rural and urban areas. But it also shows that poverty has declined in both areas much more when pensions are included in household income (before poverty rates are computed) (table 9.2).

Growth and Poverty in a High-Inequality Environment

On a state-by-state basis, the responsiveness of poverty to growth depended in part on levels of inequality and in part on initial levels of income. Across Brazil, a rise in inequality was associated with an increase in extreme poverty between 1981 and 2000.

Decomposing the Growth Elasticity of Poverty

What is the role of economic growth with respect to poverty reduction? Growth is clearly the major force behind poverty reduction, although inequality influences poverty levels' sensitivity to the growth rate. The total growth elasticity of poverty is defined as the relative change in the poverty headcount between two periods for a 1 percent increase in mean income (assuming that the poverty line remains constant in real terms).

Brazil comprises 26 states in five regions. The growth elasticity of poverty in 19 of these states was calculated on the basis of data from Brazil's annual national household survey (*Pesquisa Nacional por Amostra de Domicílios*, or PNAD). Because PNAD does not cover much of the country's northern region (seven states), that region is not included in the following analysis, which covers five four-year intervals (1981–85, 1985–89, 1989–93, 1993–97, 1997–2001).[2]

The analysis reveals that growth is more effective in reducing extreme poverty than moderate poverty. The growth elasticity of extreme poverty using the headcount measure [FGT(0)] in Brazil is −0.89, while the elasticity of moderate poverty is −0.52. The elasticities obtained when the poverty gap [FGT(1)] and the squared poverty gap [FGT(2)] are used as poverty measures are all higher—in the range of −1 for extreme poverty—indicating that growth affects the intensity of poverty more strongly than the number of poor in Brazil.

To what extent does the responsiveness of poverty to growth vary across states in Brazil? Bourguignon (2003) points out that the reduction of poverty in a given population is analytically linked to the growth of mean income and the change in the distribution of relative incomes. More precisely, the growth elasticity of poverty is an increasing function of the level of development and a decreasing function of the degree of initial income inequality.[3] When the actual poverty reduction (over the whole period) is plotted against the change predicted by this model, it appears that growth does a good job in predicting poverty reduction for some states. But in other states (like Santa Catarina), poverty is reduced by much more than predicted by its income growth, and in still others (like Piauí) poverty is reduced much less than predicted.

How much does distributional change affect the total growth elasticity of poverty? By making the change in the Gini coefficient an additional control, which attracts a positive and highly significant coefficient, the growth elasticity of poverty becomes −1. But the introduction of change in inequality in the model still does not help predict the behavior of poverty reduction in states where growth alone was not a good predictor.

The poverty reduction effect of growth is much higher when the initial level of income is high and much lower when initial inequality is high (Bourguignon 2003). In a further attempt to enhance the model's predictiveness, the change in income is interacted with the initial level of income and with the initial Gini coefficient. The interaction with initial income attracts a negative coefficient, while the interaction with initial inequality has a positive estimated coefficient, both statistically significant. Their inclusion raises the value of the income variable substantially. Inclusion of the interaction terms in the model allows the model to explain the cases it could not previously explain: despite growing substantially, Piauí had a very low initial income level that was very unevenly distributed, which meant that its poverty reduction was much lower than in Santa Catarina for a given amount of growth.

Now consider the interaction of the change in the Gini coefficient with initial income and the initial Gini coefficient. The coefficient of the interaction of the change in the Gini coefficient with initial income is positively estimated. Therefore, a change in inequality increases poverty much more when income is initially high than when it is initially low, although the increased explanatory power provided by this construct is minimal. This finding suggests that reducing inequality in the wealthiest states can raise the poverty-reducing efficiency of growth. The coefficient on the interaction with initial Gini, on the other hand, attracts a negative coefficient, though statistically insignificant. The impact of the introduction of these two variables is relatively small, as the predictive power of the model does not change significantly.

Growth Incidence Curve

Figure 9.2 presents Brazil's growth incidence curve between 1981 and 2001. It shows that growth was almost monotonically increasing with the percentiles, meaning that income inequality rose over the period. This phenomenon is consistent with a rise in Gini coefficient from 0.575 to 0.594 over the period. Income growth was negative up to the 15th percentile and positive everywhere else in the distribution. This negative growth is related to the rise in the percentage of households with zero income (from 0.71 percent of the observations in 1981 to 1.60 percent in 2001). Ferreira and Barros (1999) analyze the increase in extreme poverty in urban Brazil in the period 1976 and 1996. Their simulations showed that individuals below the 12th percentile were affected by a change in occupation to unemployment or out of the labor force, which had a stronger effect on poverty than the positive

Figure 9.2 *Brazil's Growth Incidence Curve, 1981–2001*

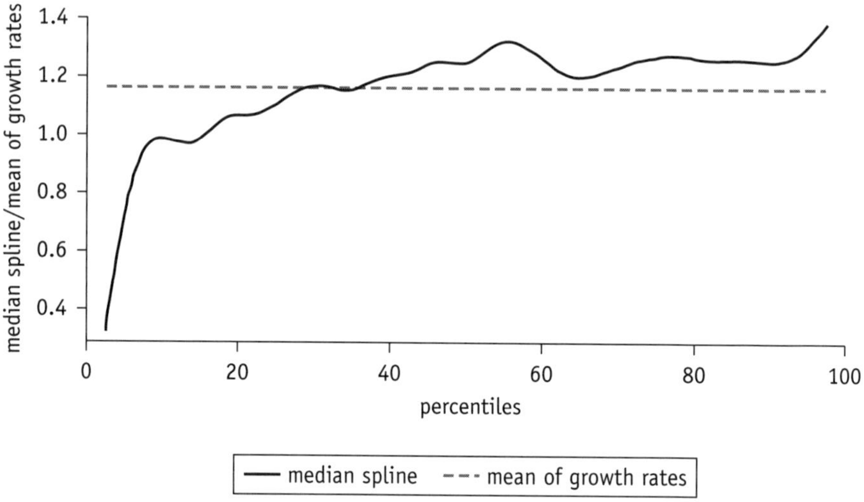

Source: Authors.

effect of demographics (decrease of family size and of dependency ratio). This phenomenon is a source of concern, because most individuals with little education and few chances to become reemployed belong to this percentile group.

Decomposing Changes in Poverty into Growth and Inequality Terms

Growth was very important for poverty reduction in Brazil, though poverty could have been reduced much faster had inequality also fallen. Changes in poverty rates can also be decomposed into changes due to economic growth (or mean income) in the absence of changes in inequality (or income distribution), and changes in inequality in the absence of growth (see Datt and Ravallion 2002). Almost all the poverty reduction that occurred in Brazil was due to the growth component. The redistribution effect was small and often associated with a rise in poverty (table 9.3).

Education and Pro-Poor Growth

Improvements in human capital endowments, through increases in education, and poverty reduction are strongly correlated. As discussed below, highly uneven access to education in Brazil is correlated not only with income brackets, but also with location and race.

Table 9.3 Growth and Inequality Poverty Decomposition, 1981–2001

Average effect	Change in poverty	Growth component	Redistribution component	Residual
Headcount ratio—extreme poverty	−0.071	−0.089	0.018	0
Headcount ratio—moderate poverty	−0.096	−0.104	0.007	0
Watts index—extreme poverty	−0.015	−0.015	0	0
Watts index—moderate poverty	−0.114	−0.07	−0.045	0

Source: Authors.

Table 9.4 Distribution of Students in Public Schools by Consumption Brackets (%)

	Primary	Secondary	Higher level
First quintile	26.0	7.4	0.0
Second quintile	26.6	12.1	0.0
Third quintile	19.5	28.0	6.9
Fourth quintile	16.5	33.3	20.3
Fifth quintile	7.6	19.2	72.9

Source: Barros and Foguel 2000.

The distribution of students in public schools by consumption brackets (table 9.4) points to the inequality of access to education in Brazil. The lowest two quintiles have a higher presence only in primary education, caused mainly by outward self-selection of children of families in the top quintile, who tend to be enrolled in private schools. Enrollment in secondary and tertiary education increases with the consumption level of the family. Children of the poorest quintile make up only 7.4 percent of the attendees at public secondary schools. The figures for public tertiary education are starker still, with the poorest two quintiles accounting for a statistically insignificant proportion of attendees, and over 90 percent of students coming from families of the richest two quintiles. While children of wealthier families, who have better-quality secondary education, gain entrance to prestigious and highly competitive public universities, children from poorer families rarely have any options for higher education other than private universities of dubious quality, which they can ill afford.

Understanding education in Brazil, particularly at the primary and secondary school levels, requires a focus on state and even municipal outcomes. Brazil has a federal system, and states and municipalities are

Figure 9.3 *Average Years of Schooling and Income by Brazilian State, 1981*

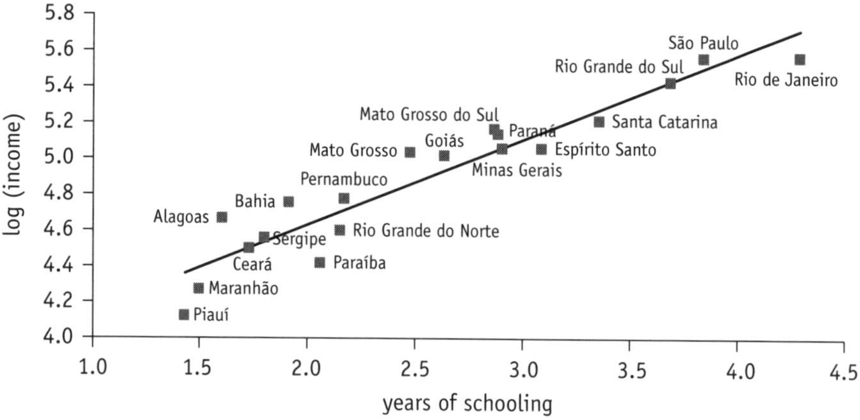

Source: Authors.

responsible for primary and high school education, whereas the federal government is responsible for public colleges at the tertiary level.[4] States and municipalities can implement measures to increase access and monitor performance so as to expand human capital endowments in their localities.

Simple correlations highlight a link between poor educational outcomes and low state GDP as well as inequality, although the direction of causality is difficult to determine. Figure 9.3 plots average years of schooling in 1981 (start of this analysis's sample period) against initial mean (log) income for the Brazilian states. Average schooling varies widely among states, ranging from 1.4 in Piauí to 4.4 in Rio de Janeiro. The figure depicts a strong positive relationship between schooling and income. States in the southeast and south, like São Paulo (SP), Rio de Janeiro (RJ), Rio Grande do Sul (RS), and Santa Catarina (SC), are among the richest and most educated, whereas states in the northeast, such as Piauí, Maranhão (MA), Ceará (CE), Sergipe (SE), and Alagoas (AL), are the poorest and least educated. Ascertaining whether high school levels are the result of high-income growth in the past or whether these levels caused this growth is difficult (see Bils and Klenow 2000, for example).

Figure 9.4 relates average years of schooling in 1981 with inequality, as measured by the Gini coefficient in 1981. It shows that the correlation between the two outcomes is negative; states in the northeast, like Ceará and Bahia (BA), are the most unequal and among the least educated, while states

Figure 9.4 *Years of Schooling and Inequality by State, 1981*

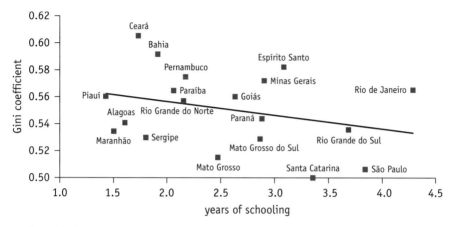

Source: Authors.

like Santa Catarina and São Paulo are the least unequal and among the best educated. Again, causality is difficult to determine: do states that have historically been more unequal tend to have less schooling (see Acemoglu, Johnson, and Robinson 2001) or have states that have advanced more quickly in terms of human capital become less unequal?

What about differences in access to education along race and gender lines? Ethnicity appears to play an important role in determining education outcomes, but there appears to be no gender gap in education. Brazil had one of the longest periods of slavery among all developing countries, which had important consequences for the Brazilian society, especially with regard to the differential treatment of blacks and mulattos. Figures 9.5 and 9.6 describe the education differential between whites and nonwhites and between males and females in each state in 1981. The white/black education differential is always positive. The male/female differential, however, is negative in the majority of states, implying that females overcame the males in terms of access to education in most parts of Brazil.

The white/nonwhite differential is higher in the richest states, like Rio de Janeiro, São Paulo, and Minas Gerais (MG), and lower in the poorest states, such as Maranhao, Sergipe, and Piauí. A possible interpretation of this finding is that labor market attractiveness increased the opportunity cost of going to school in the richest states, especially among the poorer families (of which most of the black children are members), while returns to education are lower in those states.

Figure 9.5 *Average Education by Race and State*

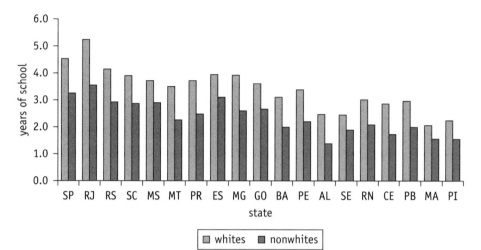

Source: Authors.
Note: AL = Alagoas, BA = Bahia, CE = Ceará, ES = Espírito Santo, GO = Goiás, MA = Maranhão, MG = Minas Gerais, MS = Mato Grosso do Sul, MT = Mato Grosso, PB = Paraíba, PE = Pernambuco, PI = Piauí, PR = Paraná, RJ = Rio de Janeiro, RN = Rio Grande do Norte, RS = Rio Grande do Sul, SC = Santa Catarina, SE = Sergipe, SP = São Paulo.

Figure 9.6 *Average Education by Gender and State*

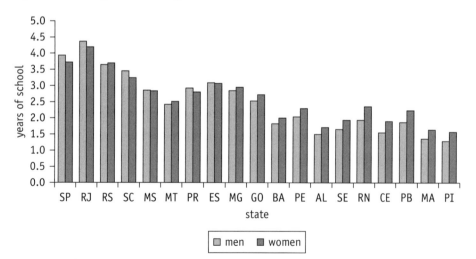

Source: Authors.

Differences in Elasticities across the States of Brazil

To understand the differences in the poverty-growth elasticity across states, one must have a model that includes changes in inequality and interactions between income growth and initial conditions, such as initial income and inequality. Which economic factors affect the participation of poor people in growth through their role in shaping these initial conditions and changes in inequality?

Table 9.5 presents the estimates of growth elasticities for different states, on average and separately for urban and rural areas. The difference in the elasticity across states, as column 1 demonstrates, is marked. The highest elasticity is in the economically wealthy state of São Paulo (-1.6), while the lowest elasticity is in Espírito Santo (-0.4).

The responsiveness of poverty trends to growth is greater in urban Brazil than in rural areas. Columns 2 and 3 show the differences in elasticities across urban and rural areas. With the exceptions of Rio de Janeiro, Rio Grande do Sul (RS), Espírito Santo (ES), and Bahia (BA) all other states have elasticities that are higher in urban than rural areas. The differences are higher in the states of the center-west and the northeast, where urban elasticities can be up to four times higher than rural elasticities.

Education and the Growth Elasticity of Poverty

As noted above, the growth elasticity of poverty is much higher when initial income is higher and when initial inequality is lower, and education is correlated with initial income and inequality in the Brazilian states. Figure 9.7 bears out the expectation that education will have an important effect on the poverty-growth elasticity and in particular that more educated states will be more responsive to growth than others. States with a higher share of individuals with a high school or higher education[5] in 1981 tend to have a higher elasticity in the period as a whole. But can a causal interpretation be attributed to the relationship between education and the growth elasticity of poverty, or is human capital correlated with other factors that are also related to the poverty-growth elasticity?

To examine how education affects the growth elasticity of poverty, the relationship can be subjected to a more stringent test, that is, relating the previous change in the share of individuals with higher education (1981–93) to the subsequent change in the growth elasticity of poverty (between 1981–93 and 1993–2001). The reasoning behind this procedure is that if initial conditions are important determinants of future pro-poor growth, changes in initial conditions should alter the poverty growth elasticity in subsequent periods. The procedure amounts to taking first differences in

Table 9.5 Growth Elasticity of Poverty by State and Area

	Overall	Rural	Urban
São Paulo (SP)	−1,594	−1,588	−1,589
	(0,147)	(0,298)	(0,158)
Rio de Janeiro (RJ)	−0,904	−0,818	−0,803
	(0,145)	(0,205)	(0,157)
Rio Grande do Sul (RS)	−0,642	−1,157	−0,680
	(0,325)	(0,378)	(0,326)
Santa Catarina (SC)	−0,962	−0,943	−1,124
	(0,188)	(0,245)	(0,174)
Mato Grosso do Sul (MS)	−1,091	−0,229	−1,003
	(0,229)	(0,275)	(0,251)
Mato Grosso (MT)	−0,571	−0,055	−0,896
	(0,191)	(0,152)	(0,188)
Paraná (PR)	−1,071	−0,151	−1,286
	(0,227)	(0,247)	(0,208)
Espírito Santo (ES)	−0,449	−0,417	−0,363
	(0,202)	(0,167)	(0,192)
Minas Gerais (MG)	−1,087	−0,735	−1,205
	(0,176)	(0,244)	(0,189)
Goiás (GO)	−0,799	−0,498	−0,854
	(0,145)	(0,167)	(0,162)
Bahia (BA)	−0,826	−0,562	−0,557
	(0,228)	(0,188)	(0,275)
Pernambuco (PE)	−0,715	−0,515	-0,622
	(0,204)	(0,203)	(0,216)
Alagoas (AL)	−0,647	−0,337	−0,673
	(0,169)	(0,123)	(0,200)
Sergipe (SE)	−0,565	−0,252	−0,662
	(0,235)	(0,191)	(0,199)
Rio Grande do Norte (RN)	−0,708	−0,457	−0,870
	(0,173)	(0,235)	(0,172)
Ceará (CE)	−0,530	−0,259	−0,574
	(0,267)	(0,266)	(0,316)
Paraíba (PB)	−0,642	−0,231	−0,979
	(0,190)	(0,274)	(0,201)
Maranhão (MA)	−0,545	−0,249	−0,511
	(0,208)	(0,234)	(0,200)
Piauí (PI)	−0,508	−0,166	−0,537
	(0,209)	(0,172)	(0,275)

Source: Authors.

Note: Estimates use five-year changes. Coefficients are estimated for income interacted with each state dummy (or state-area dummy); time dummies are included. Standard errors are in parentheses. Number of observations: 95 (state × year) and 190 (state × year × rural/urban). Headcount index uses the extreme poverty line.

Figure 9.7 *Initial Share of Higher Education and the Growth Elasticity of Poverty, 1981*

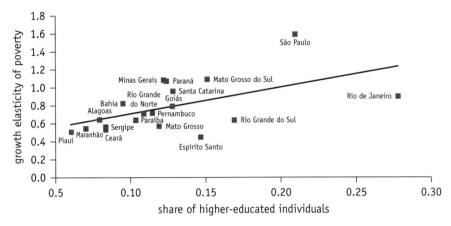

Source: Authors.

Figure 9.8 *Previous Change in Higher Education and in the Growth Elasticity of Poverty by State, 1981–93*

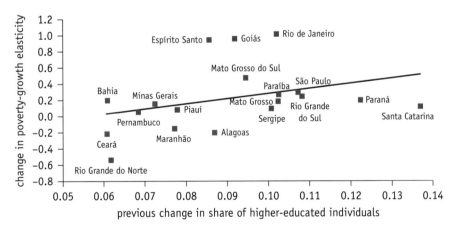

Source: Authors.

panel data to eliminate all state-specific effects that are fixed over time. If the slope of the regression line is approximately the same in the "changes" and in the "levels," evidence is produced that the relationship is causal. Figure 9.8 plots the previous change in human capital against the change in the growth elasticity of poverty and shows that a positive relationship remains and is very similar to the previous one. It appears, therefore, that this

Figure 9.9 *Change in Higher Education and Inequality by State, 1981–2001*

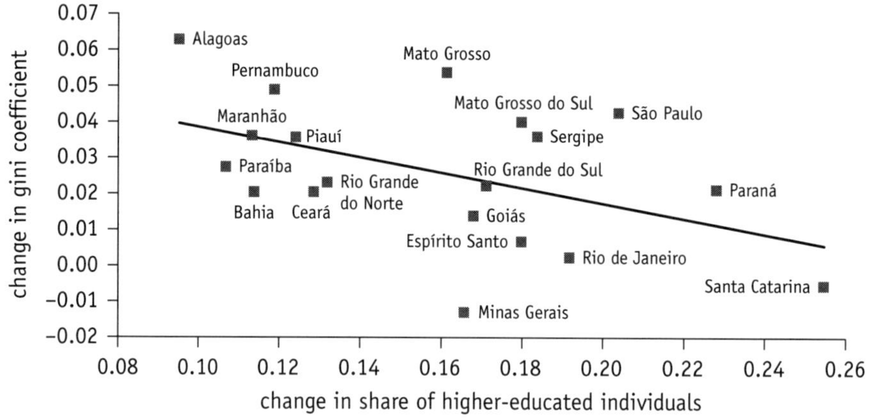

Source: Authors.

relationship runs from human capital to the elasticity, although other factors may be changing in the period, together with human capital.

As noted above, changes in inequality tend to increase poverty independently of growth trends, so understanding how changes in educational levels may affect changes in inequality is important. Figure 9.9, therefore, relates the changes in the proportion of people with higher education to the changes in the Gini coefficient in the sample period. States with the highest increases in higher education completion—Santa Catarina, Paraná (PR), Rio de Janeiro, and Espírito Santo—were also those with the lowest increase in inequality, which confirms that human capital tends to reduce inequality.

As a summary of these investigations, Figure 9.10 directly relates changes in higher education completion with poverty reduction. Clearly, states that invested more in human capital, like Santa Catarina and Paraná, had higher rates of poverty reduction, whereas states that remained relatively stagnant in terms of education, like those in the northeast, experienced poverty reduction at a much slower pace.

Regression Analysis

Is the relationship between education and poverty reduction being driven by other factors that are changing in the states at the same time as human capital increases? Table 9.6 presents determinants of pro-poor growth. Column 1 regresses the change in poverty on income growth, the lagged dependent variable, and on the interaction between income growth and average years of schooling. It shows that income growth reduces poverty, but it also confirms that the effect is much higher when a change in average

Figure 9.10 *Change in Higher Education and Poverty Reduction by State,*
1981–2001

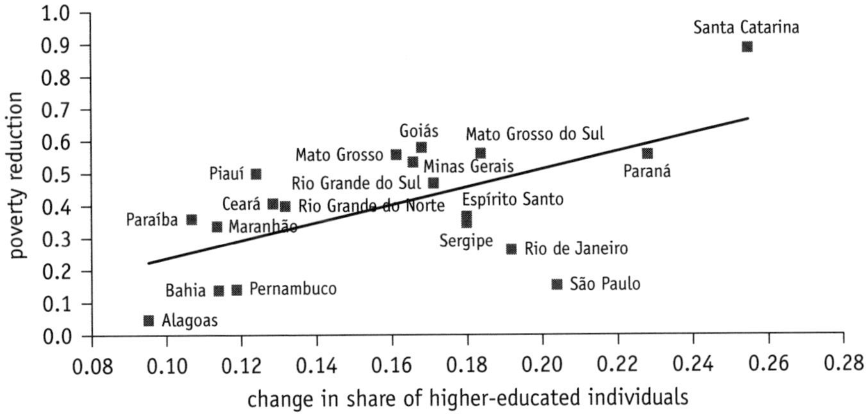

Source: Authors.

years of schooling accompanies it.[6] Column 2 includes the change in the
Gini coefficient, a measure of inequality, to show that it reduces poverty, but
it does not qualitatively change the coefficient of the interaction between
income and education.

Not surprisingly, infrastructure appears to increase the growth elasticity
of poverty. Column 3 includes interactions of the change in income with the
change of two infrastructure indicators, the share of population in each state
with garbage collection and access to sewage. The share of garbage collection appears significant in its interaction with income growth, indicating
that improvements in sanitation help growth to become more pro-poor. Its
inclusion reduces the coefficient of education, which remains statistically
significant nevertheless.

The effect of an incremental year of education on poverty does not
appear to be linear. Increasing enrollments in high school and tertiary
school appear more effective in reducing poverty than in raising enrollment
rates in primary or secondary school. Column 4 includes the share of individuals in each education group interacted with income, as an alternative to
average years of schooling, as a measure of human capital.[7] The change in
the share of individuals with a high school education and the change in the
share of individuals with a college education interact significantly with
income growth. This finding means that investments in higher education
make growth more pro-poor, which is consistent with the descriptive evidence presented above.

Table 9.6 Determinants of Pro-Poor Growth

	(1)	(2)	(3)	(4)
Dependent variable: poverty				
Income	−0.298*	−0.386*	−0.455*	−0.470*
	(0.126)	(0.130)	(0.136)	(0.100)
Gini coefficient	—	2.300*	2.388*	2.361*
		(0.503)	(0.525)	(0.443)
Lagged poverty	0.078	0.065	0.029	−0.065
	(0.181)	(0.146)	(0.145)	(0.134)
Interactions with income				
Years of education	−0.049*	−0.046*	−0.026*	—
	(0.016)	(0.013)	(0.011)	
Secondary education	—	—	—	0.022
	—	—	—	(0.093)
High school education	—	—	—	−0.362*
	—	—	—	(0,170)
College education	—	—	—	−0.280*
	—	—	—	(0.152)
Share with sewage	—	—	0.014	0.006
	—	—	(0.023)	(0.017)
Share with garbage collection	—	—	−0.115*	−0.113*
	—	—	(0.026)	(0.033)
Time dummies	Yes	Yes	Yes	Yes
Sargan test (*p*-value)	0.99	1.00	1.00	1.00
Serial correlation (*p*-value)	0.25	0.050	0.067	0.146
Number of observations	76	76	76	76

Source: Authors.
Note: All variables are in four-year differences. Numbers reflect Generalized Method of Moments (GMM) procedure (Arellano and Bond 1991) estimation procedure using lagged (*t*-2) values of the independent variables as instruments. Standard errors are in parentheses. Coefficients significant at 5 percent are starred. — = not available.

Are There Trade-Offs between Growth and Pro-Poor Growth?

Must society accept a lower level of overall growth to increase pro-poor growth? Answering this question requires a comparison of the determinants of state-level income growth in Brazil with the determinants of pro-poor growth, as shown in table 9.7. Column 1 includes the average years of education and the lagged dependent variable and shows that education significantly improves growth and that income growth is serially correlated.[8] This result is very important because it shows that human capital not only

Table 9.7 *Determinants of Growth*

Dependent variable: income	(1)	(2)	(3)	(4)
Years of education	0.299*	0.240*	0.120*	—
	(0.060)	(0.052)	(0.064)	—
Secondary education	—	—	—	0.132
	—	—	—	(0.460)
High school education	—	—	—	0.234
	—	—	—	(0.961)
College education	—	—	—	1.728*
	—	—	—	(0.639)
Gini coefficient	—	0.279	0.500	0.319
	—	(0.454)	(0.411)	(0.361)
Share with sewage	—	—	0.385*	0.387*
	—	—	(0.111)	(0.119)
Share with garbage collection	—	—	0.201	0.281
	—	—	(0.197)	(0.194)
Lagged income	0.414*	0.362*	0.146*	0.162
	(0.131)	(0.118)	(0.090)	(0.090)
Time dummies	Yes	Yes	Yes	Yes
Sargan test (*p*-value)	0.87	0.99	1.00	1.00
Serial correlation (*p*-value)	0.73	0.70	0.73	0.97
Number of observations	76	76	76	76

Source: Authors.
Note: All variables are in four-year differences. Numbers reflect the GMM estimation procedure using lagged (*t*-2) values of the independent variables as instruments. Standard errors are in parentheses. Coefficients significant at 5 percent are starred.— = not available.

makes growth benefit the poor but also increases growth, significantly facilitating poverty reduction.

Column 2 indicates the impact of the Gini coefficient and shows that changes in inequality are not related to growth in a statistically significant manner. This result is interesting in light of the literature that examines whether inequality is good or bad for growth (Forbes 2000). Because inequality is detrimental to poverty reduction and to pro-poor growth and is not beneficial to growth, Brazil could make concerted efforts to decrease its high levels of inequality without sacrificing higher economic growth.

Column 3 includes the share of households with garbage collection and access to sewage to indicate whether investments in infrastructure are good for growth. It shows that access to sewage has a highly positive effect on growth. Its inclusion reduces the coefficient of the schooling variable by half, meaning that investments in infrastructure and in human capital are positively correlated. In spite of that, the schooling variable remains statistically significant.

Which stage of human capital achievement is more important to growth? Column 4 includes the change in the share of the population with secondary, high school, and college education in each state in the growth regression. The share of college-educated individuals is the variable that attracts the highest coefficient and the only one that is statistically significant. The inequality coefficient remains insignificantly different from zero, and the share of households with access to sewage remains an important determinant of income growth.

It appears, therefore, that both high school and college education are important determinants of pro-poor growth. But only college education is an important determinant of growth. These results suggest that although education is important for growth and pro-poor growth, there maybe trade-offs associated with returns to investments in each education level: investments in high school appear to be more important than investments in college education in making growth beneficial to the poor but investments in high school alone do not improve growth prospects, whereas investments in college education are an important determinant of growth but are less effective in making growth pro-poor.

Recent Trends: Possible Explanations for Falling Inequality

Though inequality in Brazil has been memorably described as "unacceptably stable" (Barros, Mendoça, and Henriques 2000), the most recent trends are more promising. The Gini coefficient has declined steadily, though not dramatically, since 1993. Recent research has recognized changing patterns in the composition of inequality and offered several tentative, and quite preliminary, explanations for the overall decline in inequality (Ferreira, Leite, and Litchfield 2005). One possible explanation is educational improvements. However, much more research must be done to establish precise causal mechanisms, not least for the sake of informing policy makers about which reforms might positively affect equity and development in Brazil.

Trade Liberalization and Spatial Inequality

Static decompositions reveal a decreasing importance in the spatial composition of poverty, as captured in table 9.1. Regional differences accounted for 9 percent of inequality in 1993, a drop of 4 percent from 1981. The declining importance of urban/rural difference is even more striking: the urban/rural divide accounted for 17 percent of inequality in 1981, 9 percent in 1993, and 7 percent in 2004. Although these static decompositions reveal evidence of spatial convergence, they of course say nothing about the causal mechanisms behind this convergence. More research needs to be done on the effects of trade liberalization on agricultural growth, for instance, as this liberalization could quite plausibly be linked to a narrowing of urban/rural income differences (Ferreira, Leite, and Litchfield 2005).

Increasing and Progressive Social Spending

Although total social security incomes remained regressive in the post-1993 period, resulting from the continued dominance of public pension spending, increases in the volume and improved targeting of social assistance transfers may have contributed to a decline in inequality. An ability to assess the precise impact of social assistance transfers is hampered by the conflation of these programs with capital and rental incomes in the PNAD household survey category "other incomes." In other words, though the survey data reveal that the population share receiving income from this source has almost doubled, from 16 to 30 percent, this result could conceivably reflect changes in the distribution or reporting of capital and rental incomes. Given the government's attention to improved targeting of cash transfer programs in recent years (through programs such as the *Bolsa Escola* and the new *Bolsa Família* discussed below), declining levels of inequality are likely to reflect, at least in part, the expansion of cash-based social assistance programs. However, only a more disaggregated analysis of the incidence of these transfers would allow a confident assessment of their precise role in the overall decline of inequality after 1993 (Ferreira, Leite, and Litchfield 2005).

Increased Educational Access

Dynamic decompositions reveal that a decline in inequality among education subgroups was driven by declining returns to formal schooling—that is, a lowering of the skills premium identified as one of the causal determinants of inequality in Brazil. Ferreira, Leite, and Litchfield (2005) are hesitant to assign these declining returns either to a shift in supply of skills, which reflects the success of education policy, or to shrinking demand, which suggests a failure to produce and adopt skill-intensive technologies across the economy. There is, however, evidence to suggest some success of the government's more recent attempts to improve the attainment and quality of education at all levels. The most obvious mark of success has been a dramatic increase in enrollment rates. Enrollment in secondary education increased by more than 60 percent between 1996 and 2004. Enrollment in basic education in the poorer regions of the north and northeast increased by 18.5 percent and 9.7 percent, respectively. In addition, school-grade promotion rates have increased significantly, partially overcoming the disproportionately negative effects of school repetition on the poor. An expansion of education could in theory reduce underlying inequality of human capital endowments and therefore reduce wage differentials by skills (World Bank 2003).

Recent reforms in education have increased incentives for access to, performance of, and attendance at government schools. The 1996 National Education Law took steps toward improving accountability and quality by defining the responsibilities of the three levels of government with respect to provision of education services and by clarifying minimum operational standards for every public school. Primary attendance has been boosted by increased investments under FUNDEF—the joint federal-state-municipal Education Maintenance and Development Fund—which links local resources to student enrollment rates, thereby giving governments incentives to expand coverage. FUNDEB, if approved, will expand the incentives of FUNDEF into preschool and upper secondary education. The *Fundescola* (School Empowerment) program, set up in 1998 with World Bank support, has provided technical assistance and educational packages to schools in the disadvantaged northeast, north, and center-west regions. Inequalities at the higher education level have begun to be addressed by the Pro-Uni program, which provides federal loans for poor children to attend private universities.

Perhaps the most notable successes in government educational policy have been achieved through demand-side targeting. The *Bolsa Escola* (School Grant) scheme created in 2001 provided a means-tested cash transfer to poor households, on the condition that children in those households attend school. Various transfer programs were unified under the *Bolsa Familia* (Family Grant) program in 2003, thus conditioning cash transfers on a range of human-capital enhancing behaviors such as school attendance, vaccination, and prenatal care. The program appears to have increased school attendance among poor children, but its contribution to recent reductions in inequality should be the subject of further research.

Conclusions

The growth elasticity of poverty is positively related to initial level of income, which means that initially poorer states have to grow more to achieve the rate of poverty reduction achieved by initially richer states. Therefore, if all states grow at basically the same rate, regional poverty differences will increase. Special efforts must be made to raise growth in very poor states.

In terms of inequality, growth elasticity of poverty is negatively related to initial inequality and increases in inequality further increase poverty incidence. Therefore, to make growth more pro-poor, both statically and dynamically, growth must be achieved with a decline in income inequality, particularly in the higher-income and higher-inequality states.

The factors conducive to pro-poor growth are those that improve the level of income and decrease income inequality. Investments in human capital are the most important of these factors, as they tend to make growth more pro-poor and also increase the growth rate, increasing poverty reduction. Because education also tends to reduce inequality, and inequality is unrelated to growth in Brazil, there are no trade-offs involved in investments in human capital, considered as a whole.

The question for policy makers is which level of education should be given the highest priority. Investments in high school appear to be most important to make growth beneficial to the poor, but they do not improve growth prospects by themselves, whereas investments in college education are important determinants of growth but are less effective in making growth pro-poor. Future research should identify the policies that increased access to higher education in the different Brazilian states. With respect to other policy variables, the econometric exercises clearly showed that investments in certain infrastructure are also important for pro-poor growth and for growth itself. These investments also ought to be the focus of economic policies and research.

The recent focus on improving educational attainment and quality reflects the national government's awareness of the links between human capital expansion and poverty reduction. In spite of improvements, most notably in secondary school enrollment rates, major challenges remain. At an average of 6.6 years, overall educational attainment is low by international standards. Moreover, educational inequalities continue to correlate with race and residence. Inequality of educational services by area remains a pervasive problem; the worst schools are located in the poorest areas of municipalities. Rural areas suffer from lower net enrollment rates, reflecting biases in national policy, which stipulates that small schools should exist only where there are no other options. This policy has led to the closure of schools, forcing children in remote, and often very poor, areas to travel long distances to school. Further attention to policy reform and targeting across geographic and income groups will be required to eliminate the deep inadequacies and discrepancies in human capital assets in Brazil.

Notes

1. The authors thank Catherine Hull for her editorial assistance.

2. The rural area of the north region is not surveyed. There is no survey for the census years 1980, 1991, and 2000, and there was no survey in 1994. Each PNAD questionnaire requests information about households (regional location, demographic composition, quality of dwelling, ownership of durable goods) and individual household members (age, gender, race, educational attainment, labor force status, and sector of activity, as well as income as of a particular week in September and including monthly earnings from all jobs, pensions, and other sources, including interest gains, donations, and rents). PNAD's stratified sample design makes it representative at the state level and for metropolitan/nonmetropolitan and urban/rural areas. The survey has some shortcomings (see Ferreira, Lanjouw, and Neri 1998). In particular, its income measure does not accurately reflect home production and nonmarket income (important in rural areas). However, it provides comparable data across time.

3. Bourguignon (2003) uses the poverty line divided by mean income as a measure of development, but because the poverty line is the same for all states of Brazil and over time, only mean income is used as a proxy here.

4. There are exceptions to these rules: the federal government runs some high schools, and some states run their own universities, such as the University of São Paulo.

5. This measure of human capital has the highest impact on all economic indicators (see the regressions below).

6. The tests of overidentifying restrictions (Sargan) and second-order serial correlation do not reject the null hypothesis.

7. The omitted variable is the share of people with primary or less education.

8. The tests of overidentifying restrictions (Sargan) and second-order serial correlation do not reject the null hypothesis.

References

Acemoglu, D., S. Johnson, and J. Robinson. 2001. "The Colonial Origins of Comparative Development: An Empirical Investigation." *American Economic Review* 91 (5): 1369–1401.

Arellano, M., and S. R. Bond. 1991. "Some Tests of Specification for Panel Data: Monte Carlo Evidence and an Application to Employment Equations." *Review of Economic Studies* 58 (2): 277–97.

Barros, R., and M. Foguel. 2000. "Focalização dos gastos públicos sociais e erradicação da pobreza no Brasil." In *Desigualdades e Pobreza no Brasil*, ed. R. Henrique. Rio de Janeiro: Institute for Applied Economics.

Barros, R. P., R. Mendoça, and R. Henriques. 2000. "Desigualdade e pobreza no Brasil: retrato de uma estabilidade inaceitável." *Revista Brasileira de Ciências Sociais* 15 (42): 123–42.

Bils, M., and P. Klenow. 2000. "Does Schooling Cause Growth?" *American Economic Review* 90: 1160–82.

Bourguignon, F. 2003. "The Growth Elasticity of Poverty Reduction: Explaining Heterogeneity across Countries and Time Periods." In *Growth and Inequality*, ed. T. Eichler and S. Turnovsky. Cambridge, Massachusetts: MIT Press.

Datt, G., and M. Ravallion. 1992. "Growth and Redistribution Components of Changes in Poverty Measures: A Decomposition with Application to Brazil and India." *Journal of Development Economics* 38 (2): 275–95.

Ferreira, F., P. Lanjouw, and M. Neri. 2003. "A Robust Poverty Profile for Brazil Using Multiple Data Sources." *Revista Brasileira de Economia* 57 (1): 59–92.

Ferreira, F., and R. Barros. 1999. "The Slippery Slope: Explaining the Increase in Extreme Poverty in Urban Brazil, 1976–1996." *Brazilian Review of Econometrics* 19 (2): 211–96.

Ferreira, F., P. Leite, J. Litchfield. 2005. "The Rise and Fall of Brazilian Inequality." Mimeo, World Bank, Washington, DC.

Forbes, K. 2000. "A Reassessment of the Relationship between Inequality and Growth." *American Economic Review* 90 (4): 869–87.

Menezes-Filho, N. 2001. "Educação e Desigualdade." In *Microeconomia e sociedade no Brasil*, ed. M. Lisboa, and N. Menezes-Filho. Rio de Janeiro: Contra Capa Livraria.

Neri, M. 1995. "Sobre A Mensuração do Poder Aquisitivo dos Salários Em Alta Inflação." *Pesquisa e Planejamento Econômico* 25 (3): 497–525.

Pessoa, S., V. Gomes, and F. Veloso. 2003. "Evolução da Produtividade Total dos Fatores na Economia Brasileira: Uma Análise Comparativa." *Pesquisa e Planejamento Econômico* 33 (3): 389–434.

Rocha, S. 2003. *Pobreza no Brazil—afinal, de que se trata?* Rio de Janeiro: Fundação Getulio Vargas.

World Bank. 2003. "Brazil: Inequality and Economic Development." Working paper, World Bank, Washington, DC.

INDEX

Boxes, figures, notes, and tables are indicated by b, f, n, and t, respectively.